@carole_bouchard

Cover design: © Zuzanna Szyszak

Typesetting: andaollenn.com, Gwenael Dage

ISBN: 979-1-0971-7803-1

THE QUEST

Novak Djokovic's decade of chasing at Roland-Garros came to an end, unlocking history

By Carole Bouchard

CONTENTS

Novak Djokovic's career is a success story. Novak Djokovic finally winning Roland-Garros is the success story inside the success story. It came through pain, tears, doubts, nerves, flashes of anger, questioning and a lot of sweat, which meant that for the writer that I am it was the perfect story to tell. It had been an eventful and soul searching quest for Djokovic that has ended in an apotheosis, twelve months after it first ended in tears. The minds of any champions in any sport are thrilling to try to analyze, as is Novak's. How did he bounce back one more time? How did he shut down those demons that kept creeping back? Why had France developed such a soft spot for the Serbian?

In a tennis world that had been tempted to grant all the historical renown to Roger Federer and Rafael Nadal, what kind of earthquake was "The Novak Slam"? No male tennis player for 47 years had won four Grand Slam titles in a row. In the history books, Novak's name was now coming right after Rod Laver's. In probably the toughest era of the game, Djokovic had achieved the impossible after having also put an iron hand on the Tour. How do you resist writing that story? You don't.

I began my journalism career right on time for the Big 4 era. I've seen their rise to power, their failures, their flaws and the amount of work and determination they've put into ruling. The influence they gained in the tennis world, the rock star status they earned over the world, their flawless business plans and professionalism. There is no denying that Djokovic triumphing in Paris, after what in the future will be debated as the most dominating period ever, was a defining moment in tennis history. That was nothing to simply shrug off and move on to the next tournament. Nothing to try to sweep under the rug because the hero of the day wasn't the one some narratives had predicted.

I've witnessed and reported on every Parisian heartbreak of Novak Djokovic, on all his great escapes too. I've also been on most of the sites the past seasons where he would just walk over everybody. I saw how his resilience had the last word, how his holistic approach came to power, how different he was. Through the past ten years, I've also reported on most of the Big 4 battles and the changes in their internal dynamics. I had all those bigger pictures, layers and complex storylines in my head when, on this 5th of June 2016, Djokovic triumphed in Paris. And I felt I had sufficiently observed and talked to Novak, his team and his rivals through the years to have a good idea of the whole persona. So when he left Paris with the smile of the winner for the first time ever, when the guy I watched going from a prodigious outsider to a ruthless King achieved on the same day his Career Slam and a Grand Slam (over two seasons), I decided it deserved taking a step back and reflecting on what had actually happened. And that I was game to write about it.

It was supposed to just be a feature, then it became a whole adventure. There would never be a good time to get it published through the summer: too little time before Wimbledon, then Novak lost early there, Roger Federer terminated his season, then the Olympic Games took all the attention and he also got injured. Then Novak lost the US Open final to Stan Wawrinka, and quickly after that we were in a totally different landscape with Djokovic struggling and Andy Murray rising. The story was that battle for the throne. My "let's take a step back" piece wouldn't really fit in there. Along the way, the positive thing was that I had a lot of time to think about this project, to start talking to some key people and to collect good material overall. And that's when it hit me: all of this would now never fit into a feature. And I had zero wish to cut it down. I spend my seasons cutting down my features: not this time.

It was a story and a personality that couldn't do with shortcuts, and a performance that deserved better. It could also be a way to put some records straight. People who had never exchanged a single word with

Djokovic nor watched a third of his matches through the years, would come to me all season long with definitive - and wrong - statements on who he really was, what his tennis really was, what his place in the game's history was, what his relationship with his rivals was. And it started to feel tiring. As was reading variations on the "unloved champion" theme, the one "who wanted so much to be loved," the "damn, he keeps winning and that's bad for tennis" theme that had been invented just for him, or the "look, he breaks racquets and yells at people: not nice!" theme as they became the main stories accumulating around a guy who was piling up tennis records.

So all of this came together to hit me and make it obvious: that whole story was waving its arms to me, shouting "I'm not a feature, I'm a book!" And yes it was. So there I went. Here I will try to give you an idea of how Novak Djokovic had to go through a quest in order to win Roland-Garros. That this 2016 French Open victory became the culmination of one of the most impressive periods of domination in tennis history. The, for now at least, high point in the career of a champion one needs to dig deeper into to understand before judging his place in the Greatest Of All Time list or the influence he's had on the game and its actors. Winning in Paris sent the Djoker into another dimension, and it is this path and final leap that I'm inviting you to share in this book.

You're not going to walk alone with the chatty French that I am: don't be afraid! As the time has now come to share this book with those who will be interested in it, I just want to thank the people without whom said book wouldn't have been the same. Those who gave it life, information, food for thought, and layers of understanding. First of all, of course, a massive thanks to Novak Djokovic who accepted right away to give me an interview for the book. Also for the access he gave me to his team. A team that I also want to thank hugely: Marian Vajda, Gebhard Gritsch, Miljan Amanovic, Boris Becker (despite the fact that the German legend was not working anymore with Novak at the time I asked to talk to him), Elena Cappellaro and Edoardo Artaldi. In those talks, I happened to also need to look at the scars, to recall some demons, to come back with more questions: Novak and his team didn't close the door nor send me to hell. I'm grateful for the trust.

I'm of course also grateful to the great Rod Laver who gave me some time with such kindness. And among all the coaches, players, fitness experts and "tennis world" people that allowed their voices to be featured in this book, I need to thank some who have always been available through the years for me: Patrick Mouratoglou, Paul Quétin, Christopher Clarey and Thierry Van Cleemput. This book has also given me the chance to meet some great tennis experts, and among them I owe a big thank you to Darren Cahill, Niki Pilic and Guy Forget for sharing their tennis views and anecdotes. I've been convinced for a long time of the crucial place of mental work in professional sports, and in tennis in particular, and going into this Djokovic quest has only reinforced that certainty. On this mental road, I met someone who threw a huge light on the topic, and on different key moments or ways of speaking adopted by Novak, so I want to thank Catherine Aliotta from the sophrology training institute in Paris.

All the quotes you will read in this book mostly come from exclusive interviews I conducted, the rest coming from press conferences I attended and a small part of them from material published elsewhere and sourced. The goal was to provide you all with an original and unique story, built on never before read content and rich with exclusive looks behind the scenes. I hope I have delivered! And here I want to thank Robert Lysiak for the correcting job he did on the book and also the editing advice he offered, with an enthusiasm that was a great boost in the last stages. And if you love the cover as much as I do, you have only one person to thank: it's Zuzanna Szyszak for her very wonderful art work.

In 2014, after nine years of good service, I decided to leave the French national sports media group L'Equipe. I'm not a desk person, I'm a reporter. That's something I knew when I decided to quit law school, something I was convinced of when I picked Political Sciences and Communication as a bridge between law and the journalism school I would attend after. I did the internships then, the summer work in local newspapers. I did the newbie tasks I didn't like but that were the mandatory steps. I did the freelancing jobs. I did the way too early shifts or the way too late shifts, the days that just wouldn't end. Out of passion for my field, I did the "don't count your hours nor whine about the too-low-for-my-liking wages." I had been patient and was rewarded, finally traveling the sports world to report on site. To directly witness the stories and talk to their actors. To see what was happening backstage in order to better know and explain what would happen on stage. Or that's what I was thinking until late 2014.

Often people ask me a polite version of "why the hell did you leave L'Equipe?!" I'll just say that I had worked very hard and for a long time to deserve becoming a sports reporter. I was more than qualified and had proved it. I wanted to go forward, not backward. Being a journalist isn't a fairytale anymore those days, but pragmatism wasn't going to make me give up my goals. So I took a leap of faith in myself, in the sports industry, in the relationships I had built there, and became a freelance journalist again. What I've learnt since that jump is that freedom is a luxury that is worth some sacrifices... and that I really love it.

So in this "thank you" moment, let me take some time to thank all the people and media that have put trust in my work since I took that jump. They know who they are, in France and abroad. And all the male and female players, coaches, colleagues, agents, publicists, tournaments and Tour people who have never said "no" when asked to talk to me, to help, to answer questions even when they didn't like them or had something else to do than talking to the French wandering the players' areas with her recorder in hand. I can't say that without a shout out to Nicola Arzani from the ATP and Eloise Tyson at the WTA who despite the thousands of emails they received, always kept an eye on that French person.

But you know who should be the first person to trust you? You. It all starts in the level of confidence and trust you decide to put in yourself when many are saying you shouldn't. In the mountains of Kopaonik, Jelena Gencic told a little boy called Novak Djokovic he would conquer the tennis world one day. She trusted herself. A decade later the same Djokovic would land on the main Tour, announcing to everybody that he was there to become the n°1. He trusted himself, and to this day the Djoker has never stopped believing in himself. And that's why on that 5th June 2016 he completed his legend.

Painful Routine, Higher Stakes

He was there again, standing on the Roland-Garros podium. It was his year, all signs had been pointing to it. Finally, he would get his Career Slam. Finally the elusive Grand Slam title would elude him no more. He would walk to the other end of this podium, raise the trophy, "la Coupe des Mousquetaires," over his head with a roar, and then listen to the Serbian national anthem being played in the stadium. His day of glory. And as the crowd was indeed on its feet, chanting his name, "Novak! Novak!", clapping like there's no tomorrow, all the tears he had been fighting hard not to let go, were now running down his cheeks.

But they weren't cheering his triumph: they were cheering for comfort. And he wasn't crying tears of relief and joy, but of both pain and gratitude for the love. Not too far from him, he could see the trophy he wanted so badly...in the hands of Stan Wawrinka. When he then looked down at his own hands, he saw the finalist's plate. The loser's trophy. Again! Heart: Broken. Soul: Crushed. Again!

For the third time, - the second in a row - Novak Djokovic had lost, on this 7th of June 2015, a French Open final. Again, he could hear those predicting he'd remain the cursed one in Paris. Beating Rafael Nadal, the nine time boss of the Porte d'Auteuil in the quarter finals? Useless. Being the best player on Tour since January? Useless. He failed again, beaten by an opponent playing as in a dream, by a semi-final played over two days and by his own nerves. That should have been it. The end, bye bye, ciao. Paris, we're over.

It was actually going to be the opposite: on this exact day, through those same tears, that's when he started to win Roland-Garros 2016.

When the Parisian crowd gave him a two minute long standing ovation while he was standing as the loser again on the podium, it was surely the first time in a Grand Slam final that love was pouring down from the crowd like that for him. It was even stronger than the previous year in 2014 when he also received a strong ovation while the finalist's plate was put in his hands after his loss to Rafael Nadal. Feeling his pain, the crowd was sending a virtual hug. Tears had been close that day but at the time he found a way to keep them from running wild.

Not this time. So he cried after mouthing "merci," bowing down, putting thumbs up. The applause grew louder and louder, including Wawrinka's. The "Nole! Nole!" chants louder, and the eyes redder and redder. Sports crowds are sometimes weird: they seem to need to see the champ being heartbroken before finally fully connecting to him. "It was one of the most honest awards' ceremonies when he really cried and the whole crowd just lifted him up and I think he remembered," acknowledged his then head coach Boris Becker.

So it's maybe on this 7th of June 2015 that Djokovic found the last key that would make him win Roland-Garros a year later. And also from this point forward that his longtime coach Marian Vajda, who has been with the Serb since 2006, decided to build the next campaign, despite the broken hearts, not fully sure how it would all feel twelve months later. "It was very bitter... The loss, the way he lost, how many times he had already been in the final. It brings you thoughts like 'will it ever happen again?' Emotions are mixing inside of you. But in my mind when he finished the final I said 'this is the point where we have to start from. It's not the end of the world, not the end of your Roland-Garros hopes: you still have one more chance.' That was my speech to him all the time. Next year is very close, you have a chance. Novak also had in the back of his mind that somehow he had to accomplish it, but would it ever happen? That was the question."

So on this day Djokovic would find a way to turn this third loss in the final into something less traumatizing. "I fell short, I didn't win that match," he'd say. "But what happened afterwards, the appreciation and respect I got from the crowd and that standing ovation really touched me deep inside. I was so looking forward and so eager to come back and to be part of this event again. That's where it actually got to another level of connection." Paris hadn't broken him, the quest was still on, and would rage even stronger twelve months later.

Through the same resilience that would make him forget about his heartbreak, he found a way to go and win a third Wimbledon title just three weeks later. Oh obviously the seed planted then was a weak echo in the hours after this disappointment. Or even through the three weeks until Wimbledon. I really thought he would actually still be in recovery when he arrived on June 28th for his pre-tournament press conference at Wimbledon. One of the reasons being that he looked truly hurt and empty through his post-final press conference in Paris, despite all his efforts to cover it. I remember asking him how he would bounce back on such short notice before London, trying to sound positive in order to get the best possible answer in those circumstances. "Twice when you lost here in the final, you bounced back immediately at Wimbledon. Do you think it will be tougher this time or is there something of a routine which can help you move on pretty quickly?" His answer started with a cynical laugh and went on with the biggest possible irony: "No, it's going to be very easy. I mean, I'm going to Wimbledon and winning a trophy. (Laughter) Of course it's going to be difficult. But, again, my mind is not in London at the moment, really. I just got off the court and I need some rest. That's all." A few weeks later after Novak's Wimbledon victory press conference, Serbian colleague Sasa Ozmo would tell me with a laugh: "Hey, just like he told you in Paris: 'I'm going to go and win Wimbledon!'". Indeed. But when we first met again on the eve of the third Grand Slam of the season, I really had a hard time imagining it. Djokovic hadn't played a single event since the French Open and was also beaten at the Boodles exhibition right before the start. So I was really expecting a still grieving aura.

Instead, Djokovic strolled into the main interview room with the same confidence he carried from Melbourne to Paris, and even smiled while answering questions. But the heartbreak, Novak? "Before Roland Garros, I'd lost only two matches. I had one of the best season starts in my career. Of course, Roland Garros finals wasn't easy. All in all, it was another great tournament. But I needed some time to just mentally recover, rest. More than physical rest, I needed that emotional, mental rest to recharge my batteries and get myself in a proper state of mind so I could start all over again. It took me some time really to recover

15

and to rest after Paris. I didn't want to think about tennis too much. I spent time with my family, just did other things."

All very reasonable, but we weren't ready to believe he could be that reasonable so quickly after having all his hopes destroyed. Surely, it couldn't be that easy. So Novak, really, how could you recover from THAT? "That's the match that I wanted to win, but it didn't happen, mostly because I lost to a better player that day. I had to admit, no question about it: I could only just congratulate him because he was the one that was taking his chances, stepping into the court, being brave, coming up with some incredible shots. He deserved to win. Maybe I could have done a few things differently. But it's all behind me now. I'm experienced, and something tennis has taught me over the years, is to move on, and to be able to do that very quickly. You need to be able to reset very rapidly and get yourself a new motivation and inspire yourself to keep on going. This motivation and faith has to be even stronger than it was three weeks ago. I've been in this particular situation before. It's brought me a lot of mental, emotional strength. Because of the matches like this one against Stan, I have become stronger and I've learned how to grow in the process."

Again, not ready to believe that, so one more question in the 'Novak, really, how do you cope without doing a Goran 911' scenario. "Right after I lost the match, of course, there was this sense of disappointment. There is no doubt about it. I felt that for some days after. Because I have a family, I have different things in life, different interests, I've managed to move on because of the experience of learning how to handle these particular situations and circumstances. I managed to get the necessary reset in my mind. The traces may stay, let's say, for some time. But you always try to train your mind to look on the bright side, to move on, to leave what happened in the past, and just take it as a lesson, and something that will give you strength."

And as much as Wawrinka had killed him that day, he was also the one that had helped Djokovic stand up again. "I felt something I never felt before in any Grand Slam final with any of my rivals that I played against before: this connection with Stan. I thought we shared these unique moments on the court and we showed to the world that even if we fought for the biggest title, we still had respect for each other and appreciation. The way we greeted each other at the net, then after when he came to my bench, I appreciated it very much. I think that shows his greatness, as well. That's the way it's supposed to be. That's what I felt and I think what people experienced that day."

Djokovic didn't create this connection with Stan just as a coping mechanism. Every person who was on the court that day felt it, every person who'd been following those guys on Tour for years felt how real it was. So no one should be surprised to read here how emotional it had also been for the Swiss to have beaten Novak that day. "For me that was overall quite a surreal moment," he told me during the 2017 Australian Open, accepting to travel back in time to share what really went through his mind and heart from the instant he clinched the title. "Of course first because I won, because it was Roland-Garros. Then also because one of the first clicks in my career had been a loss against Novak at the Australian Open in 2013[1] (a fourth round lost in five hours, 12-10 in the fifth set) with an amazing moment spent on court. I always had a ton of respect for him and we always got along really well, often practiced together. I've already had many great episodes of my Grand Slam career against him, like also my first semi-final, at the US Open in 2013. So yes this Roland-Garros final was full of emotion. When I won the match point, there's this emotion but my first thought was 'don't make him wait at the net;' Those are maybe minor things, but at this moment the emotion that got out was respect. And there were those words we shared at the net too... Yeah obviously it was also a great and special moment for me as well."

Yet, many will be surprised to read how tough it had also been for "Stan The Man" to have taken away the Serb's dream. In an individual sport where many shield themselves inside a bubble of selfishness, Wawrinka couldn't help feel something he still struggles to publicly truly identify. I had a hunch that day of the final, but never found a good time to ask Stan if I was right or if my brain was imagining things. Here in Australia after so many months since that Paris final, and also as he had won another Grand Slam title at the US Open at Novak's expense, it looked like a good moment. It looked like maybe now it

---

1. "Djokovic - Wawrinka joins list of recent tennis epics", The New York Times, January 01, 2013 (*http://www.nytimes.com/2013/01/21/sports/tennis/21iht-open21.html*).

wouldn't be too much to ask. So I said it out loud: "Correct me if I'm wrong but I couldn't help feeling that in this amazing winning moment for you, there was still a little part of you that was sad for Novak…"

I knew right away that I did well to wait months and months to inquire about that. Stan took a long pause, searching for his words with an embarrassed smile. His face turned a shade redder and he had his now infamous shy laugh, the 'I know what you want to hear, you may even be right but nope I won't tell you' one. Around 20 months after that match, it was still a touchy topic. Yet, he took an honest plunge: "To be telling myself to avoid making him wait at the net and to see how down he was… Let's say…That I won't say it because it would kind of suck to say it. Let's tell it like this… But I've always tried to be the same guy in victory or defeat, to always keep the same respect for the opponent." He shot me a 'I won't say more but now you know' smile, eyes shining and that was enough. I mentally patted my hunch on the back.

As for Djokovic, a year after that loss he would only say that the three weeks between Paris and London hadn't been easy at all mentally, keeping the details of the depth of the hole he fell into for himself. But getting out of it and finding a way to get the positive out of the heartbreak was also important help for his 2016 Paris quest.

One sure thing: Novak Djokovic will-power can do wonders. My first tennis memories of The Djoker go back to the epic 2005 US Open match he won against Gaël Monfils in the first round (7-5, 4-6, 7-6(5), 0-6, 7-5), with the medical time outs, breathing issues, and all the changes of momentum you can insert. The only thing I remember years later is this pure drama, this packed crowd which looked like it had no idea what the hell they were watching, and the sight of that 18 year old Serbian guy who would just not quit, who would try and do anything to get the win. And would just grab his opponent after match point for a huge hug. Monfils' face reading like a totally stunned "How the hell did you pull that out?!" Popcorn.

I had found impressive the way he handled his first Grand Slam final at the 2007 US Open despite the loss. And his run to the 2008 Australian Open title had been fascinating as we were in the midst of the "Fedal[2]" era. Then I think I met Novak for the first time in 2009 at the French Open, with a vivid memory of him entering the packed main press conference room after his third round loss disaster against Philipp Kohlschreiber on Court 1 (6-4, 6-4, 6-4), throwing an "Ah, now that I lost, everybody's coming!" with a smile.

From the get go, I had the feeling that this one was different. You call it destiny, you call it born to be great, you call it whatever you want to. I never changed my mind, not even when he struggled in 2009, or forgot how to serve for months in 2010, or when his mind seemed to refuse to win a Grand Slam final between Roland-Garros 2012 and Melbourne 2014.

But really during this Wimbledon 2015, it became obvious for the whole world: Novak Djokovic is different. His resilience has few equals, as he has already bounced back from basically everything thrown at him through his life on and off a tennis court. Some players are all about short term success: he's all about higher purposes and perspective. Some will doubt themselves after one single big loss: he'll never ever start. He can shake, he can choke, he can lose, he can break racquets and benches, go through the worst tantrums and soul searching, but he won't be broken. And he'll still look at the pack thinking he can best them all. As Rafael Nadal once said with a usual eyebrow up: "Novak always comes back. You don't know when, but you know he's never going to give up and he's going to find a way back."

So in May 2016, Novak Djokovic came back at Roland-Garros. With his head high and a smile. Again, he's the number 1 player in the world. Again he had dominated the season until then. There's no revenge feeling, no negative emotions as he'd call them. Just a burning desire to finish the job. The quest for perfection, again and always. And this relentlessness is a performance in itself. As if it wasn't mentally complicated enough, pressure wise, the Serb was not only fighting for this elusive Grand Slam title: he was also on collision course with one of the most celebrated feats in tennis: winning the four Grand Slams

---

2. The nickname given to the Federer and Nadal rivalry. As you'd find "Rafole" for Nadal - Djokovic, "NolAndy" for Djokovic - Murray and "Fedovic" for Federer - Djokovic. Tennis fans got game when it comes to nicknames!

in a row. No one had done it since Rod Laver, who did the calendar Slam twice through his amazing career in 1962 and 1969. In an era where Djokovic keeps getting compared to Roger Federer and Rafael Nadal, here came a chance to add a line to his book of achievements that they had never crossed. A chance to assert one more time and in the strongest possible way that he was now ruling them all. In Paris, Novak Djokovic was facing tennis history and his career history as he never had to before. It was all about him, it was all in his hands.

CHAPTER ONE

And So It Begins Again

He had been thinking about the 2016 French Open finals for twelve months. A red mark in the calendar stuck out somewhere within his brain cells, despite all the denials and the strategies to avoid the clay-made elephant in the room. "Now I have put myself in a position which I wanted to be in, of course, ever since last year's final" Novak Djokovic calmly announced to the press on this 3rd of June after his semi-final win against Dominic Thiem. After spending two weeks trying to stay in the moment, and denying that he spent the past year with the French Open somewhere in his mind, the Serbian let the mask crack a bit on this Friday. Actually he also did it right after his first match, telling the crowd at the court Philippe Chatrier that he was starting "the most important two weeks of his career." To deal with this pressure, some good amount of denial was obviously needed in between. Yet, after clinching his spot in the final he could let his claws out freely. Yes, he spent the past twelve months planning how he'd come back in the French Open final to wipe the loser's tears from his cheeks once and for all.

As everything in Novak Djokovic's career, it was a long term plan for domination. Nikola Pilic, more known as Niki Pilic, still remembers very well what it was like to train the young Djokovic in the days spent at his academy in Munich. He took him in when Novak was 13 years old and he could talk for hours about the will power of the Serb. "Once I gave him a wild card for a 10k Futures: he wasn't ready for that obviously, but he didn't play badly. He was young, and knew how hard it was to win ATP points and that he had to work. So he said 'I have to work, I have to work.' I taught him to change his service: wrist action, wrist action, wrist action. He was practicing every day. This is the will to be better. He will always try to do something better. It is something you have to be born with. You cannot learn that."

As you can't learn burning ambition like the one Djokovic has. Pilic remembers: "He won one Challenger and his father and I were eating lunch at my academy. And his father congratulated him. Novak's answer? 'Father, you know when we said you should congratulate me.' Even then he was thinking: 'Congratulations is when I win Grand Slam titles.' And it wasn't an 'if' but a 'when.' He's always been like that. Always fighting, always with a strong will to win."

A strong will that he was now applying to the French Open, and Pilic can testify about how much Djokovic wanted that title. "It was very important for him. I know because I spoke with him many times: he said 'I have to win Roland-Garros. I started to play on the clay and there's no reason why I shouldn't also win Roland-Garros.'" So for years now, Djokovic's focus kept coming back to Paris.

With the relief of now owning this highly coveted trophy, the Serb could dwell less painfully on how mentally challenging this quest had been for him. It had been eight months since he finally seized the Paris trophy but when Novak talked about it, it felt like it was yesterday. He was still as happy and excited as he was at the time. Still as elated and satisfied. Still as relieved. "It was a learning curve I think, Roland-Garros, for me in every sense. Not only tennis wise but in life as well, how I needed to approach things psychologically. And in the course of the last five years up until 2016, I was very close to winning the title several times. But I just missed that final step and when I kind of looked back and analyzed why that had happened, I thought that a lot had to do with me putting just too much weight on my shoulders. Myself. Because whatever anybody else was doing wasn't in my control. What was in my control was my reaction to that. And my reaction at the time wasn't balanced I think. I wanted it too much.... In some way too much.... Of course I wasn't the only one but with that as the only Grand Slam title that was missing for me to win, and as I was coming back each year the tension was building, right? (He smiled). So it was just adding up and adding up."

And it's not as if he could escape from the situation even if he wanted to. Because this talk he was having with the press in the main press interview room of Roland-Garros in early June after beating Thiem, he had basically already had in January in Melbourne. As he had every season since 2012, when the French Open became the sole box to check in his Grand Slam résumé. You see, players aren't the only ones who love patterns: the media do too. And in the tennis news cycle, Djokovic fighting for his Career Slam in Paris had become one of the most famous patterns of the year.

As is that of Djokovic habitually holding the trophy in the Rod Laver Arena in January. From 2011 to 2016, "Nole" only lost once Down Under. Once. A tournament which was also the first Major he won in 2008. So since he collected his first Wimbledon and US Open in 2011, sitting down with the press after his last match in Melbourne had nearly always meant two things for the Serb: the Grand Slam Watch was on as was the Career Slam Watch. There was absolutely no way he'd get out of the main press conference room without the words Roland-Garros being uttered. That was the next Grand Slam leg, that was the one he never won, that was the only obstacle remaining in his way. That was one of our tennis thrillers and no way were we going to let it go. For four years, from January to May, the Serb had been asked about Roland-Garros.

In 2016, all went according to plan. He won his sixth title in Melbourne: he already held the Open Era[3] record with five titles, but now joined Roy Emerson in the overall records. The feat was amazing, even more so in this era. And the Djoker was the happiest we had seen him during these two weeks. Way more than when he won a 100 unforced - errors - marred match against Gilles Simon! The tournament organizers provided Champagne for the press, so when Novak entered the interview room he saw most of us with a glass in hand. He laughed. But refused his own glass. He gave great quotes, didn't look especially emotional about this new Grand Slam title as it seemed more like a mission accomplished kind of feeling. He's the boss in Oz, status intact. It made me think that now maybe only a French Open win could really shake him enough to crack the public persona image he had built.

---

3. The Open Era starts in 1968.

As Andy Murray told me in Madrid during an interview in 2015 right after he won the title, "Novak and I are very emotional players." And he's right. Contrary to the machine-like comparison Djokovic has earned, you can totally read emotions on his face through matches or practices.

And there would be a whole article to write on the different looks he shoots towards his coaches' box during matches. I'm pretty sure some of those side-eyed looks have frozen his former head coach Boris Becker from time to time, whereas his historical coach Marian Vajda has experience with him and barely flinches anymore. But, with Novak, all of those feelings are constantly worked on, evaluated ("do I need to let the rage go now, do I need the adrenaline rush now, must I keep it together or it's going to be overwhelming?") and then dealt with. It's more work than instinct but it has become such a routine that it flows naturally.

But even more as he doesn't naturally show his emotions a lot in public. There would be flashes of anger, pride, hulk moments, ecstasy, but they would only last a few seconds. And he's known for giving the best loser speeches on court and in front of the media. He's also going to answer most questions he's asked in press conferences with the same calm and reflection to make his point, even those that clearly annoy the hell out of him.

For the latter he has developed a pretty efficient system of talking without really saying anything you'd be able to use against him. He still can get entangled in controversies and snap when his patience has run its course, but we're very far from the same Djokovic putting Andy Roddick down at the 2008 US Open. Or who said in 2006 after retiring against Nadal at Roland-Garros, down two sets in their quarter final, that it was a pity as he felt he was dominating. A classic that won't ever leave his legend's scrap book by the way.

Some would even say this provocative side of the Djoker is missed. But he's no Connors, Lendl or McEnroe: Djokovic takes no fun or pleasure at being the locker room bad guy or the public enemy n°1. That also explains why he has cut down his brilliant impersonations and most of his on court and off court spikes of provocation. This, and a desire to be taken seriously and not as a clown. He took on his duty like a politician, understood how this business was working and so became the professional he is.

He also takes great pride in being an ambassador for his country and the game. Not to forget that he'd been the kind of World n°1 that enjoyed a king's status: he dominated his kingdom with a smile, but he still dominated it. From time to time you'll hear him say he regrets there's not more fun on Tour, and you'll see him do some tricks at practice, like the Rafa forehand impersonation, or delight the crowd during exhibitions. But for the rest, it's now mostly all under control.

Let's take the 2013 French Open semi-final loss against Rafael Nadal where it seemed he couldn't lose that match. He looked broken and in shock when leaving the court. But he came before the press very composed, giving thoughtful answers, being very reasonable. At most he was caught taking a deep breath between English and Serbian questions. Dealing with a heart crushing loss as a professional. Barely human, right? Yet, I was to later learn that this same Djokovic had apparently been frozen in shock and disappointment in the locker room after the loss. Reminder: his first coach, mentor and "second mother" Jelena Gencic died during this French Open.

The day he learnt it, after beating Grigor Dimitrov in the third round, all his media commitments were cancelled. I was told he totally broke down learning the news. Yet after his next match he met the press and gave great, emotionally controlled answers about Gencic. As he seemed to cope well, questions came back regularly for days and weeks, as if the restraint for someone's grief wasn't needed there. And the same happened after his loss to Nadal: he seemed fine, so let's go.

That's how good he is at keeping an iron-willed public persona. What he went through that year in Paris would have knocked down many players and made them look fragile. But Djokovic, consciously or not, refused to show that. Is it a "you won't break me" pride? A "strong men don't cry" education? A coping mechanism, "that's the only solution for me not to lose it for a long time?" Only he knows.

Also what a long way from the despair he was in after losing to Rafael Nadal in Madrid's semi-final in 2009 despite having three match points. That day at the press conference he looked exactly like he was feeling: destroyed. Again: that's work. So, this is to say that in 2016 in order to break this armor and to also really visibly move him again on a tennis court, I could only see one contender: Roland-Garros. Because he had no coping mechanism yet for controlling emotions there after a win, as he had never experienced it. Because in Paris his scars were still burning.

When Murray qualified for this first French Open final, he was close to tears on court. Asked why such a huge outpouring of emotion, his answer was clear for anyone not considering those Big Four guys[4] as "players from another planet": "To reach the finals of the French for the first time, that's a big moment for me. It's not an easy thing to do. I never really expected to be able to do that." Djokovic had won nearly everything, so there were not a lot of "first times" left. Paris was the one to rock his world again.

During this last 2016 Australian Open press conference, where Novak had his trophy next to him, there was a moment that opened a window onto his unfiltered world. The inevitable Roland-Garros question came at the very end, and he was asked how hungry he was now for Paris. At this exact moment his eyes shone, he smiled widely, looked the reporter directly in the eyes and said: "Very." Then went back to his "wolves" metaphor (that the ones trying to get to the top are hungrier than the one already there): "But a wolf needs to eat a lot of different meals to get to Paris. Paris is a dessert."

And he never was publicly closer to what was going on inside of him than at this moment: the quest was on, lived like a bloody chase with one single option: winning. Roland-Garros was his battle against the world and himself. His test of character. His defining moment. And for now he looked as if he was enjoying the idea, not fearing it. Like every sports legend, Djokovic is a bit of a masochist: he loves to suffer, he loves the fear, he always asks for more pressure.

Every journalist following the Tour closely has at least once heard him say: "Pressure is a privilege." For sure he doubts, for sure he's afraid but at the end that's the thrill of the battle that takes over. "I worked very hard and envision myself to be in a position to be the n°1 in the world and have this kind of expectation and pressure so now I can't complain," he said at Monte-Carlo in 2016. "I actually enjoy it. I asked for it, was ambitious throughout my career, wishing to be

---

4. That's how Djokovic, Nadal, Federer and Murray are called.

where I am at the moment. Yes, I do have pressure but I'm not the only one, and pressure is part of what we do and it means that you're doing something that is working, that you put yourself in a position to play and fight for the biggest trophies in the sport. Thankfully I haven't lost too many matches in the last couple of years and I've been playing the best tennis of my life, coming as a result of many years of dedication. I just try to keep going, I don't pay too much attention to the ranking or points I have to defend: that time is behind me. Now it's just about maintaining the level of performance, the game that I have because I know that if I can do that I have a very good chance wherever I play to get far."

As he was thinking of himself as the wolf leading the pack, he also didn't allow himself to be happy for too long. "I can't allow myself to relax and enjoy," he explained in Melbourne. "Of course I want to enjoy, and I will, but it's not going to last more than few days. After that I will already be thinking about how I can continue playing well throughout the rest of the season. That's kind of a mindset that one needs to have if one wants to stay up there. 'Cause I think you need to work twice as hard when you're up there."

Some could find it a pity that you wouldn't let yourself enjoy a Grand Slam title to the fullest, but Djokovic wasn't at that stage of his career anymore. He was not winning a Grand Slam: he was collecting one more piece to build his legend. One more line on his résumé. One more proof for when posterity would come to judge his place in tennis history. And one more Grand Slam trophy getting him back in the chase towards Nadal (14) and Federer (18). Novak doesn't play this game to be anything other than the best. After all, when he was 6 years old, Jelena Gencic told him that one day he'd be among the greatest players in the world, and it stuck then grew in his brain through the years. He's been the best player in the world already, so what about the best ever? But there was no way to ever achieve that if there remained this little corner of red clay in France that kept refusing to submit.

I believe every champion is haunted by a special feat he or she is pursuing but can't achieve. The better they are, the higher the stakes and the goals. And whatever they have already achieved, this one thing that still eludes them looks like the dark cloud. Yet, who would dare say that Pete Sampras' career was flawed? Nobody. Still, it hasn't been complete, as the American never achieved the career Grand Slam, never won the French Open. Maybe as he didn't seem to care, everyone else did. Novak Djokovic cared about Paris. He cared about his career Grand Slam. He is the biggest perfectionist: as long as it's not perfect, he's not going to be fully satisfied. He once said in Bercy in 2015: "Nobody can be perfect, but if you go for perfection you might reach excellence." Mix this character trait with his ambition and his competitive nature, and you realize that Roland-Garros had been marked as the land to conquer at all costs. This little reminder that his career was not yet perfect.

It was not an obsession as he always rejected the word, "Because it doesn't come from the right emotion in the heart." It's more both a love interest that needed convincing and proof of trust, combined with a key that would unlock the last stage of his quest for greatness. Again, no one would have come to Sampras telling him he failed. Even if he never once played a French Open final. Yet, people and the media came at Djokovic talking about this Paris malediction, this constant failure that put a shadow over his career.

His three finals in Paris weren't something to be proud of, but only it seems the reminder of how he was still not complete nor worth being in the list of the greatest players of all time. With, at the time, 11 Grand Slam titles and 29 Masters 1000. With 4 years out of the last 5 on the throne of the ATP. No, Roland-Garros was the last obstacle for those still denying his place in history. And no doubt that Djokovic, knowing it, was even more stubborn about winning this damn thing. Because we talked perfectionism, ambition, and competitive spirit, forgetting the last ingredient: pride. Djokovic has high expectations for himself, for how his career has to be shaped: and that doesn't include letting anyone have a reason to doubt his greatness. That doesn't include a single piece of the puzzle being missing. That doesn't include Roland-Garros defying him. Despite having won more than what 99% of what other players would dream of, he was haunted by the missing piece.

He wasn't the first to arrive in Paris, which was logical after the rough week he just had in Rome. He played and won an amazing and brutal quarter final against Nadal, then an even more amazing and more brutal semi-final against the Japanese Kei Nishikori, before losing in straight sets to Andy Murray, in the rain. "Utterly Knackered" were the words for the one who had been denied a fifth title in a Foro Italico where he's treated like a local. Speaking fluent Italian will do that.

To add to an eventful Italian week, he succeeded in injuring himself: in the first game of his semi-final, he tried to hit the sole of his shoe with his racquet to get the clay out, but missed and instead whacked the internal face of his left ankle. As a result, he cut himself and bruised the bone: painful. As the discomfort grew along with his frustration, he'd give some side-eyes to his box that looked like: "Really?! Why?! Why so dumb?!" Injuring himself stupidly like that two weeks before the French Open was infuriating. In his relationship to Paris, it could even trigger an "I am so cursed" syndrome.

More seriously, that's an injury he would carry through the French Open, where really he didn't need any niggle to bother his body and so his mind. "It was bothering him a lot," revealed his physiotherapist Miljan Amanovic to me in March 2017. "It was a serious bone bruise. He wasn't able to have a shoe, to practice normally. He was playing all the time with a protection. He played a few matches with it at the French Open, until the quarter finals maybe. Day by day it went better, but it was painful and it was at the worst place because every contact with the shoe was there. But with the adrenaline..." He went through this with gritted teeth, as he did that week in Rome where he finished tired but maybe not as damaged as he could have been. Off he went for some rest and family time. The Parisian frenzy could wait.

So the place was already buzzing with practices, tensions, expectations, photographers, camera crews and journalists when Novak appeared for the first time on a court there. This was the Thursday before the event, May 19th, and there he was in a white Uniqlo T-shirt where three hearts of different colors had been drawn on the chest, "NOVAK" written over them. On this empty court Suzanne Lenglen, he started his preparation with the new French hope Lucas Pouille. Around the same time on the centre court, and so at the other side of the stadium, his arch rival Rafael Nadal was hitting with the Belgian David Goffin.

On the eve of the draw, everyone was just wondering one thing: where will Rafa, fifth seed on the entry list, land? In 2014, it had been in Djokovic's quarter, leading to a manic countdown. If Andy Murray was the most in form player with Djokovic, the French Open recent memories were all about three guys: Nadal, Federer, Djokovic. Their epic battles entered legendary status in Paris, and since 2012, it had basically been all about the Spaniard versus the Serb with two finals (2012, 2014), one mesmerizing semi-final (2013) and a 2015 quarter final that looked like a transfer of power...until Wawrinka decided otherwise.

The mighty lefty was then once again seen as the obstacle on Djokovic's road to the one title that still eluded him. In that context, knowing when the mouthwatering blockbuster would take place was a key piece of the script. Forgetting that Stan Wawrinka, the defending champion, could also change the landscape depending on where his n°3 seed fell. Reality sometimes can't compete against fantasy, especially when Rafa again looked close to his vintage self during the past few weeks with a title in the Monte-Carlo Rolex Masters (Masters 1000), another one in the Barcelona Open ATP 500 and this thrilling Rome Masters 1000 quarter final against Djokovic just before Paris.

This hope for a titans' showdown grew even bigger after Roger Federer withdrew from this 2016 edition. His withdrawal would be made official a few hours after both his nemesis' practices, around 5.30pm. After his back injury in Madrid, sustained during a practice with French player Jérémy Chardy, he tried to play Rome, miraculously winning one match against Alexander Zverev but understandably losing the second against Dominic Thiem. It was obvious how much discomfort he was in. As it was obvious that things weren't getting that much better when he tried to practice on Wednesday for 20 minutes before the rain came. So it wasn't really that much of a surprise when he decided not to take more risks on a 34 year old back.

For the first time since 1999, the Swiss wouldn't play the French Open, also ending his record of 65 Grand Slam appearances. Here is the message he posted on his Facebook page at the time: "I regret to announce that I have made the decision not to play in this year's French Open. I have been making steady progress with my overall fitness, but I am still not 100% and feel I might be taking an unnecessary risk by playing in this event before I am really ready. This decision was not easy to make, but I took it to ensure I could play the remainder of the season and help to extend the rest of my career. I remain as motivated and excited as ever and my plan is to achieve the highest level of fitness before returning to the ATP World Tour for the upcoming grass court season. I am sorry for my fans in Paris but I very much look forward to returning to Roland Garros in 2017."

With the shape he was in, no one really believed Federer could go all the way in Paris. In addition, the main feeling of a big part of the tennis community was that the only thing he'd succeed in doing would be sending Nadal, 5th seed, into Djokovic or Murray's quarters. Guy Forget, the tournament's director, summed up those mixed feelings: "He's feeling better: his knee is better, his back is better. But not to the point where he can compete with these guys. And Roger plays to win tournaments. Not having him is a disappointment for the tournament, as when you love tennis you have to be a fan of Roger, but I'm sure an amazing champion will still be crowned on Sunday. Also, maybe Rafa is seeing a little sign from fate in this for the draw (smiles). Also maybe it will give a more balanced draw. But I think that Novak, Rafa or Andy knew that Roger wasn't feeling that well." So as much as the sadness of not seeing Federer in Paris was real, so was the relief on some faces at the idea of Nadal becoming the 4th seed.

One titan was down, three remained with two having a long history in Paris. A Grand Slam tournament nowadays is more than a tennis tournament: it's a show. And for a show, you need a great cast, drama, tears, fears, suspense, heroes, villains, outsiders, usual victims, unexpected events. Also to get into a show or talk about a show, you'd want storylines and narratives. Nadal-Djokovic gave you everything. So if you're looking for epic, you want those two battling it out on the court Philippe Chatrier again, at the latest possible moment so the stakes are at their highest. A modern sports' version of the gladiators. 2013 raised their rivalry in Paris to another level and everyone would gladly take another slice of this each time it was possible. Like it or not, this sport is built on great rivalries, matches with tons at stake, over and over again. So the "they can meet before the final!" about Nadal and Djokovic had become one of the Roland-Garros gimmicks. Both camps dreading the possibility while trying to put on a good face.

On the eve of this first pressure spike, all was quiet on the grounds. So quiet that one didn't dare disturb it. The calm before the storm. The last moments of ease before two hectic weeks. You could feel the tension slowly but surely mounting. Sure, the qualifying rounds had started but they weren't happening on the main courts, were set at the back of the stadium and wouldn't provoke massive commotion before the final round. In the alleys, staff were fixing the last details, setting up everything for the biggest tennis event of the year in France.

My main goal in those first days in the stadium was basically not to be run over by one of the trucks. For the top players: it was tuning-up, period. They were all in the starting blocks, eager to make sure they were fully ready, trying also to put away the nerves before the first round. Andy Murray described it really well in one of his daily columns in the French national newspaper "Le Parisien" that (full disclosure) I was recording and translating. In his opinion, it was a tricky period. "I know that for sure the day of my first match or the night before, I'll definitely have some nerves. I get probably more frustrated in practice; like you can hit 20 great shots and then one bad one and you're like 'oh f..ck'...That's bad. It's what's difficult I think for the teams at this period, because the players are so anxious to be feeling great before the tournament starts. So I might want to do an extra half an hour or hour's practice if something is not feeling quite right. But also I've played a lot of tennis so I need to stay fresh as well. It's sort of difficult for the team to say like 'no, you don't need to hit any more serves, you don't need to do anymore in the gym, you need to relax now.' And that's what's tough the few days before."

Hence the reason those last practices aren't always what one would call relaxed. When I sneaked onto Lenglen to catch up on Djokovic on that Thursday, no one was chatting lightly or joking. It was around 1.30pm and they had been at work half an hour. I even felt the need to walk the stairs slowly in order to avoid making noise as this big Lenglen stadium was so quiet. I heard the balls being hit, that's it.

The media seating is - both fortunately and unfortunately - right at the bottom so no way you can go incognito there. You basically sit behind the player on the court. No one else was there, so I decided to start watching from the stairs, before other colleagues arrived so it made it less "stalker-ish" to go and seat myself. I also sneaked in the day before in the afternoon to watch Andy Murray at work with David Goffin. Practices tell a lot about a player's mindset or shape or what he's working on regarding his game, and so the issues faced, the tiny flaws he's fighting against. I take it as a part of my job to go and watch them as time and time again it has given me information that I wouldn't ever have guessed from just matches and interviews. So right after their Rome battle and right before the start of their Paris campaign, it was a mandatory thing to go and play the spy a bit.

Right from the start, the weather was terrible. Djokovic was warned: Mother Nature had no intention to make it easy for him. If he wanted to clinch the trophy, he'd also have to fight against the elements. A quest shouldn't be a walk in a sunny park. A quest should make you suffer. Go and ask Hercules if he had fun through his twelve labors. From outside, it looked like a good practice for a first one. Not as intense as the one I witnessed from Murray, but focused on the Djokovic basis: the timing.

You could see that the focus level was high by how demanding Novak already was. Vajda and Becker kept being solicited to correct a backhand position here, or a forehand and return there. There were lots of discrete discussions among the team through this practice. But if from outside it looked like a normal day at the office, it wasn't actually really the case as Boris Becker explained to me. Those days leading to the start of the tournament had been anything but peaceful. Becker recalled: "I remember that first practice with Lucas Pouille...It was sort of raining but not, and Novak had something with his shoulder so he didn't want to serve, and it was a very nervous practice. I could tell he was on edge. We managed to practice, to play one hour and a half and I think the more he practiced the better he coped, the more relaxed he got. But every day up until the first match was a tightrope."

A tightrope that Marian Vajda had been wondering about and worrying about for months, as the Slovakian coach wasn't sure of how much pressure Djokovic could really take in Paris. "Novak already had 11 Grand Slam titles behind him so I had the belief he could do it again. For me as a coach, the question was to how strategically do the whole year without having it all the time in his mind, with the press and everything... How can we handle it? He's a guy who can really handle these things and he's very determined and disciplined but still... If we focus too much on Roland-Garros, will it destroy his mind, will he go down? Will he be too nervous before? And everything that happened before, every practice before Roland-Garros was exactly like that: he was questioning all the time! Obviously he sees himself as a champion, he sees him potentially winning it: this is the picture, which is great. But it's a dream. Underneath, there are little things you need to catch and climb, and again and again, but then 'boom' you fall again: it already happened three times!" The always passionate Vajda still looked like being in a cold sweat while explaining the anguish Novak had gone through. We were in Monaco in February, comfortably set, but on his face all the pain of that month of June 2016 was back. Shaking his head at how hard it had been to just mentally remain in the event.

A few weeks later, as I was catching up with Amanovic, who has worked with Novak since 2007, he had no issue going back in time to that nervous period. They were all still marked by this fortnight, in a very touching way. Amanovic is a serious but friendly and easy going figure around the Tour, as he has also become a usual shadow to Djokovic. Cap with the "D" of the boss on head, broad shoulders, he's always around at practice or warm up to attend to Novak's body needs. You'll see him jump towards him at the first signal, whether it is for an arm that's itching or for a towel that needs to be given or a drink or some reassuring words. Miljan is just there. He's always in the box during matches suffering along, bringing support, sharing the joy. As he told me to sum up his relationship with Djokovic: "I know him like my pocket." So yes, the nerves in Paris had been real and Amanovic could still remember how it felt. "It was tough. Every tournament is tough. But just this question 'Is it this year?' was the one making it kind of unpleasant. Yet, if he was not to winning that one, was it a big deal? I don't think. But in the perspective of somebody who already did a lot, who won all the other Grand Slams, he was missing this one. And here that year the difference was also that this was the one to do 'the Four In A Row', that was a special one. And all of a sudden this pressure came on his back."

The team still did well to keep it among themselves on that first practice as through the whole tournament. So Lucas Pouille during that first practice didn't notice any of this. A few hours after that session, I asked him how it went and the French hopeful was pretty satisfied. He also said that hitting with Novak in Paris that year had a special touch: "That was very nice, even if it was in the rain a bit. It's really pleasant to be able to hit with him on this court. That was a good first session for me. But yeah hitting with him, it's even greater now as he really wants to win here, it's the last trophy he's missing: you can feel how into it he is. We had a great time with a lot of quality so it really went well and it's the best way for me to get ready for the first round. Yeah he asked me what kind of drills I wanted to do but at the same time we all want to do kind of the same ones so... we worked on the diagonals, made each other move and played some points at the end. A classic! (smiles)"

This first practice was also the moment to be fully reassured of his fitness. He had left Rome really tired and with a bad bone bruise inside his left ankle. So on this Thursday, he prolonged his practice with some physical work. And maybe he should have warned his bodyguard beforehand. Running up and down the stairs close to the bottom side of the court was one thing, even if I decided it entered "no way I'll ever try this" land when he started to jump up and down on one foot, then repeated with the other. But when Novak decided to run all the way up, in reach of anyone from the public, the imposing bodyguard in a suit had no other choice than running behind the Djoker. The sight of that bodyguard running up and down Lenglen's steps with an obvious internal side-eye remained one of the funniest images of this French Open 2016.

Novak's fitness trainer since 2009, Gebhard Gritsch, was like the rest of the team: nervous. So he didn't see anything funny from that first contact with the Parisian clay. This work on the stairs was actually done to catch up and also to make sure that really they had thought about everything. Djokovic isn't the only perfectionist on the team! "Leg strength, power and explosivity are a key factor and I wanted to make sure that everything was in place. So normally we'd have done it two days before but we didn't have enough recovery time, we knew that. In my head it was 'he must peak at this tournament' so it was part of the plan to give another stimulus for his legs to be ready. Because that French Open was the main thing of that year: we planned towards that, to make sure he'd be in top shape. And on clay regarding footwork, you've got to be in top shape. You never know, you might need to work very very hard, do lot of running... And it's not only about that tough match, it's about the fact that if you're not in top shape, you then can't recover for the next one."

Gritsch is a common and highly respected figure on the Tour: you wouldn't be able to miss his tall stature and bald head when he's around. The so very experienced Austrian always gave the impression of being in control, of being stoic. You'd watch him in Novak's box through the most epic matches and most of the time he'd sport this focused and calm face. So I was quite stunned to hear him casually tell me he had been a bundle of nerves before the start of that French Open. As much as Vajda and Novak. "Honestly there was some high level of nervousness in the team, because that was the objective and... How many times in his life would Novak have this chance? So maybe this is it. He needed to win this one. So I think everybody was quite nervous; there wasn't the usual calm in the team. Also Novak wasn't calm himself. In a team it's like that: if one isn't calm, nobody is calm (laughs). It was very challenging mentally." There's really been something rather touching to listen to all of them admitting without any issue how mentally rough the fortnight had been. No one tried to play the super hero part, the "we marched in total control to history, fully confident in everything." And it had probably saved them all to have zero issue to recognize that emotion and work on it.

This first session also gave way to some funny moments that would set the mood between Djokovic and this 2016 French Open, and that would no doubt help him to deal with his own stress. At the end of his practice sessions, Novak has this habit of making his team and often also his training partner of the day play a tennis version of the French game "la pétanque" with tennis balls. Each person, behind the net, would throw a ball and the winner would be the one whose ball ends closest to the baseline. It is serious business. After this practice with Pouille, Novak even invited the staff preparing the courts, to their delight. It would remain a custom, as would his signing autographs for fans before leaving the courts, his waving to everyone and this feeling that he was playing at home.

On that Thursday he even stopped to take selfies with some, to high five others, all of this after having also sent balls into the crowd. "A lot has been going on in my mind ever since I arrived in Paris," Djokovic would later say. "But I felt like this year when I arrived it was really different from any other year. The relationship and connection I had with fans and with people around that are contributing to the organization of the event, that I see on a daily basis, from security to ball boys, ball girls and all the people around, it was just different, you know." Despite the stress, the whole team was actually really glad to come back to Paris, as Gritsch explained: "It is quite amazing, but the funny thing is... I also play tennis and we all grew up on clay courts. So when we come to Paris, it doesn't matter what happened, we just love the clay courts. It's a beautiful game: this is what tennis is all about. So because we love it, it makes it easier."

I chose not to attend the draw at 11.30am on Friday the 20th, basically right when I saw the practice schedule for that day. Nadal was hitting with Murray on Lenglen at the same time as the draw, and Djokovic with the Croatian Borna Coric on Chatrier. Sorry, draw, you lost the power of attraction battle here. I would anyway get the draw sheets soon enough; my phone would buzz with the first "OMG, can't believe that x and y could face each other in x round" soon enough. Also I already knew Rafa would land in Novak's side of the draw. How? Because it's always like that. I'd have been surprised if he hadn't landed there.

So I made my way to the Lenglen court when everyone else was off to "Le Club Des Loges" for the draw. If everyone is off to watch and report on the same thing, you're probably better off somewhere else to find valuable things to report in tomorrow's papers, if you have the choice. On Lenglen, Nadal was there with Toni, Murray with Jamie Delgado. No one else was in the stadium as it was at the time forbidden to the public. It would be open later to spectators, who would have to seat themselves on the sides only. Which led to a funny moment as the security guard decided that it meant I couldn't sit in the media section. And that Andy Murray's agent, Matt Gentry, had to move too. Despite both of us having clearance via our credentials. That were hanging around our necks. Of course we refused to go, of course we told him to check with his supervisor and of course we were right.

That has to be one of the routines of the tennis season: "You can't stay there. Yes, I can. No. Yes, just check. I don't need to. Yes, you do. Oh ok it seems you can stay. Yes, I know." Although my favorite "security guards" story from Roland-Garros has to be the one in 2015 where Roger Federer was refused access on Lenglen because he didn't have his credentials on, and the guys didn't recognize him. Let me tell you that it didn't go well. At all.

So Andy and Rafa were hitting together and it felt like a solid one during the period I watched. Rafa's forehand seemed a bit touchy, but it had been for a while. Murray seemed as intense and focused as the other day: absolutely locked in. In retrospect I should have paid more attention to the white tape on Rafa's left wrist. You see players with tape all season long so I guess your brain gets too used to it. Muzz' (Murray's) brain would also notice it but without dwelling too much on it either. "I knew he'd been having problems with the wrist because he had it taped when I was practicing with him the week before the tournament," said Murray through his daily columns after Nadal withdrew before the third round. It was quite a heavy taping. The conditions were very heavy, and sometimes when he was hitting the forehand, he was kind of shaking the wrist, and grimacing a bit. I knew he was having problems with it, but obviously you never know how bad it is." We're way too used to Rafa being injured but being able to play great tennis in spite of it. And at Roland-Garros, we tend to decide that whatever happens, Nadal will be the one to beat here. Federer once said he created a monster, but he's not the only one to have done this in the past decade.

In the meantime, Djokovic was at work on centre court with one of the next generation's gems: the Croatian Borna Coric. Novak had been playing a bit of a mentor's role with him for a while, agreeing that the similarities between them were quite real. I watched Borna hitting with Goffin on court 1 on Tuesday and he was a disaster: balls were flying all over the court, rarely inside of it. He was going nuts. But on this Friday against Novak, from the part I saw, it was a great session. The ball striking quality was excellent and Borna was pretty pumped. The full Djokovic team was reunited as his physiotherapist

Miljan Amanovic, working with Novak since 2007, was now also there, whereas Stefan Duell had taken this part the past few days. Novak looked relaxed and hyper-focused. His looseness while hitting was superb, which with him is the sign that his head is in a good place, that nothing is coming between his mind and his shots. He was hitting as clean as ever, meaning that for now he was winning his internal battle against pressure and stress.

In the midst of this practice spying job, what finally kicked in for me was those top players' practice rituals: all season long you'd see Djokovic and Murray hitting together, Nadal and Murray too, or Wawrinka and Djokovic, or Federer and Wawrinka. And when I was again thinking of how interesting it was to watch those big rivals basically working together, my brain got lost in one question: have I ever watched Djokovic and Nadal hitting together? Nadal and Federer? Federer and Djokovic? Nope. Maybe it happened back in their young days, but from recent memories since they were all together at the top of the game, I couldn't remember a single time. Maybe I missed it... But if I hadn't missed it, what was it saying about the Big 4 dynamics?

Muzz gave probably the most honest answer about it, in his usual deadpan way of saying things: "Well, they normally beat me so maybe they're a bit happier to practice with me." Was Murray, consciously or not, deemed harmless in the big finals so that there was no issue sharing the practice court with him? Or with the eventual tactical and technical advice the coach would give, or the eventual pains the physio would attend to?

A player like Goffin never hid the fact that he made a point to train with those guys in order to learn from them. So was this Big 4 practice habit saying a lot about how they thought it was actually "3 + 1"? I got some massive raised eyebrows from Nadal when asking about this practice situation, and a firm denial of any kind of "never with Novak or Roger" rule. "I don't have a problem practicing with anybody. I am always open to practice with any player, no? I don't know. I didn't prepare the practice. That's the real thing, no? With Toni and his coach I think in Rome or Madrid they fixed the practice for that day, and that's it. For me, I really don't care. I can practice without any problem with Novak or with Roger. No problem."

Asking Novak, he found a way around speaking about Nadal and Federer, to focus on Andy. Still admitting that ranking and rivalry might play a part at some point. "I mean, no particular reason. I've known Andy for a very long time. Yes, certainly things are different now when we are n°1 and 2 in the world than they were maybe five or ten years ago when we even played doubles together at the Australian Open. But we still kept a very respectful friendly relationship off the court, and on the court, of course we do want to win against each other, but it's never against the opponent, never with any intention to do anything against your rival. As long as it's like that, of course I'm more than happy to practice with him."

What came back from Djokovic and Murray was also the fact that practice between the top ones meant a guaranteed high level. "That's probably the best possible hit I can have, you know, best possible preparation for any match because our practice sessions are like official matches," said Novak. "Honestly, we practiced in Madrid recently and we played a set and a half. We both felt like we played a match, you know. So it's good. Not all the time, I guess, because it's not easy to always keep that kind of high level of concentration and intensity when you're playing against one of your top rivals. Sometimes it's also not easy to practice against one of your biggest rivals, because there is always, I guess, the element in that practice which mentally you don't want to seem like something is wrong with you. You always want to be at your best. But on the other hand, from the other perspective, it's actually good that you are trying extra hard and putting out extra effort, because then you train better. You put more quality, more intensity in the training. But of course it's something you're looking forward to and to see where you are and things that you need to work on."

A little spy game never hurts. Murray agrees: "Sometimes I haven't practiced with either of them for a while, but, yeah, I have hit with them over the years a lot. You know, especially sort of before the big events or at the beginning of the year. You don't actually learn loads about their game when you're practicing with them, but it's great practice. Why not get the best practice possible before big events? Intensity is high obviously when you're playing against the best players. You know, you want to practice well. And there's a little bit more incentive there in the practice. It helps me, I think."

In this word "help" maybe lies the main reason why Nadal, Federer and Djokovic weren't sharing the practice courts: why would they take the risk of helping each other when each of their battles for tennis history has been one long and hard nerve wracking battle? No reason. I'm curious to see how this practice habit will evolve now that Murray has proved that the little bro could still steal his big bros' toys. In their first tournament of the 2017 season, in Doha, nothing had changed yet, as Novak posted a picture of him and Andy on Twitter, thanking him for a great warm up. It's quite fascinating that neither the ranking battle, nor the Grand Slam finals matches nor everything at stake on court between them has had any negative effect on their off court relationship. At this level of professional sports, it's pretty rare.

Far away from those considerations, a big part of the tournament had already been played. The draw was out. As I already told you: I wasn't there. So: thank you, replay. The 2015 champions, Stan Wawrinka and Serena Williams, weren't the ones doing the draw that time, as the French Tennis Federation (FFT) had chosen to get involved in Paris' bid for the 2024 Olympic Games. Hence why French track and field icon Marie-José Pérec, triple Olympic champion (400m in 1992, 200m and 400m in 1996) and Tony Estanguet, triple Olympic champion in canoe, now vice-president of the IOC athletes committee, were in charge. Then FFT president Jean Gachassin stated the obvious: "Through the years, it remains a moment we're waiting for impatiently."

After the women's draw was sorted, it was the men's turn. On the screen, a picture of Stan Wawrinka holding the trophy after last year's final was set between the two sides of the draw. Unseeded players were placed electronically along with some calming music, and then Pérec came to sort out the tokens that were inside the "Coupe des Mousquetaires," under the supervision of Stefan Fransson and Rémy Azémar, supervisor and assistant supervisor. It was time to decide which one of the third and fourth seeds would land at the top of the draw and so with Djokovic... And Pérec with her right hand got the number 4 out. Provoking a discrete but sonorous "woaaaaaah" through the ranks. A kind of sorry smile could be seen on Pérec's face. It was official: Nadal on Djokovic's side. Obviously.

The landscape for the Paris drama was all set up. It would have been fitting to suddenly see and hear Elizabeth Banks throwing her now infamous "May the odds be ever in your favor" line from the "Hunger Games" movie. This or the "There can be only one" from Highlander, Adrian Paul version if you ask me.

After the shock that can be a Grand Slam draw, a perfect scenario demands seeing the faces and reactions of those involved. And, right before a Grand Slam event, one also wants to weigh those contestants' emotions, stress levels, confidence levels, to see who is upset by his or her draw, who can still smile, etc. So Roland-Garros tradition sees the media day happening right after the draw. Main top seeds, men and women, come one after the other to talk to the written press and radio and television reporters in the main interview room situated in the media centre inside the centre court building. At 4pm, it was Djoker's time, right after Nadal and Murray. Business as usual in Paris for Novak: "How do you feel this year for this one Grand Slam title you've never won? You're 29 now, any sense of urgency? Could you imagine it not happening?" And again Djokovic set the mood for his 2016 campaign: don't hit the panic button, be Mister Zen as long as you can.

So could he picture himself never winning Roland-Garros? "I can, because so far it hasn't happened," he laughed. "So I'm imagining it every day. But I'm also imagining myself, you know, being the winner. So let's see what life has organized for me... But if it doesn't happen, there is always another year, because I don't have any intention of slowing down yet. On the other hand if it never happens, I need to be very humble and realistic and see my results and career: I need to be satisfied with what I have achieved so far. Even if my career was done tomorrow, I made some achievements that I must be proud of."

We were so far from the same Djokovic who, in 2013, made the interview room staff announce that he wouldn't answer any questions about Nadal and this potential semi-final. Who looked so stressed out right from the get go. In 2014 he looked better, until he ended being a ball of nerves for the final against Rafa. In 2015, he had no issue talking about Rafa who had landed in his quarter, but would still fist pump nearly every point won in the last two games of their match (7-5, 6-3, 6-1), even crossing himself several times and looking up to the sky.

We won't ever know how it would have ended this time, but one thing was sure: Djokovic was no longer afraid of the idea of facing Rafa in Roland-Garros. As if he accepted that the only person who could make him lose here now was himself.

Yet, he wasn't of course denying the pressure building around him: it's just that this time he looked like he had found a better shield for it. "Of course the expectations are big not just from my side but from people around knowing that this is the only Grand Slam I never won. Of course people, you know, are very eager to find out whether or not I can make it this year, and that kind of anticipation was present also in the last couple of years. So it's not the first time I get to encounter this kind of sensation and pressure and so forth. I played ten matches in two weeks, which is the maximum I could get out of Madrid and Rome, and it was a perfect way of getting the match play that I needed before the French Open. So I can comfortably say that in terms of match play I'm ready."

That's the feeling I had that year about the vibe that would be around Novak through those two weeks: it would all be about him and his demons, but this time the safety net would be stronger. He was arriving as the undisputed boss: winning Melbourne, Indian Wells and Miami back to back, then Madrid, then reaching the final in Rome. Murray was a threat, obviously, but his record against Djokovic in Grand Slams was in favor of Novak. With Federer out and Nadal still searching a bit for his vintage self, everyone had decided this title was for Novak to lose. And the crowd, faced with the potential of witnessing history being made, had also decided it was his time. No one since Rod Laver (1962, 1969) had won four Majors in a row. No one since Jim Courier in 1992 had won the first two legs of the Grand Slam season. And only seven players had ever completed a Career Slam.

And despite even bigger pressure than the years before, it was in 2016 that Djokovic found a way to handle it better than in the past. It would still be emotionally complicated but yet there was among this natural tension a little touch of serenity that wasn't there before. "I feel like Roland-Garros has contributed a lot to my maturity mentally, and I guess to my comprehension of my mental ability and strength," he would tell me months later. "I felt that 2016 was a perfect time for me to achieve that. But this time in approaching it (especially the latter stages of the event), I was not carried away too much. I was excited to be in the semi-finals and finals but I wasn't too satisfied...I wasn't too peaceful about it, but I wasn't too hectic about it. I just kept the right balance and I wanted to stay there. It was an effort! I had to use the experience from before, I had to work every day mentally with myself, listen to my inner voice and kind of convince myself that I had the ability to do that, which I felt and believed, but at the same time if I didn't do it, it was not the end of the world. Whereas the approach was quite different the years before: it was like it's now or never. As a top player I've been enjoying this privileged status but with it you're also paying the price of pressure and expectations that are constantly there, from yourself and from all the other people. And so to add more to that is not necessary. It's always a kind of juggling I believe: just the right amount of intensity but yet composure. It's life-forming. And trying to find an optimum state of mind in everything that you do. That's why 2016 Roland-Garros was right at the peak of my own capabilities in every aspect."

It was also it seemed at the peak of the crowd's appreciation of who Novak was and of what he was trying to achieve. From his first practice to the final match point, he'd be watched as the one walking to his destiny in a warmth I have never witnessed around him before in those events. Had he suffered so much here for them to think "enough!"? Maybe. But his opponents, the weather and mainly his own demons would still test him until the very end. Yet, he had to feel even stronger that year as he had been on a rampage for at least 18 months.

CHAPTER TWO

Ruler Extraordinaire

When you're about to face your biggest career hurdle, it's nice to arrive in full confidence at the bottom of the mountain. Of course it had already been the case for Novak in Paris, especially in 2011 and 2015, but this time one would say the stars were aligning even better. Novak was ruling the Tour for a good 18 months. Sure he had lost the French Open final against Stan Wawrinka in 2015 but before that and since he was close to unbeatable. Truth be told, the fact that this 2016 Roland-Garros could be "The One" was making even more sense in this domination context. It felt like the last obstacle before the master achievement, the last crown for a player whose dominance was already setting him among the greatest rulers of the history of the game.

Since winter 2015, he had played the finals of the last five Grand Slams, winning four of them: the Australian Open 2015 (against Murray), Wimbledon 2015 (against Federer), US Open 2015 (against Federer), Australian Open 2016 (against Murray). As he had lost the final in Paris against Wawrinka, it meant that he played all Grand Slam finals of the 2015 season, in which he also contested 15 straight finals. He won nine Masters 1000 in this period and clinched the ATP World Tour Finals title for the fourth time in a row, a feat no one before had ever accomplished. When he arrived in Paris that May 2016, he had collected 16 titles through this rampage and had only lost three matches since the start of the season. Around La Porte d'Auteuil, the Man On A Mission was also looking like one of the Avengers.

And it wasn't just a thing coming from the media as the whole locker room was starting to feel hopeless and resigned. In Rome 2015, on the draw that was kept in the players' lounge, one of the guys had written Novak's name in the winner's box. The tournament hadn't even started. In January 2016, Gilles Simon echoed the lasting feeling before facing the Serbian in the fourth round of the Australian Open: the ranks were getting tired of being annihilated: "Players are starting to have enough of this," the Frenchman said in L'Equipe newspaper[5]. "Everyone feels a bit humiliated. It's not that Novak has become arrogant but I know a lot of people will push for me in the locker room. Nearly everybody." Simon is on good terms with Djokovic so it wasn't coming from a bad place.

It's mostly that the Djokovic period of dominance was turning into a trauma. Through the 2015 season, Novak counted 31 wins against Top 10 players and had beaten each and every one of them in the same year. No one had done it before. Simon would indeed push Djokovic to his limits, in a five set match (6-3, 6-7, 6-4, 4-6, 6-3) that will remain in history for the 100 unforced errors the boss hit that day through what was a tennis version of a nervous crisis, and this for four and a half hours. "He got all the mistakes of a whole year! For all year!!," can still laugh Vajda while remembering that stat. Simon was voluntarily playing lifeless balls in the middle of the court, returning one after another ball back and Novak was just going ballistic. After the match point, he didn't even smile: that's how mad he was.

But the hard reality for the rest of the pack was that even on a terrible day, Djokovic could still get away with the win. So as much as he was upset by his level of play that day, he knew that he had probably depressed the locker room even more: "In terms of level, it's a match to forget for me. But again, I won it, so it's pretty good. When you're playing that bad and still manage to win..." Asked to comment on Simon's words about the locker room hoping he'd lose, Djokovic decided to let the Djoker inside of him answer. "Which locker room? Yeah, I read that but he didn't specify which locker room." The colleague insisted and reformulated the question, but still got a Djoker

---

5. "Contre Novak Djokovic, Gilles Simon pense avoir le soutien de tout le vestiaire.", L'Equipe.fr, January 23, 2016 (*http://www.lequipe.fr/Tennis/Actualites/Contre-novak -djokovic-gilles-simon-pense-avoir-le-soutien-de-presque-tout-le-vestiaire/627328*).

answer. "Again, I don't know which locker room he's talking about. Women's locker room? I'm pretty popular, I know that," Novak said, laughingly.

That's the only thing he would say about the miserable condition of his rivals. Their frustration wasn't his business. That's also how Djokovic had been for years now paving his own path to domination, and how one can understand that when he arrived in Paris in 2016 the confidence taken from the past 18 months was just adding new evidence to what he had already achieved for so long, and to the belief he always had in himself. The last huge boost for someone who for a decade had been convinced of belonging at the top. Novak Djokovic couldn't be stronger than he was when he set his first foot in Paris in 2016. "In 2015 until that French Open, he was at the peak of everything," is how Gritsch saw it. "From 2011, there's no doubt that he improved his game a lot, and sure everybody was trying to improve too, but for the first time in his life I think he had the feeling that nobody could beat him. He achieved such a level of game that he knew that if he played at his top level he'd win."

A couple of months after this latest Australian triumph, I would ask his coach Marian Vajda about the consequences of this huge amount of confidence Novak had gained during a year at least. A period he told me at the end of the 2015 season that was stronger than the already fantastic 2011: "Novak is much more solid than in 2011. Much more confident. Much more experienced. I think it's much better this year because he proved it with much more dominance."

This dominance was still going strong in March 2016 when we talked. "He's really maintaining his game, his level every time, every day, every practice," said the Slovakian coach. "He's always looking for a good preparation, even though he has played a lot of matches, but especially in the matches he always finds a good rhythm and a good focus. He loves to play matches, he's a competitive guy. His motivation is amazing, fantastic: he wants to win every match. He sees the perspective but can also focus on the present so this is great. Motivation comes from the results as he's winning, but also he's not overconfident: he could be overconfident after winning everything, right? (laughs) But this also can be counter productive. Perspective gives you a lot of confidence."

The key was also to keep going in making him work on his game: "There's always something to improve, even when you work with such a player: one day he's losing the rhythm on the backhand, maybe next day his forehand isn't working. We have to always work on his skills, on what is the most perfect performance of Novak and try to reach that level. If he's a little off, we try to find the best motivation to get there. And mentally he can do it, it's amazing: he always can get there, to the best level in practice and then doing it in the match. And he's not very happy when he's not doing it so it's amazing how he always wants to do everything a little better. He knows where he can get. This is Novak: he wants to win all the points, doesn't get satisfied with one point (laughs). Probably that's why he's so strong. He's very motivated, and both feet remain on the ground."

Before the start of the clay season, Djokovic had already built a comfortable cushion of confidence. By winning titles but also by the way he won some of the matches leading to the trophies. Back to January and his first tournament of the year in Doha, he won a classic over Rafael Nadal in the final (6-1, 6-2), absolutely trouncing the Spaniard, hitting winner after winner. It was his 16th final in a row and to sum up the impression he left, nothing could be better than quoting the guy who had to go through the beat up: "It's difficult to imagine anyone can play that good," said Rafa at the time. Voilà.

No doubt it was the same feeling for Roger Federer after their semi-final a short while after in Melbourne. Long was the day of the 100 unforced errors, as Novak clinched the first set of what should have been a blockbuster, 6-1 in 22 minutes! I was seated right in front of the Swiss colleagues in the stadium for this one: the shock was real. Totally caught off guard, Federer was like the boxer cornered and taking punches. Novak was returning like in a dream and hitting passing shot winners I was not sure were even possible to make. After a second set won 6-2, everybody in the arena was just left with mouths wide open. Nobody toys with Federer, except Nadal on clay, but that's what Djokovic was doing. Someone had reached the last level of the PlayStation game.

Unable to handle the speed from the baseline, Federer changed his strategy when the beat up of all beat ups was looming. He took some pace off, started to slice his backhand way more to try to kill his rival's flawless timing. And it worked for a set (6-3). But that's all he would get, as Djokovic regrouped and adjusted soon enough to clinch the fourth set and the match (6-3). A master class put on The Master. Unreal. Federer didn't beat around the bush after that match: "I've seen Novak play this well before. It's tough when it's from the start because obviously you've got to try to stop the bleeding at some point, you know. Because he returns very well, like Andre Agassi. He can get one or two sets all of a sudden. Those sets run away very quickly. Before you can really sometimes do something, you know, 45 minutes and a lot of tennis is being played and it's tough to get back into it. I found a way. Started to play better myself. Made a bit of a match out of it, which was nice. When he gets on a roll, it's tough to stop. Novak right now is a reference for everybody."

Top players are used to raising their level in the last rounds of a Grand Slam tournament, but it wasn't that Novak had raised his level: he was a totally different player than the one who had qualified for the semi-finals. Confronted with one of his greatest rivals, he had let all his claws out: no more over thinking, no more lack of focus, no more routine mistakes, no more choking. Totally locked in. "I've had matches where I've played similar tennis," he said after that match. "But I think against Roger, these first two sets have been probably the best two sets I've played against him overall throughout my career. When you're playing one of your top rivals, somebody of Roger's résumé, of course it requires a lot of focus, determination, and a different preparation for that matchup than most of the other matches. So that's why I came out with I think a great deal of self-belief and confidence and intensity, concentration. I mean, I played flawless tennis for the first two sets, no doubt about it."

You couldn't find anyone not impressed by Novak's level, and the great Rod Laver himself was astonished: "Looking at the mistakes, I think Novak had maybe five mistakes in those two sets," the Australian legend said. "It was just quite incredible the speed he was getting around the court and being able to hit great shots down the line, just an inch inside the line. I don't think Roger was negative in hitting any groundstrokes. It looked like he was doing pretty well with the groundstrokes when he came to the net, but Novak had all the answers and he played beautifully."

After a 2015 season that was already among the greatest ever played, the Serb was showing the whole tennis world he had no intention of slowing down. With this win over the Swiss, he was now leading the confrontations against Nadal, Murray and Federer for the first time in his career. On the court that day after beating Federer, Djokovic talked about making sure that his "convictions would be bigger than" his "doubts": it's a good summary of how he took the leadership.

In the Australian Open 2016 final, Djokovic would see his confidence growing again after defeating Andy Murray (6-1, 7-5, 7-6(3)), but after the first set he really had to dig deep and that match was neck and neck. Those two were at their very best and some of the rallies were insane, like their 2015 final here. Once again, Novak would have the last word, a record sixth title in Melbourne and his Grand Slam titles count was now 11. It had been the perfect launch pad for the season of course but mostly for the French Open, Novak's goal of the year. He had the first leg of the Grand Slam season in the bag, and was now off to get the second one.

And indeed the months to come would be all his, despite a retirement in the quarters in Dubai against Feliciano Lopez due to an eye infection, and a grueling Davis Cup match won against Mikhail Kukushkin of Kazakhstan in five sets, 94 unforced errors and 5 hours of play. Then Djokovic would win the Masters 1000 of Indian Wells against Milos Raonic (6-2, 6-0), with a new win over Nadal (7-6(5), 6-2) in the semis, and the Masters 1000 of Miami against Kei Nishikori (6-3, 6-3), looking like someone who had forgotten how to lose. He'd lose only one set through these two events. It was the fourth time that Novak succeeded in the Indian Wells - Miami double, something he had already been the first to do three times in 2015. There was just no stopping him.

When asked about this "Djokovic era," some top coaches of the Tour, among them many who had tried to make their players beat the Djoker, just stated what had become the obvious: when Novak is at his best, there is just no way around or through that guy. The Swedish coach Mikael Tillström was in Gaël Monfils box for the 2016 US Open semi-final the French played and lost (6-3,6-2,3-6,6-2) in front of Djokovic. For him, it's the non stop pressure put on by the

Serb that makes all his opponents crumble or hit their heads against the wall. "The better you serve, the faster the ball comes back," he told me after that match in New York. Not angry, not desperate, just realistic in admiring the mastery: "Then you're forcing and forcing, and so missing. Then the scoreline becomes the stress. He puts a lot of pressure so suddenly it's 5-0. It's not easy to play your best tennis against Novak because of the pressure he puts on you: you hardly ever get an easy service game to hold. You're constantly under pressure. It becomes 'What am I going to do?' and if you don't change something it can become very ugly. He's really tough. Agassi had it on his best days, Roger too: they put this type of pressure where you don't know how to win one game. Also his returning is so lethal that it's almost like he's serving to you on the baseline: that's how fast the ball comes back. First two shots against Novak: that's where everything changes. Novak does that to you, makes you feel like your best shot isn't there and makes you always be the one chasing."

I remember the Canadian player Milos Raonic also explaining that Djokovic wouldn't give the same ball twice, and that he wasn't having patterns you could build on, and worse that he was making a point of having no patterns you could build on. Raonic has one of the biggest serves of the Tour, and still is 0-8 in their head to head with only one set won. In 2014, in the final of the Masters 1000 in Paris in November, Raonic lost 6-2, 6-3. Indoors, with a serve that most of the players can't even touch on Milos' good days. So what happens against Novak? He just starts returning as if he knows in advance where the ball is going to land, and sends it right back at Raonic who then starts to question each serve he hits, and then gets dispatched from the baseline as he can't match Djokovic's footwork. Of course then Raonic would come to the net... to better be pierced by relentless passing shots. A case in point of the Djokovic "Method To Destroy An Opponent" even when the guy is much taller and bigger than you.

And Djokovic has a different plan for every other type of opponent, as there's also a chameleon in him with a good side of chess master. For Thierry Van Cleemput, who is coaching Belgian star David Goffin: from 2015 to the French Open 2016, "Novak was maybe, we'll never know, the best ever during this period." And the technician that Van Cleemput is can't do anything but marvel at what Novak has brought to the table: "In Djokovic, there's something that is extraordinary and that can't be matched: his timing. He has a tempo that can't be compared to anyone else's: he's always in the right rhythm. He also has this ability to adjust very quickly. I've known him since his young days and I sometimes saw him searching in the wrong direction but very quickly he would focus again on his strengths to get everything he could out of his own potential. So yes he can play as well on clay as on any other surface, and from the moment he decides he won't miss anything anymore, he won't. I saw it with David (Goffin) at practice so many times! You feel David is playing amazing, and he is, but he's not winning any game because on the other side it's even better and Novak won't miss." Van Cleemput even dates the start of Djokovic's dominance back to 2014. Like the Serbian picked up where this wonder of 2011 had left him, erasing seasons in between where his doubts had once again gotten bigger than his beliefs in the last stages.

I know that some colleagues left Rome, after the May 15th final won by Andy Murray, thinking Novak Djokovic showed again that he was vulnerable on clay. There was a bit of truth there: Novak showed moments of vulnerability between Madrid and Rome. Nadal after all had been up a break in both their sets in their Italian quarter final. Nishikori could have won in the semis too, and Murray pushed him in Spain and beat him in Italy. Not to forget that the Djoker lost in his first match on clay in Monte-Carlo against the Czech Jiri Vesely. Sure he was looking more nervous than the previous months. Someone even asked Murray after his semi-final if he was also finding that Djokovic wasn't playing as well as last season: "The general feeling is that he is not playing as well as last year or has not the same confidence.". Novak had lost only two matches this season, but when a player is dominating like this and has been playing that well for months, it seems you can get picky. I went out of Novak's quarter and semi-final in Rome thinking: "Yes, clay is still challenging for his nerves but lord how good were those matches that he still won at the end?"

And Murray shared my feeling as he seemed a bit intrigued by the question before answering. "I mean, if you call Djokovic's level "not as well as last year" and he still has beaten you all the time, that's not really looking optimistic for your future! I don't know, to be honest. I saw a little bit of yesterday's match: I think it was a very, very good level, for sure. But I think Novak has played extremely well this year. You know, maybe he's not played perfectly in all of the matches he's played, but he's winning and that is a sign of someone that's very confident. So it's really impossible to say. When he's played the big matches at the end of tournaments he's improved his game. Maybe the start of some of the tournaments he's not start-of-the-tournament fantastic, but he's finished most of them very well." His main rival wasn't going to be fooled into thinking or hoping Djokovic's level would drop. He's been on the receiving end of enough of Novak's returns to know better than that.

And I still thought the same after this final between them in Rome. Not only because Djokovic was obviously exhausted on that Sunday, having started his semi-final at 8pm the day before, and ending close to midnight. So I wasn't exactly sure what to take out of this match, except the fact that those two guys would be the heavy favorites in Paris. Murray, his back now co-operating, had found a way to make his game efficient on dirt. And he had worked so much on his serve lately that it was back to being a huge weapon.

More importantly, he finally believed he could win in Paris: it was written all over his face. Through this 6-3, 6-3 victory against Novak on his birthday, he had been so steady in his will. He had showed Novak that the door would be closed. He had ruined every initiative of the Serbian, be it by an ace, a huge defense or a fantastic counter punch. There had been no way through him for a Djoker whose legs weren't reacting fast enough that day, damaging his accuracy too much. It was also raining so the court and balls were heavy, making it even more impossible to find a crack in Andy's game. Arguing with the umpire would do nothing: they would be playing under the rain. After this match, it was as clear as in Madrid: Novak's only option to beat this version of Murray was to be at his very best, going lights out.

Here was maybe the worst news for Djokovic, added to a resurgent Rafael Nadal. So he should have looked worried, right? He should have looked tight? He should have been annoyed at how the Rome final went? He should, but he didn't. And that's why I left Rome thinking that this guy was, after these past couple of weeks, exactly where he wanted to be before Paris, Rome title or not, rivals or not. He got the match play, he was pushed to his limits, his mental strength was tested. And as a bonus he also got in Madrid the Masters 1000 titles record: 29 (He would go to 30 that same season after winning in Toronto). And as a second bonus, he became the equal of Bjorn Borg and Pete Sampras with 64 singles titles.

There wasn't the slight sense of worry or concern on his face when he came to meet the press after the final, already ready to take the first flight home. And it wasn't a posture at all: his brain had already switched to Paris and was looking at Rome as if his last test was done and conclusive. He was lucid enough to acknowledge he couldn't stand a chance in this final: "To compete with Andy in long exchanges and rallies that we do have in our encounters, that required a lot more energy and a better performance from my side, which didn't happen. Not taking anything away from Andy's win: he deserved to win and deserved to win the entire tournament, because he was the best player." And then, that it was all still boding well for Paris: "All in all, it was very good two weeks after, you know, dropping out in Monte-Carlo early. I needed this kind of result, winning one tournament and playing a finals is great. I got what I was looking for, a lot of matches, and confidence and, you know, I spent a lot of hours playing on the clay, which now, leading up to Roland Garros is exactly what I need. Hopefully it's going to help me perform well in Paris."

Any doubt that could have inserted itself in his mind was already brushed off: "I already had enough time spent on the clay courts. Now it's just fine-tuning. It's getting those energy supplies that I will need for later on. You know, my confidence level is high because of the matches, many matches that I have won this year on this surface and all the other surfaces. So I don't feel that I'm doubtful or I'm shaken up by this loss." He didn't look as if he was trying to convince himself here; he was basically sending out a warning, a "game on" statement.

He was maybe even more confident at that moment than some members of his team, as Boris Becker didn't leave Rome totally serene. "Great week but shit final, excuse me," he'd tell me months later to sum up the event. "So we felt a little bit nervous about how he would pick it up." But still probably less nervous than all the team, Novak included, felt when they landed in Madrid in the first week of May, after having been ousted in the first match on clay at the Monte-Carlo Rolex Masters.

Since 2013, the only Djokovic you could see in Madrid was this big picture of him in the "Celicioso" bakery, selling only gluten free products. For the rest, no trace of the Serb at the Caja Magica since his second round loss against Grigor Dimitrov in 2013. He had won here in 2011, then joined the protest against the blue clay in 2012 and lost in the quarter finals. In 2013, he had badly twisted an ankle at a Davis Cup tie but still managed to win in Monte-Carlo against Rafael Nadal. A little earthquake, that totally turned him into "public enemy number 1" in Spain when he landed there. Against Dimitrov, he had the whole arena against him from start to finish, and couldn't resist several times telling them what he thought about it. He was not to be seen on centre court again before 2016. Novak has always denied it was because of how he was treated that day: truth is that he had a right arm injury in 2014 through the Monaco event, and had played a lot at the start of 2015. Madrid being played in altitude on totally different conditions than Roland-Garros didn't help.

But in May 2016, Djokovic made his comeback on Nadal's turf and sounded pretty upbeat about it. "I'm excited obviously to get back on the clay courts," he stated during his first press conference in Spain. "I didn't do that well in Monte-Carlo; that wasn't really a fun time on the court, so I hope I can have a few more matches during this week. I was really looking forward to stepping on the court and competing because I haven't played a competitive match on clay courts for three weeks. I needed some match play... So I'm glad that I arrived here earlier, had some very good practice sessions."

He was indeed in a tricky situation as he had only played one match on clay, and badly needed to get comfortable again on the dirt before Paris. Losing early in Madrid would be a bit of a disaster for his preparation, and so for his confidence. So there was an obvious relief when he won against Borna Coric (6-2,6-4). His coach Marian Vajda didn't deny at the time that they were in a bit of a time trial. "Clay is always special. Clay: it's different, you have to adjust and sometimes it's harder than other times. If he plays more matches, he'll get used to it. Clay is hard work. You cannot play 'boom boom boom': no chance. This was more clay court match today, I liked it. After the loss in

Monte-Carlo, he had one week off: he was tired. I think it helped him, cause he rested a little bit more. We started the preparation ten days ago."

Vajda was pretty intense talking about the situation the team was in. Paris was looming, no doubt, and so the pressure too. "Obviously, it's the French Open he wants to win, so obviously there must be some kind of pressure as he hasn't won it yet. But he has to feel better on the clay by playing more matches before coming to Paris. Maybe he's a little bit more nervous now, but once he gets to Paris, having more matches on clay and getting used to it, he'll be relieved. He needs to first find his clay court game, has to be patient. Clay, it hurts." I wish there was a way here to show you Vajda when he uttered the last sentence: eyes locked in, a clenched fist, and no smile. It was clearly the face that Novak was now confronting in practice every day: yes, it's going to hurt but no, you're not going to complain and go around it. Boris Becker had also made the trip, but just for a few days of practice and he was to leave the next day.

Despite the mounting pressure, you could feel the effect of the amazing start of the season on Novak: the confidence won the past few weeks through another victory in Melbourne followed by doing the Indian Wells - Miami double for an unprecedented fourth time, where he also beat Roger Federer's prize money record with an impressive 98,2 million dollars at the time. On June 1st he would become the first professional tennis player ever to reach the 100 million dollar prize-money-in-a-career mark. So the loss in Monte-Carlo had only been a tiny scratch on his confidence mattress.

His mood was mostly joyful with a light-hearted humor. For example, he - as all of us in the Madrid press interview room - was dying in the heat. For some reason, AC was persona non grata there. But being the n°1 player in the world gives you some leverage so as he asked if there was a way for them to let him breathe, the AC was turned on. And then we all understood why it was off before: the price to pay for freshness was a lot of noise. All looking at each other in a "yep, that won't do" way, we heard Novak asking in a laugh "Is it air con or a spaceship?" prompting laughter all around. A joking Novak is a serene Novak. The evening of the 4th of May after his win against Coric, he would also be seen with his brother Marko at Santiago Bernabéu for Real Madrid's Champions League game, finding a way to hug Nadal there in the process but also to pose for pictures with Ronaldo, the Brazilian legend.

This peace of mind would be confirmed through the whole tournament as he would then easily defeat Roberto Bautista Agut (6-2, 6-1), dispatch Milos Raonic (6-3, 6-4), and pass his first big test with success against Kei Nishikori (6-3, 7-6(4)) with an impressive level of play. Only in the money time of that match would he show that pressure could still get to him. At 5-4 and 40-0 Novak had three match points to qualify for the final and end what had been a routine display of dominance. But he missed on an open court at 40-0 and then crumbled until the loss of his serve, despite four match points. He'd be shaky until the end, losing three straight points in the tie-break from 2-0 then finding a way to convert his fifth match point. At the end, it was a very good win for building his confidence on clay. "Knowing that I missed four match points, I then was really solid after that. I think mentally it's good to go through these particular situations for confidence."

Now back in a Madrid final, he had to face a resurgent Andy Murray, who since the birth of his daughter in February and a rough time at Indian Wells and Miami, was coming back strong on clay, having played the semi-finals in Monte-Carlo and making a new wave in Spain by beating Nadal (7-5, 6-4) for the second time in two years here. Apart from the title, there were other things at stake for both of them in this final: Murray was at this time trying to keep his n°2 ranking, and so being sure to avoid seeing Novak in his side of the draw in Paris, and Novak had a shot to match the 64 career titles of Pete Sampras, and to get to 29 Masters 1000, one unit better than Nadal to get the record back.

As the 2016 tennis season trend required, it was raining the day of the final but it stopped just at the right time and the roof was opened before the Djokovic - Murray final. That would be the first of their three acts on the dirt this season and for that one, as the road to Paris was well on the way, it was also about the mental edge one was going to win or lose against the other. Novak started like in a dream (6-2), as he pulled Andy apart: too fast, too accurate, too aggressive. But like in a repeat of their tennis relationship, Murray came back on Novak's heels (6-3) by showing the same resolve he would display all season. Being a wall but also taking his chances, he would also show how much his serve had really improved since that back surgery at the end of the 2013 season, as well as his movement.

In a blink, he took the second set (6-3) whereas Novak's focus was all over the place. Djokovic wouldn't feel comfortable against Murray until the end of the match but he would still find a way to cross the finish line first. Up 2-0, he committed two double faults among the rest, but he regrouped to take a 4-2 lead, the foot pushing on the gas pedal: backhands down the line, forehands like missiles. But that was the thing: he had no margin anymore. Murray was bringing back everything, pushing Djokovic to aim for the lines. On the red, he was also pushing the Djoker on the edge, confirming their French Open semi-final the previous season. Novak was now fully aware of the Muzz-on-clay threat for 2016. Even more that he had all the issues of the world to have the last word over him. Sure he'd been up 5-2 and had a match point at 5-3 after a double fault from Murray. But an ace killed that hope, and Novak found himself down 0-40 while serving for the title at 5-3.

He was tight but still had a nice cushion of confidence, masterly built since January, so back he was at 40A. He would have to save three more break points before getting a second shot at the trophy in a thrilling last game. That he would miss thanks to a terrible forehand in the middle of the net. That forehand reasserted itself by sending a winner on Andy's seventh break point. And at Novak's third match point, the release would come after a forehand in the net from Andy. A smile, a deep breath of relief and Djokovic would cross himself and look at the sky, hitting his heart with his right hand.

On his way to Paris, he had taken a very important victory during this week in Madrid: he now got the match play and a level of confidence fully restored. "It came at the right time," he would say after the match. "I had an amazing opening four months of the season. Early exit in Monte-Carlo, but it happened for a reason, because I needed some time to really recharge my batteries. Three weeks was more than enough to get some freshness and new breath. It will definitely serve as a great confidence boost."

In the same red T-shirt and white shorts that had seen him win that Sunday in Madrid, he would lose a week later in Rome to the same Murray, but both would leave Italy with a smile. They had displayed an even much better level of play through that Italian week, had sent a clear message to the rivals and were gearing up for Paris as the biggest favorites. They were ready. It was even easier for Djokovic to get over that loss as he knew that he had been put under the worst conditions possible, which wouldn't be the case in Roland-Garros: no way to play until midnight there and to be back the next day in the afternoon.

Also, he had faced and passed two amazing tests in back to back matches against two amazing players who had all the tools to crack him. There is little doubt in my mind that being pushed to the brink by Rafael Nadal and Kei Nishikori in Italy gave Novak the last drop of confidence in his game and his nerves that would in the end be crucial in Paris. He had been tested to the limits of both his body and his mind but hadn't surrendered: knowing what was waiting for him at Porte d'Auteuil, it was a bigger relief than clinching a new title in Rome. This year he had also played the three clay Masters 1000 for the first time since 2013 and was getting out of this for the most part undamaged. He had done everything he could to give himself the best possible preparation: there would be no "what if" feeling.

Yet, he had been close to arriving in Paris in neither such good shape nor state of mind. First came Monte-Carlo and this loss to Vesely in a match where, to put it simply, he wasn't ready at all. And it came as no surprise to his rival and friend Stan Wawrinka who had practiced with him before the start of the event: "It was the first match on clay for him," Wawrinka said at the time. "He wasn't playing really well. He was hesitating. He tried to play well, but he was not really into the match. I think he had a tough time in the States and to win back-to-back at Indian Wells and Miami was quite impressive. He spent a lot of energy there, came here early, practiced. He was playing very well but we could see that mentally and physically he was a bit tired. I think now he will be able to rest, practice and he will be ready for the big challenge: the French Open. That he lost in the first round will not change anything. On the contrary, it might help him rest a bit earlier."

A blessing in disguise? Novak mostly hoped it would put to rest a side of his recent reputation: "There is proof that nobody is unbeatable. It happened so many times in my career that I'd lose a match. It's not the first time. Obviously it's not easy to lose the match in terms of accepting it. But I have to congratulate my opponent, who played well and aggressively. And I was playing really, really bad. Really a poor performance... Practice week went well but I didn't feel that freshness the entire time. Eventually this was going to happen, and everything happens for a reason. I'm going to get some more time off, which I look forward to. Really, I had two days off after the beginning of the year. You never like to lose and kind of think that that's going to help your future. That's not the way I am. I don't calculate. Of course, Roland Garros is the big one on clay. This match today will not disturb my preparation for the rest of the season and what's coming up. I'm still confident. I still feel I'm playing the best tennis of my life."

He proved to be right. As it also maybe put extra pressure on him to do well in Madrid. Back on the wall in terms of getting enough playing time on clay, he was already locked in, focus-wise, since April. Yet, Patrick Mouratoglou wonders if it wasn't the opposite: if, by losing in Monte-Carlo and then in the Rome final, Djokovic's brain was somehow trying to trick him this time. "Novak arrived as the huge favorite in Paris the past couple of years: he was the n°1 in the world and was regularly beating Nadal in every clay tournament. But it kept ending badly... Mentally he wasn't approaching it nor playing it the right way at all. Like the 2013 semi-final or the 2014 final. So this year he did things differently, but I don't know how conscious of that he was. I don't think it was conscious actually... This time he arrived as the semi-favorite, because he didn't play as well as the years before. I felt it coming months before Paris; he was so nervous during the practice sessions, even before the start of the clay season. And it's logical: once the clay is looming, he knows why he's going there. So I think maybe he took some pressure off his shoulders by not playing as well as he used to on it."

Gebhard Gritsch was among the ones thinking that maybe the way the preparation went in 2016 indeed helped Novak's mind, as he'd explain to me. "I had the belief that it was better for him not to dominate all the tournaments before so he didn't have the pressure of all the media and everybody coming to him saying 'You're in top form, you need to win this one!'" Novak, through most of his career, has been extremely strong mentally but here it was different and it's so difficult to keep it up, because the pressure gets bigger and bigger, not smaller and smaller. You win more and you'd think it'd get down but no, especially in situations like this where you really think 'wow, I need to grab this chance now!'"

Djokovic indeed had to tango with danger again in Rome where the lefty Brazilian Thomaz Bellucci blasted him off of the court in the first set (6-0) of their round of 16. In the previous match, Stéphane Robert had also made him work on his tennis (7-5,7-5) and his mind as the atypical Frenchman drove him quite nuts more often than not with a game Novak couldn't predict at all. On his way to Paris, he wasn't in the mood for an UFO landing his way. Against Bellucci, he replaced the anger and frustration by self-deprecating irony: he put both arms in the air after winning his first service game at the start of the second set, and wouldn't let go of an ironical smirk. Being handed a bagel, as tennis people use to call a 6-0, didn't really fit well in Novak's 2016 French Open quest. So for some time until he took the lead in that match his face looked like a non stop "See what you've done? Are you proud of yourself? Universe, could you please tell me which trick you're playing on me again?" smirk. But he wasn't doubting he could turn this around: he was just astonished and massively displeased at finding himself in that situation.

Displaying one of his great abilities, Novak started to make some tactical adjustments, changing the ball quality he was sending to Bellucci, changing the hitting zones, and little by little starting to really dictate his will to his rival. So he had the last word (0-6, 6-3, 6-2) on a match that, had he lost it, could have created a tiny dent of doubt in his mind before Paris. On the contrary, now he was reinforced in the trust he could put in his game and also in his nerves. Then Nishikori and Nadal would be the last pieces to complete the formula that made sure he would feel ready to conquer Roland-Garros.

How do you know where you really are when you haven't been pushed? Sure if you destroy every opponent on your way, you gain great confidence and know you're for now way above the rest. But as you've never been tested, how are you going to react if somehow on the most important path someone takes a direct shot at you? Thanks to the Japanese and to his nemesis, Djokovic would know before his greatest challenge that even in that case he had the answers. That if his whole game was as lethal as since the start of the season, his spirit now was matched it. On a surface that demanded utmost patience, resistance to frustration, and lucidity, he had succeeded in setting his spirit in the right place. And who better than one of your greatest rivals to put your head and game right on top? No one.

I remember Andre Agassi saying that when he would face Sampras, the shape they were in or the ranking they had or how they had played in the tournaments before their battle wouldn't matter at all. "It's the rivalry," summed up the whole situation. Agassi said that it only took Sampras to see him on the other side of the net to raise his bar to the max. There are a lot of similarities in Djokovic's relationship with the rest of the Big 4, and this quarter final against Rafa would confirm it again. Two bulls locking horns, for hours.

French player Edouard Roger-Vasselin, who was still in the double draw, happened to be in the locker room with Novak and Rafa before their new battle. Impressed enough by what he saw, he tweeted: "Being in the lockers for their preparation ahead of the match is an incomparable privilege. #Rafadjoko #mental #guerrier." One more time, the journalist that I am regrets the "what happens in the locker, stays in the locker" players' law.

Nadal would start like a storm, taking advantage of windy conditions that were upsetting Djokovic's timing. He was his vintage self when hitting that forehand, and came close to a double break at 4-1 in that first set, but that's when Novak's "I won't get dispatched by him" gut feeling kicked in. In their rivalry, the Serbian was now the one dominating and that had massively calmed his nerves when he had to face Rafa one more time. As had the fact that he was probably the only player now with an efficient game plan to totally neutralize Nadal's main weapon: that lefty, powerful, heavy-on-the-top-spin, forehand.

That game plan included going boldly at the forehand, flirting with the lines and playing backhands in half volleys from the baseline: not for everybody's talent and nerves. Slowly but surely, Novak settled down and started to level that first set (4-4), going up 5-4 in a wonder of crossed backhand winners that pushed him into full Hulk mode to celebrate. Novak had awakened his own voice in Nadal's head. Rafa's best weapon kept being sent right back at him as once again it would land on Novak's best one. It was a new fight between the Mighty Forehand and the Almighty Backhand. The lefty was now misfiring a lot on his forehand, but the end of that set would see him fight like crazy, throwing everything he could at Novak. Who would answer back each time. That meant that the level of play was now crazily high and entertaining, with amazing points following outstanding ones.

Hence, when Djokovic finally clinched the first set (7-5), it was on what would be one of the best points of the season. Nadal was the attacking one, Djokovic close to the tarp and fighting like mad to put one more ball back. Rafa moved forward on an overhead: not enough. Then came forward again on a drop shot backhand volley, just to see Novak, after an exchange of out-of-this-world reflexes, nail a high forehand volley. Set, Djokovic. Roar and over the top celebration, Djokovic. Crowd: wild. This time, the Djoker was entirely back for the first time since Miami.

The importance of this match on Novak's route to Paris was not to be minimized, even less as he ended the first game of the second set by throwing his racquet on the ground then on the chair breaking one side of said chair in the process. A break had created this. Drama wouldn't leave that match, as Nadal would later call the trainer and tell his box that he couldn't feel his left foot anymore. The tape was apparently too tight so fortunately no extremity died that day and the match could resume. Nadal would get five set points with many big chances to close those points out but in vain. Including a terrible forehand drop shot. On his first break point, Djokovic would be back to 5-5 and then be as clutch as one can possibly be until the last point of this match (7-5, 7-6(4)), where he played ping pong with Nadal before finishing him off on a crossed backhand.

Rafa had proved that he was indeed coming back strongly now, but even on his best surface he was still coming up short against Novak against whom he had now lost 15 straight sets. In terms of mental edge, that wasn't a stat any top player wanted to have against another one. The Djoker had a huge smile on his face, going from one ear to another: one more piece of the puzzle on his road to la Porte d'Auteuil. "It felt definitely special to be on the court today playing against Rafa for several hours, two sets, very long. Thankfully we didn't play Grand Slams, best of five. Who knows when this match would have finished. Certainly winning against Nadal on clay doesn't happen every day, so it is one of the ultimate challenges if not the ultimate challenge we have in sports. So I'm going to take this as a boost of confidence, no doubt, for the rest of this tournament and then of course for the French Open. And also take into consideration Nadal is in form, you know. I think he's been playing much better than he did in clay court season last year. He won Monte-Carlo, Barcelona, he won many matches on clay courts, started to feel more comfortable on the court. He misses less and he's more aggressive, so I think I won against a Nadal that played at a high level today, and that's definitely giving me satisfaction."

As would beating Kei Nishikori the next day after an even bigger thriller (2-6, 6-4, 7-6(5)), pushing Djokovic close to the edge of falling off the cliff. "The quality of the match, I thought it was phenomenal, really," Djokovic would end up saying. Left ankle whacked on the way, nerves raw as flashes of pure rage would take him over from time to time. At 4-4 in the second set, where both players were in PlayStation tennis mode, Novak was a 0/10 on break points. On the verge of absolutely losing it. Yet, he would find the way out again, converting his first one on set point. Clearly struggling to keep it together as the Japanese was still painting the lines.

And Novak blaming and cursing the whole universe, even more when he missed two points for 5-1 and found himself at 4-3, breaking a cord at 40A. For the record, he didn't even notice it; the umpire had to tell him before he was about to serve. That's the kind of mental state Djokovic was in. On fire, Nishikori came back at 4-4, and then we were again with Roland-Garros looming in the corner: was the Djoker still made of steel even on clay? Even as his biggest tennis trauma was now waiting for him in a few days? At 15-30 on a double fault, he didn't look about to win. But as so often in his career, Novak avoided the danger at the last second with some miraculous shots as his drop shot ended a winner thanks to the net. Djokovic's mother, Dijana, crossed herself on this one.

Nishikori would save a match point at 4-5 then lead 3-1 in the tie-break, as Novak was on the ropes. Some would tell you that it's when he's the most dangerous. Nishikori agreed after losing five points in a row to be now down 3-6 in that decisive tie-break. He'd save two more match points but at 6-5 a good serve and a forehand sent Djokovic into the semi-finals. He had been on this court for three hours of struggle, knew that it had cut his chances by a good half for the Sunday final against Murray. But he had powered through another tough one and there was no doubt anymore as to how strong he was going to be in the only city that mattered in this part of the season: Paris. He was still feeling this way after losing the final, and by the way under rainy weather that in retrospect was a perfect preparation for Paris too. Roland-Garros could come his way, he was up to the task. Game on.

CHAPTER THREE

Going Through The Scar Tissue

Novak Djokovic, despite all that was going in his mind, still had a way to look at peace in Paris that year. Obviously a result of the constant balance he was working on, of that perfect "in the moment" state he was fighting hard to stay in. So when he succeeded in remaining in that bubble, he really seemed so well. As I crossed him in the hall of the interview area, he was walking with his agents, two bodyguards behind him, and was told by an ATP representative that he now had to go to another TV studio. It was Saturday, mid-day, June 4th. The day before the final, before what could be the most important moment of his career. He could be tight, he could already be in his bubble. He could ask for the whole world to keep quiet around him and refuse to see any intruder.

But, instead, the number 1 player in the world was strolling into the media centre, totally laid back. At the moment he walked by me, I was waiting for the Canadian junior marvel Felix Auger Aliassime to meet the press. One thing you learn as a journalist on the Tour is to avoid disturbing players in their "off media time." Even more so before a match. Even more before a final. Even more before a Grand Slam final. You happen to share the same space at this time by accident: you act as if they aren't there. There's a time for everything and there's a "no way now" time for everything too. So even if Novak and I were used to greeting each other, there was no way I was going to intrude there.

It was the same I guess for the two colleagues that were here near me. I was even reinforced in my feeling as members of his staff and of the ATP accompanying him had their "please don't disturb" faces on. Not to mention the two bodyguards, obviously. Yet, that said a lot about the mindset of Djokovic on the eve of this huge day, that he still shot his biggest smile and a "Hi, how are you today," waiting for an answer. I'm fine, Novak, thanks a lot. I'm not the one who in 24 hours will walk onto Roland-Garros' biggest court for a shot at history.

During the evening, he'd go on to post a video on his Facebook page of him and his team playing heads up in the house they were renting during the tournament. Clearly, nerves hadn't kicked in. I remembered at this moment how Nadal in 2012 revealed that he had watched Sangoku (Dragon Ball Z) the night when his Roland-Garros final against Djokovic had been interrupted in order to have a nice sleep. To each his own.

That same Saturday, Djokovic would have a 45 minute practice right before the women's final. I'm by the way still not sure if the final between Serena Williams and Garbine Muguruza would have started on time, at 3pm, if Stefan Fransson, the supervisor, hadn't politely come on court Chatrier to signal Djokovic that it would be nice to finish the drills. The former French hope Guillaume Rufin was the practice partner. I had witnessed all previous Djokovic pre-French Open final practices and warm up sessions, and the previous three had a common point: Novak was tight. He'd miss way more than usual, wouldn't find his rhythm at all even on his backhand - which is usually the red alarm - and would look totally turned within himself. No jokes, no smile, no chatting. He'd just do hand gestures to the team if he wanted something. Or at the maximum, shout orders to the sparring partner. Any word told to him by the team seemed to be an intrusion, and any miss by the sparring partner an outrage. After that, towel on head and off to the locker room on his own. Usually I'd walk out after watching this not being too optimistic about his chances.

I saw nothing of that this year at that moment, only a calm and determined player who was looking at the finish line with envy. When he arrived, blue t shirt and white shorts, the whole team was already there waiting for him, actually also taking selfies to immortalize the moment. His brother Marko was hitting with the sparring partner to kill time. And I would soon see through Novak's practice that he was really looking good. Gone were also those annoyed looks to Marian Vajda after another backhand miss, as both of them seemed to spend two weeks getting this crucial shot back in shape, and it started clicking before the quarter final against Tomas Berdych.

I still remember how suddenly super clean Novak was hitting that shot through the practice before that match. Which is quite fascinating: seeing the number 1 player in the world battling with his best shot. With a shot that is on the "best two-handed backhand of all time" list! When you see lesser ranked players hitting theirs all over the place for ages without getting mad... And without the coaches doing anything... But then here's Djokovic looking disgusted even when he hits it inside the court. Brainstorming with his coaches, showing them he can't find the good height to hit, or can't find the angle he's used to hitting. This is like an engineer trying to get the best Formula 1 car correcting a 1 mm flaw. This is a champion knowing where his bar is, and deciding he won't accept anything under it even if it's good.

His compatriot and former World n°1 Jelena Jankovic once said jokingly that her backhand was paying her bills. Certainly, Djokovic could have said the same, adding that this shot also won him Majors and the throne, as well as a special place in Rafael Nadal's head as it had grown to become absolute kryptonite to Rafa's forehand. So there was no way Novak would sleep in peace if he was feeling that something wasn't clicking as it should. Thor doesn't go out without his hammer, Djokovic doesn't go to the tennis battle without a perfectly tuned backhand.

I had this talk with Novak at Monte-Carlo in 2014, and two years later as he was counting on that mighty backhand one more time to bring him tennis glory, it was still totally accurate. "Today in modern tennis you have to be a very complete player in order to be at the top of the game. Because today you have many more players who are better from the forehand side, and most of the tennis matches are won on the forehand, being able to move your opponent around the court, but also on the backhand side you need to be very solid and able to threaten your opponent from that shot, and that's where I got a lot of success during my career. It's one of my weapons." A weapon he's frequently been accustomed to do battle with: "Of course there are times where you feel better or worse with every shot and this is the same with my backhand as much as it is natural for me, as much as I have confidence in that shot. There are periods in every year that I go through where I don't feel so confident nor comfortable hitting that shot, but the most important thing is to reset your mind and work on it. It's a work and a process: you can't be born with any shot. I might have a talent for certain kind of shots like the backhand that in terms of movement seems natural for me but you have to continuously work on it in order to have it at a high level of performance."

And he was right again about it in 2016, as he destroyed Berdych with it, then would do the same to Dominic Thiem's unbelievable one-handed backhand in the semi-finals, which wasn't a given, as the Austrian was in very fine form and a clear threat in his path. Sometimes a little change can have drastic consequences, as what would have happened to Djokovic's career if he had stuck to his childhood backhand? Because this masterful shot we've been admiring for years nearly never existed and is actually one of the first big decisions the young Djokovic made in his career: "I started with a one-handed backhand, yes. Because my first serious coach, Jelena Gencic, she wanted me to play one-hand backhand. When I was 7 or 8 years old I started to hit that backhand and I played it fine! But I was a bit frustrated because that's when I started playing tournaments. It was my first year playing local tournaments, and all the players figured out that I was small and skinny and had a one-handed backhand so they all played high looping balls on my backhand and I couldn't do anything so that's when I thought about it and started to play with two hands." It's probably the one and only time Novak ever said "no" to Gencic, to whom he owes so much, but that may have changed his destiny entirely.

So on that Saturday before the final he was crushing the ball on both sides with an effortless attitude. He was hitting as clean and deep as one could. Finding every zone he wanted. There was of course way more focus in this practice but the mood wasn't heavy at all. He would talk to Vajda, would listen to Becker, would ask this drill or this ball from the sparring partner, French player Guillaume Rufin. But all seemed smooth. The whole team gathered for their now usual group cheering, and Novak went out, smiling at the crowd, waving. "Man on a mission" were the words coming again to my mind. And I thought: "Good for him because I've just watched Andy Murray destroying the ball some minutes ago on this very court." For the first time, I had no doubt Novak would play his best tennis through the final. Wasn't sure he was going to win of course as I did find Murray very impressive in his semi-final against Wawrinka and also through the warm up. But this time I was really sure that Djokovic would be able to play his game.

But despite his game being exactly where Novak wanted it, now that the final was looming the stress level was getting close to its peak, trying one more time to get the better of Novak, to shake those demons awake. It would not succeed on the day before the final, not succeed on that Sunday through the warm up nor for the start of the match. After all, he had now fixed his mighty backhand, the one area of his game that needed to be on top that day so all was well, no? The little voice in his head telling him his best weapon maybe wasn't to be fully trusted had been silenced for good this time, so what was there to worry about?

"Nothing," would be the answer at the start of the final. Indeed after one game of this crucial match, no stress was visible and the backhand was working like thunder so I was feeling good about my intuition. After the next four games, not so much. Because after playing an amazing return game to break Andy, starting with a stellar backhand drop shot, getting to 0-40 on an also stellar forehand drop shot followed by a backhand pass down the line, and all of this perfect scenario finishing with a huge forehand return that pushed Murray to miss, that's when nerves decided to kick in for Djokovic. That's when the demons he knew so well found their way back into the light.

And not just a little: suddenly he wasn't able to hit a forehand above the net nor inside the lines. He couldn't hit a first serve. He couldn't find a single hitting zone nor of course execute his game plan. He was stuck. Going from full control to hitting the wall in twenty minutes (1-4). Months after, he still couldn't really explain what had happened after that first game when I asked him. "It's a very good question! To be honest I still don't have an answer to that question even in my mind," he told me before trying to put words on what remains a kind of disbelief. "Because it was kind of a trance that I was in, really. Because once the match started I was...I don't know if anybody can be 100% ready for something, but I was as close to that as I can be, in every aspect of my being. Emotionally, mentally, physically, spiritually, whatever: I was THERE, you know."

His eyes wide open and shining, Djokovic was still pretty intense when reminiscing that day. "I started first game, so good, great, broke his serve at love: playing amazing. And then I missed one or two balls and then (he laughs) I guess just the occasion and everything just got to my mind. And so before I actually got centered back again, the first set was over." No one, not even Novak himself, could have seen this coming in that proportion after the way he had started the event.

This attack of nerves would have indeed been impossible to see coming from his first round, except for Marian Vajda who even before the first ball hit in Paris knew that no crisis was totally out of the question. We knew he'd be nervous, but few would have guessed how much he had actually suffered. And so that at any point the scars could be opened wide again. After ten years spent with Novak, after sharing the pain of those French Open losses, he could see that something was wrong with Djokovic. And this for weeks actually.

"That was the toughest preparation of my life with him," he told me after a huge sigh. "Mentally, keeping him ok and pushing him to practice, to stay focussed, every day. This was the toughest because the memories kept coming back and back and back and they were all negative. Nothing positive. Before the tournament it was incredibly tough, he was very very nervous. That was hell in his mind. But the more hell it was in his mind, the stronger he was in the matches. Somehow he got together and was able to forget about the negativity. But the toughest thing was still trying not to think about what it all meant, and this during 14 days."

That's surely why the team was at the start relieved when they saw his draw. With all due respect to the opponents he faced, let's be honest here: he had the perfect first rounds to get into this tournament, to find his rhythm, footing and grow his confidence level. Yen-Hsun Lu, Steve Darcis and Aljaz Bedene are solid players, with possible flashes of brilliance from the Belgian, but for the n°1 player in the world trying to win his first French Open, it's called a good draw. No big servers, no super powerful rivals, no "impossible to hit through" clay specialists that would test his patience. Against those three, he'd have the advantage in basically everything: hitting harder, playing faster, keeping the intensity longer. Against them, he'd also get many chances to break or to get a break back. The pressure wouldn't be non-stop. So it would be mostly on his racquet.

And despite all the stress going on, that was something Vajda never doubted: Novak's tennis was at its best. "In the practice with Novak, there are some things, some remarks that make you tell how ready he is or not. He was ready, that was just the mental. But he had enough matches, enough practice, he was solid on the strokes. I always have this sentence: whatever done before, I release myself during the tournament. We did so much, everything was done. All the work was done."

That would indeed be shown in his first round against Lu on the Tuesday, May 24th. He was looking good at his morning practice, had a nice chat with Tsonga at the end of it on this Chatrier court and left after having signed balls for some fans. You could feel anticipation in the crowd at seeing Novak start a new campaign in Paris. Rafa and Roger aside, he was the main storyline and it had taken on the crowd too. Also, it seems, people were ready to witness history being made in Paris with this non calendar Grand Slam at stake, even way more than they were in 2012 when Djokovic was in the same situation after this wonder of a season in 2011 and this legendary 2012 Australian Open final.

This time there was really electricity in the air right away in Paris. So when Novak entered court Philippe Chatrier for his first match, he got a big reception. He should have played the second match after the 11am start but it was Andy Murray who ended playing right after Angelique Kerber as he was entangled in a two day fight against Radek Stepanek. So Djokovic had to witness his main rival getting out of trouble before starting his own quest. Actually, even better: he had to warm up for his first match at the same time as Andy, who was hitting with Lu! Who said inseparable?

When it was finally his show time, he appeared in a dark red T-Shirt, with black lines around the shoulders that went down his sides, with black shorts with red lines on the sides as an opposite echo to that of the shirt. Looking very elegant and boss-like, he launched his 2016 French Open against a player who a few days ago was still playing a Challenger in Bangkok on hard court. Yes, you read that right. Tough to have a better deal to shake off first round nerves. And actually the first set Novak played in Paris that year wouldn't be his best ever, as could be expected. Lu was pumped by the occasion and determined not to get his ass kicked in front of the whole centre court, so he was bringing lots of balls back and going for his shots. On the other side of the net, Novak was looking a bit bothered and frustrated. Being up a break at 4-3 didn't help as Lu got it back right away and went up 40-15 on his own serve.

That's when the Djoker got out of his box for the first time. He decided to switch off the safe option that for him is to defend and grind his opponent down, and instead switch on the aggression. It would basically be a symbol of his whole Parisian campaign: he wouldn't win it by playing it safe, but only by going for it. It was going bold or losing. Head under a towel after clinching the first set 6-4, he got back into this match pushing even harder and moving forward. He also displayed some great drop shots on the way, ending up being absolutely unplayable for Lu in the third set with a 5-0 lead, and so winning the match easily (6-4, 6-1, 6-1). Too strong, too fast, too accurate: if anyone can play ping pong on a clay court, it's Novak Djokovic. "I just needed the time to kind of get myself engaged, kind of get used to the conditions and the new court," he later told the press in a bright red jacket. "Second and third set were really good, I thought I found my rhythm, whereas the first set was up and down."

He had just claimed his 50th win at the French Open, and it was again the feeling of a calmly determined Novak that would prevail, as he was smiling throughout the press conference and even had this revealing joke to tell a Belgian colleague warning him that Steve Darcis, his next opponent, was called The Shark. "Oh, really? Well. I have a nice answer in my head, but I will keep it to myself. I love sharks," he joked with the face of the hunter on, smile out. Some species of sharks are endangered around the world and at this moment it felt like the Belgian was among them.

Indeed, Steve Darcis wouldn't find a way through Djokovic on that first week's Thursday. Wouldn't claim a single set. But the talented Belgian still succeeded in making several things clear about Djokovic's level and state of mind early in this tournament. He was 100% focused, 100% stubborn on making this year the one but he wasn't immune to the consequences of this pressure. If one event derailed him through a game or a set and he wasn't in the mood for it, it could really send him into what I'm used to calling "MessLand." Also: one-handed backhands were really on his blacklist. That's how from 3-0 up and an opening for 4-0, Novak ended at 4-4 30-40 in that first set after a crossed forehand winner from Darcis. Feeling some nerves on the other side of the net made the Belgian believe there was really something to be done out there on the Lenglen court. "I knew I had the style to cause him trouble with my backhand slices for instance," said Darcis. "I felt he wasn't that serene. He looked nervous, he was making unusual mistakes. Tactically, I played a very smart match."

Back to the wall, the Serb again remembered he was a shot maker and hit a wonder of a forehand down the line taken so early. He'd go on to hold, then save a point for tie-break before taking his chance on an amazing cross court forehand return to earn a set point. A sliced backhand miss from Darcis would gift the set to Djokovic (7-5). Crisis aborted. On a day where he kept the black shorts but switched his red T-shirt for a white one, he'd become more serene as the match went on, serving better, finding more depth in his shots. Sure he'd lose a break in the third set, and a match point at 5-3 but he'd close it out at the end (7-5, 6-3, 6-4). "It wasn't an easy match for him even if he won in three sets, said Darcis, finding some solace in that defeat. He was a bit annoyed and upset so I'm still a bit happy to have put him in this state even if I lost. Too bad I don't get to play matches like this every week, because these are the ones that really make you improve."

Yes, Djokovic was tested, yes he shook a tiny bit and got frustrated but he got the win in the end, displaying a good amount of cold blood under pressure. Next time he would see the court Suzanne Lenglen would be, unexpectedly, for his semi-final against another one-handed backhand. And he wouldn't take this as good news at first.

For now, on this May 26th, sporting a black cap with Roland-Garros written in red, he was grading his performance of the day, and it wasn't getting very high marks. Unless we were talking about the scorn scale attributed to it. Good enough for a second round, but surely going all the way would require doing much better as soon as possible. The Djokovic bar is rarely set anywhere far from the top of the ladder. And the ladder itself seems to always get somehow taller. "I'm pleased to get the job done in three sets, but, you know, there were things that I definitely didn't like in my game today. Too many unforced errors from the first or second shot in the rally. I allowed him to come back in the match in those sets because I was managing to drop my serve very easily. So hopefully that's not going to happen in the following rounds. The matches will get tougher, and, you know, it's kind of expected at the beginning that you are a bit rusty on the court, and hopefully things will get better."

And back on Chatrier, they would. In the third round, Djokovic didn't encounter many issues to get over the British Aljaz Bedene (6-2,6-3,6-3) on Saturday May 28th. His main one would be to get it done before the sky would be too dark for them to play. He did it, basically needing candles to see the yellow ball and the white lines, but still managing to get over that third hurdle. All smiles at the end, in total communion with the crowd. He didn't know it at the time, but he was soon to have to dig deep in order to avoid another heartbreak in Paris.

You can't understand the magnitude of Novak Djokovic's triumph at Roland-Garros, and the amount of stress he had to go through to finally get his hands on the French trophy, if you don't understand how thick the scar tissue was there, how he went into a journey and learned the very hard way. In a sport where you often talk about mental blocks and how tough it is to go through them, his win in Paris is a case study. It's not only him: after ten years of working together, and ten years of failing Porte d'Auteuil, his coach Marian Vajda shared the burden. Roland-Garros had inherited the status of a sort of taboo. Maybe if you don't talk about it until you have no choice anymore, then all will be fine.

In Indian Wells 2015, I was interviewing Vajda about Novak's shape and mindset at the moment, and also about the fact that Marian was back on the team after Becker handled the past months. He was basically jumping around out of joy to be back, "full of energy" as he said at the time. And that's this same super happy Marian Vajda who would suddenly plead with me not to talk about Paris now. "Please no, we'll talk about it when it comes!" I can't even remember if I was actually thinking about talking of that as we were only in March, but me being French was surely a red alert for Vajda! We laughed and moved on to other topics.

So in 2016 when I chatted with him again in California about how Novak was coping physically after a very dramatic Davis Cup weekend, I finished with a joke, telling him he surely was happy that I hadn't even pronounced the words Roland-Garros. He put his hands in the air, saying "yes, yes, thanks!" with a smile. Another member of Djokovic's team actually put hands over ears as a joke, when hearing the two words. In March, Roland-Garros was a private joke. But a telling one: the One-Who-Must-Not-Be-Named.

Gerhard Gritsch wouldn't deny it at all: the French Open started to look like a malediction upon them all despite all the love they had for it. The scar tissue was thick: "Not only for Novak as the whole team's biggest disappointments were always in Paris. Each time we thought we did everything... We wanted it so badly and somehow it just went through our fingers... It was crazy. And he was ready! The match with Wawrinka didn't go his way but it happens, and Wawrinka played great. But we almost felt that there was something higher, like a curse. Maybe, maybe, he accepted it and thought it wasn't going to happen and he had to live with it. Maybe that relaxed him a little bit because you can't control the universe."

As Djokovic entered Paris' second week, he wasn't there just to win a tournament. He was there to have one more tango with all of his French demons. Because it's not only that he lost at the French Open. It's also about him collapsing there, about him getting so close to the title that he was nearly able to touch it before seeing the trophy and so the dream taken away. It's about all the times he had chances to go all the way but missed the last hurdle, about those matches he should have won but lost. It's not about winning or losing, it's about the suffering and the trauma. No other tournament has laid bare the tiny scratch in Novak's confidence, and his self doubts, as much as Roland-Garros. No other tournament has hurt him more. No other tournament has made him cry that much. Between him and the French Open, it had long ago stopped being just a professional affair. It was and remains deeply personal. And as with anything personal, it could let a good dose of the irrational enter.

There seems to be a rule where Djokovic and Grand Slams are concerned: there will be a match coming directly from hell. It was against Simon that year in Melbourne, it was against Andreas Seppi in Paris in 2012, being down two sets, and against Jo-Wilfried Tsonga, saving four match points that same year, also Andy Murray in the 2015 semi-finals over two days, and against Kevin Anderson in Wimbledon in 2015, down two sets. He'd win those matches but after many scares, mistakes, tantrums, tennis versions of "near death experiences." Those were matches where his tennis would struggle most of the time and where the victory would only come from a big heart and a hatred for defeat with occasional flashes of genius to avoid the fall.

Why were they even more special in Paris? Because there you could multiply each of these factors by three. That's the power of the irrational finding a way into your personal affairs. This year at Roland-Garros, everything decided to fall on his fourth round against Roberto Bautista Agut. The Spaniard's game was labelled dangerous right from the start: big forehand, great fitness, great footwork, able to be a wall but also to go for his shots, big competitor. As Novak crossed him in the player's lounge, that Monday when play was washed out, he jumped on him for a hug, laughing while saying "Vamos a jugar! Vamos a jugar!" ("come on, let's go and play" in Spanish) to a Bautista Agut looking as if he had no idea what to do with the n°1 player in the world shaking him by the shoulders. Good fun.

Novak had trashed "RBA" 6-2, 6-1 just a few weeks ago in Madrid and was up 4-0 in their head to head, so maybe it was giving him a sense of comfort. But that would be the last time for the next 48 hours that he would find anything fun associated with the Spaniard. Boris Becker had a foreboding about it, as if he could smell trouble looming. "I was nervous," he admitted to me. "I respect Roberto a lot, he's one of the great fighters of the game and I don't think he gets enough credit. So I was afraid of this match, then the weather didn't help." Even as we spoke about it months later, the German still looked as if he was there again on Chatrier, in Novak's box, suffering along. Surely, he'd have loved to have been wrong about the way this match would go!

For a real "Djokovic Match From Hell" several ingredients have to be there, and this time it was like the Universe threw everything it could at Novak. So as Monday, May 30th, had been washed out, the tournament had to give ticket holders their money back. Needless to say, having a second washed out day in a row wasn't an option. Players would be on court at some point, rain or not.

After a full day of rain, it was still going on when I arrived on site that Tuesday, but as I took the player's lounge route to access the media centre as on every other morning, the vibe there was that there would indeed be some play. When? No one really knew. And the faces were concerned. Not a single coach wanted to see his or her player out in this weather, as it was labelled the "anything can happen, and mostly anything terrible" day.

Novak was supposed to be on court at 11am, but he and Bautista Agut would end up setting foot on Chatrier around 12:15. No one was in denial here: it was still raining. Djokovic had opted for dark shorts and a white shirt, with red lines around the shoulders then going down on the sides. Heavy clay, big and heavy balls, slow court: this equation acted on Novak's game like ice on fire. Not good, despite the fact that he won the first point of that match on a 30 shot rally. It would be one of the very few moments he'd be in control in this first set. He couldn't move properly, so couldn't hit properly and so couldn't keep a cool mind. Djokovic could still sigh and grimace about that day months after. He wasn't denying the struggle it had been: "The conditions were wet and slow, and Roberto is the kind of player that likes these kinds of conditions, because the ball's bounce is low, it's very slow and he has a great anticipation on the court, gets a lot of balls back in play. I felt, especially in that first set that I lost, quite stagnant in my legs. I didn't have this dynamic movement and I needed that. So all of these circumstances affected me."

Terrible sensations, timing off, uninspired and annoyed body language: up there court side, both Marian Vajda and Boris Becker knew that it'd be a very long and painful path. When Novak was starting like this, there was no hope in him finding his cosmic tennis anytime soon. It'd be a grind. When I started to talk to Vajda about that match, his first three words were: "Oh my god..." So as Novak was all over the place, Bautista-Agut was taking this rain as a savior: he had all the time in the world to play, to turn around that backhand in order to dictate with his forehand and make Djokovic suffer.

Also he was being very smart, mostly putting balls in the middle of the court after noticing that Novak's brain just couldn't find a way to cope with that. Down 4-2, Djokovic still got one break back, just to lose it right away. That was it with his patience towards the organization and basically the whole universe. Angrily, he demanded the supervisor come and check the state of the court. Demanded for the match to be interrupted. Was denied. Two games later though they would stop the match, but Novak was now down a set to Bautista Agut (3-6). Funnily enough, the conditions at this time were basically the same as when they had started this match. "There are things players don't like, that's all," stated Vajda. "And here it was completely against him. Because when it's slippery, for Novak it's very bad, especially for his movements. But luckily it stopped."

It was 12:50 and in only half an hour, there was the first big dent in Novak's quest. And he would have close to three hours to dwell on it before coming back on the court. The players' lounge was as packed as the locker rooms might have been so there was no way to escape to stress-free places. Anyway, there was someone who didn't want him to escape to a quiet place, who was waiting for him for a "once in a coaching lifetime" pep talk. Boris Becker decided that day to cross the untold line between him and his charge as he was feeling that disaster was on the way.

"It was really slow, Novak was out of sorts. He lost the first set, was struggling, then there was a rain break. He walked off, furious," remembered Becker as if it was yesterday, looking me in the eyes to really make me understand that the word "furious" was not exaggerated. "And then I remember having one of the most personal speeches to him. Really looked him in the eyes, we stood very close and I really felt that I needed to tell him the complete truth now. And then he looked at me almost shocked, like how dare I speak to him like this. And he knew it came from the right place so he just swallowed it." What was said at this moment won't be disclosed, as Becker reminded me of the "what's told in the locker room, remains in the locker room" rule. But facing a furious Djokovic and picking that time to put the fist on the table might not be on a lot of people's wish list.

Anyone who has been around Novak enough knows that he has several kinds of stares when things aren't going the way he wants to or when he's just not in the mood. They're going to come and go as fast as lightning but they're still useful warnings. And among them, there's a "enter here at your own peril" stare that usually makes people do a U-turn, so Becker must have really felt that this match was going to end Novak's quest to step up despite the red alarm. "I think because we already worked two and a half years together, I knew there was trust and there was respect. Sure it helped that I was a former number 1: I think that's how I got into it. But because of the two and a half years together, I was allowed" - he insisted on the word - "to speak to him like this, because he would know it meant something. He went out, managed to win the second set, the weather got better so it was a little bit faster and then it was easier. But it was the most difficult match of the tournament." Later after this match was over, Fabrice Santoro while conducting the usual on court interview would tell Novak he looked so disciplined in the second part of that match, and you could see him smile when he answered: "Well, I have to be like this or I'm going to get some tough talk in the locker room from my coaches." Thanks to Becker we now know it wasn't just some post match banter.

Before play resumed, the same Becker went out on the court to see what was going on as both Novak and Bautista Agut were made to wait in the corridor. Unbearable for Djokovic to be just there waiting when inside of him he was boiling. So he entered the court, white jacket on dark shorts, and displayed one more time how both entertaining and bossy he can be. He borrowed an umbrella from the crowd, tested the ground, and to please the public had a little "Gene Kelly Singing in the Rain" dancing moment. Smile on, he slowly made his way to the umpire's chair, waving to the crowd, and isolating his face from the camera with the umbrella, surely asking umpire Cédric Mourier a polite version of "what the hell is going on? Am I going to play or not?"

A last look at the sky, he gave back the umbrella and he was back in the corridor. The Djokovic way of putting on an efficient show, and surely easing his own nerves too. He was maybe one set down, but he was still the King. Shortly after, the game would resume. And this break, added to the Becker speech, really did Djokovic good: intentions were better, he had stopped complaining about the conditions of play, and he was finally going for the jugular. But there's another rule for a "Djokovic match from hell": he will have many opportunities, he will convert very few, hence he will wreck many nerves. Once again, Novak put on a classic out there: many break points not converted (5 to be at 2-2 instead of 4-0), finally one taken (4-2) but lost (4-3), and taken again after saving a 4-4 point through a wonder of a point where he yelled his lungs out. He gave his all on this one and on the next one to break: taking the ball early, he hit a splendid crossed backhand, then a crossed forehand that pushed RBA to miss. Game over? Not for the universe.

Up 5-3, Djokovic broke one string at 30-15, then another at 40A! I was in the media seats on the side of the court when he gave a "This is really happening" shocked look to his team at this moment. A long and confused look, probably rightfully wondering what he had done to deserve this much bad luck today. Or started to think there was really a curse upon his head in Paris. An inside out forehand out on break point would put Bautista Agut back on serve at 5-4. At this exact moment, all was set for the irrational to take over Novak. Sure he was doing better than at the start of this match and was fighting to keep his head above water. But the internal battle was so strong... He was now a set down and two breaks lost to an opponent that wouldn't go away. Conditions were killing his game. The sensations were bad. Disappointment was around the corner, and he met it so often in Paris that he was beginning to smell it again. Having witnessed many of those lost battles, I could too.

If Djokovic on this gloomy afternoon, harassed by this stubborn rain, was starting to even think of those tough times, it was the end. "Yeah it could have crossed his mind in a match like that, like 'It's happening again!', considered Vajda. "Yes, I think you are right. In every Grand Slam he has something like this, but this was a special one." How could he forget what had repeatedly wounded him? You could count at least ten of Novak's losses in Paris that have scarred him. And you could also add a good eight matches where he shook so much he nearly lost and only got out of them after epic battles of nerves. That made nearly twenty memories ranging from touchy to traumatic, something he was again carrying with him through every match. The dramatic scenario of his semi-final against Nadal in the 2013 edition had to jump to mind, as this one embodied perfectly the Djokovic soul crushing experience in Paris. Rafa would end winning that one in five sets (6-4, 3-6, 6-1, 6-7(3), 9-7) in 4h37 after being down 3-1 in the decisive set. Novak probably thought he had it, Nadal probably thought it was going away, until this point when up a break at 4-3 on what looked like a routine volley at 40A, Djokovic ended in the net. He'd lose that game, the momentum, a huge part of his composure and then the match. "Disappointment is my only feeling," he would say after that epic match.

And on this loss would be grafted so many painful things, as this 2013 French Open had been seen like a mission for Djokovic. He would win that one for Jelena Gencic, who passed away during the first week. "She didn't know she was going to die probably, but she told Novak when she saw him last time that she would be the happiest woman to hold that trophy. When she saw Novak the last time, she told him she wanted to take a picture and have the whole collection," recounted Marian Vajda[6] then about the only Major win that Novak was missing. So "Nole" wouldn't only lose a semi-final that day against Nadal, he'd be prevented from honoring Gencic's wish. Roland-Garros would then become even more personal for him and so even more emotionally tough to deal with. Because the issue was, that it was one more scar on the body.

There had been this quarter final against Melzer in 2010, lost despite being two sets up, and that would put him so down that he would put in question his whole career after that, entering one of his biggest doubting moments but also becoming a crucial turning point. There had been this 2011 semi-final lost in five sets against Federer despite being unbeaten since the start of the season, there had been that 2012 final lost in two days against Nadal while he was already fighting for the Novak Slam that year. "It was tough to move on from that one," Djokovic would admit some time later in Wimbledon that year. "But now I try to tell myself that I haven't missed a date with history, but that I played my first Roland-Garros final which means I've moved forward."

But it wouldn't stop there, as there would be the 2014 final against Rafa again, where Novak would win the first set and then see the

---

6. "Novak Djokovic's French Open Chase", NYT, May 18, 2016 (*http://www.nytimes.com/2016/05/19/sports/tennis/novak-djokovic-french-open-roland-garros.html?_r=1*).

Spaniard take over, even throwing up on the court as he had apparently had stomach issues that day. He would lose on a double fault, exactly like in 2012, to Rafa's greatest relief as Novak might not have seen it that day but the Spaniard had been on the edge. He even had to call the trainer for cramps after the end of the match. "I was exhausted, I gave everything I had. It was the hardest match physically that I've played here over the years. I was just empty," he'd say, hinting that he couldn't have handled a fifth set. And to cap this overall Djokovic heartbreak he would then lose in 2015 against Wawrinka despite having beaten Nadal in the quarters and looking so good. As if there would always be something or someone coming to make him trip on the last step.

Djokovic could be the Iron Man everywhere else for however long you wanted, but on the Parisian clay there would always be a moment where he'd get abandoned by his armor. And everyone knew this, starting with himself. So while he was watching Bautista Agut about to serve to get back to five all in this second set, and while he next had to begin this mano-a-mano phase from the baseline, exchanging punches and playing with the lines, there was absolutely no way he could even tolerate to be on this court in this situation if he hadn't developed a coping mechanism to deal with this tennis trauma.

He hadn't been the only one at the top of the game to have this kind of mental block when it was Paris time. Patrick Mouratoglou recalled how it hadn't been easy to convince Serena Williams that she wasn't the cursed one at Roland-Garros, where she had won in 2002 but then struggled for a decade. "When I started to work with Serena, she told me: '...whatever: mentally I can't do it in Roland-Garros. Mentally, when I'm there I sink.' And that became a mental block because human beings are like that. When facing the same situation again and again, the same traumatic thing keeps happening - and losing in a Grand Slam for them is a trauma as they always think they're the favorite - then the trauma only gets bigger each time it happens. It's like a snowball that keeps growing. It's not easy... One has to be resourceful to put it aside. In those moments, you feel physically marked by the mix of the place, what's at stake and the previous losses. You physically feel that you're not good. To change this, you need to reprogram everything, it's the only way. One needs to create similar situations where it finishes well, it's the only solution."

One French player had the honor to live a big part of this 2016 quest from inside of the Djokovic team: Thibault Venturino. The Frenchman started to practice with Novak for the second week of the tournament and until the semi-finals as he had to leave before the end. "Through the first week, those players prefer to hit between themselves but the further they got the more they want to have their own practice," he would say about why he entered the scene. As in Bercy, the French Open had decided to offer a sort of sparring partners' service and Venturino was one of the favorites of the Djoker team. Both men knew each other since 2014 when Venturino was already sparring for the stars of the Parisian Masters 1000. "I had just hit with Federer so that was what one would call a great day!" he smiled when remembering it. "We practiced for 1h30, it was pretty nice, we had chatted a bit. I got along well with Boris Becker too: he seemed to like me, I got lucky. So as each time it went well, they're now used to ringing me up if they need a sparring partner at some point." Becker would confirm that he was very fond of Venturino: "great guy, great player!".

And so Venturino saw how it was sometimes tough on the Djoker to just go with the flow. "From the first time I played with him in the second week that year until the semi-finals, yes you could feel the pressure mounting, which is normal. And with him it's easy to tell when he's stressed out. He takes things to heart a lot and with a team like this, with so many people and things behind him, it was huge here for him. Despite the fact that he had won nearly everything except Roland-Garros. He's a pretty emotional person I think so each time it's going to come back. As long as he didn't get this release of winning the French Open, I think it was very hard to live for him."

So there had obviously been a long term plan around Djokovic to make sure the wounds were really healed in order to get it right this time. Boris Becker had lost two French Open finals with Novak and it seemed that for this third time, hoping it'd be the charm, he had decided to really make him confront the naked truth, the demon in the eyes. Shock therapy. "I think it was an advantage for me having been in Grand Slam finals," he told me when I asked how they dealt with the scar tissue this time. "I knew how nervous you get and how important it was so that helped me understand the players' behavior. They should feel a safety net around them where they can absolutely be themselves. For those two weeks, everything is allowed. You're supposed to put your pants down, you're supposed to be completely honest otherwise we can't help you. And if you weren't from the business you wouldn't understand. If you've never been under such pressure you wouldn't understand. I think that was our secret."

Becker definitely sounded like the one always ready to go and get things out of Djokovic, to take the direct road to the issue whether Novak liked it or not. A nice balance and mix, surely, with the rest of the team who through the years had learnt to maybe be more careful about the Serbian's mood swings. "Over the years we learnt to deal with him," smiled Gritsch when I asked him what had been the best option with Novak considering the tension, pressure and scar tissue in Paris. It is a very fine line. "Obviously we want to make sure he's at top level and so we need to communicate, and we have things to say that are very important if we have to adjust technical or mechanical issues, but with Novak it's a skill to find the right time. When he is not open, there's no need to talk (laughs). It doesn't make any sense. And because we've been with him for so many years we have quite the skill to wait as long as we need, you know (laughs)."

And all this work hadn't started in Paris, not even in 2016. Again, that's a work that started right after the 2015 Roland-Garros. You don't start from scratch at the start of a Grand Slam event when there is so much baggage. You already carry many seeds with you a long way. Becker had even decided at Wimbledon 2015 to make sure Djokovic would face everything with head held high after losing to Wawrinka, as he told the New York Times[7]: "I organized another practice with Stan because of that. I told Novak: 'That was clay, this is grass, it's a new tournament, and you've got to practice with the guy who gave you a very disappointing loss.' And Novak did it, and once they practiced,

7. "Novak Djokovic's French Open Chase", NYT, May 18, 2016 (*http://www.nytimes.com/2016/05/19/sports/tennis/novak-djokovic-french-open-roland-garros.html?_r=1*).

they joked about it, and it was over. Paris was over. So there are ways about it, how you overcome situations. But in order to overcome them, you have to face them. You have to talk about them. You have to deal with it. You can't run away."

Not everybody was sure it would work in London, as Gritsch recalled how painful the start of that event had been for Novak. "Boris threw him into the water (laughs). We were talking about it and I wasn't really sure if it was going to work or not. And Novak maybe at the beginning was also not happy about it, because it was a big jump... But at the end it worked out. It was amazing because when Novak came to Wimbledon, he didn't want to play. He wanted to do anything else but play tennis. Boris and I were talking to him... We started slowly and somehow the practice sessions were better than he expected. He started to enjoy a little bit. He was not happy in the matches, still, because you can't forget these things so fast."

In this general strategy for Paris, Becker agreed that there was a need to lower the pressure. "How?" I'd ask him. "You have to stay in the moment, and it's not important where you are. That final of the 2016 French Open wasn't won on that Sunday afternoon, it was weeks and weeks before. When you went through the repetition, the practice, when you went through an Australian Open final. It's all a part of the path, of the background. If Novak had lost in Australia, he would have been a different guy. So I think all those little bits of the puzzle are sometimes underestimated by people, players and coaches. So I thought the team did an unbelievable job to come to the final and not be surprised about it, not be nervous about it. Novak wasn't nervous, he was ready. In the practice sessions and between the matches, yes there was a lot of tension, a lot of emotional baggage, but he has a good team around to protect him so he could flourish."

It's no secret that Djokovic is a firm believer in mental work, meditation, yoga, and sophrology techniques like visualization and breathing work. "As you work on your muscles in the gym, mentally you also have to work," he told me in Monte-Carlo that year, as for him it was as obvious a thing to do as practicing his forehand. For Catherine Aliotta, director of studies at the Sophrology Training Institute in Paris who works regularly with athletes, olympians among them, there was simply no way Novak would have even been able to come back on the court Philippe Chatrier without this work. The scar tissue was too thick. "For athletes, everything is creating an anchoring system. So it's the analysis made after the loss that's going to anchor either the ability to bounce back or the collapse. Added to this, here, there's an emotional side to those defeats due to their scenario and context, which means many events got combined at the same time. He suffered and he lost. When defeat is associated to a strong negative emotion, it's harder to get going again the next time. This is that emotional side that makes me fail to rise to the occasion and so I can't get anything out of this match. This will create a negative anchoring on a court or a tournament, a fear or an anticipation meaning that it's harder to emotionally deal with all of this. Behind each defeat I need to imprint something positive. That's what helps keep the same motivation, which is tough. So he needed to take something out of what happened. You need to deal with everything linked to that trauma which is also tied to a match where a lot was at stake. If you don't do that, you don't come back, that's the thing." And this feeling that can come of having a kind of malediction upon one's head needs to be taken seriously: "That's something one needs to fight against. Even more because one feeds those beliefs. One needs to anchor an ability to bounce back at all cost."

What could possibly be the positive Novak found out of those crushing losses that made him come back again in May 2016? He's been giving a big part of the answer each time he's been asked to talk about the 2015 final, the one nearly everyone was sure would be The One and that escaped him again. The only things you would get out of him about that day were the connection he had with Wawrinka after the match point at the net, when Stan came to his bench, and also the love he felt from the crowd. Those moments shared were the only things he would talk about at length. It was even stronger than after the 2014 final, but the option was the same, as I could see through a talk with him at Indian Wells 2015. We were talking France and so Roland-Garros came up and I asked him if it was still fun to come back to that place where he had some of the biggest losses of his career. He answered yes right away, and in his answer you have probably the biggest parts of how he coped with those defeats in Paris.

First of all, it's life helping him to get better: "The matches that I have lost, against Nadal especially, over the years were not easy for me to take, not easy to digest but it's all a learning experience and I know that life is challenging me and allowing me to have these opportunities to grow. So I'm trying to take it in a positive way, where I'm going to use these losses as a lesson, as something that allows me to improve, to grow, to understand myself and what I need to do better next year. That's my mindset and my approach."

Then, the human factor was a beautiful thing to take out of those losing days: "Roland-Garros is always one of my highest priorities. It always is. But in 2014, when I lost in the final, I experienced one of the nicest moments of my career when the Philippe Chatrier stadium was applauding me and there was a long ovation. I had tears in my eyes because it really touched me and because the French crowd is not easy to win over to your side, so for me as a non Frenchman to have this kind of support and appreciation, is definitely something I will never forget, something that actually encourages me even more to keep on going and fighting and hopefully one day winning."

In 2014 he had sworn not to give up, on court during his speech: "Until the end of my career I will try to win at least once here." And even Nadal had been moved on the podium: "I was very touched when the crowd applauded Novak for so long. That was a real proof of love," he commented after the match. So those were the images "Nole" would again carry with him after the 2015 loss, with the difference being that it would be even stronger: a longer ovation, wilder tears, a stronger connection. That was the Djokovic way of making sure he'd want to go back to Paris to try again to win it. That was what he would cling to when the scars were burning.

Catherine Aliotta takes it as a very effective way of keeping his head and motivation in the right place. So effective that it totally could have been a part of the method used by him to deprogram those painful defeats in order to imprint something positive. "He needed something to nurture his intrinsic[8] motivation after all of this, and that was the job of the debriefing work done with the coaches. Imperatively, at some

---

8. An intrinsic motivation means that it is personally rewarding. One performs an activity for its own sake rather than the hope of getting an external reward. One does it to have fun and to be competent in what one's doing.

point, he needed to be told 'look you've been very competent at this', or 'look how you connected to the crowd': it fed this motivation. The pleasure in pleasing people, the exchanges felt, my opponent's respect for me when he greeted me at the net: that's something that pleased me and not the outside world. It needed to be nurtured because it's what was going to make me come back, and that's also what we were going to work on if we were in a mental preparation using sophrology. It'd be about thinking about it regularly, anchoring it into specific motions with specific exercises to deprogram that stress, that anxiety towards a tournament, a court or an opponent."

And to succeed in all of this and come back one more time, Dr Michelle Cleere adds that one has also to mourn once and for all the past missed opportunities. Dr Cleere is an elite performance expert with a PhD in Clinical Psychology and a Masters in Sports Psychology. She's also a member of the United States Professional Tennis Association and has worked with many tennis players. "When you come back to where you've failed, there are two sides to the coin: I'm going to come back stronger, I'm going to make it happen this time. Or, I'm going to fall apart. Djokovic has continued to be strong through that: getting better and getting stronger. But in the last steps, it's a bit like a PTSD. There's always also this little bit of doubt in the back of your mind. 'I got so close the last times, am I going to be able to make it happen this time?' When I work with players in those situations we talk a lot about what has happened and then about how to let go of that. Everything has to be its own thing: you can't play the French Open based on how you played the French Open last year. In between you're going to get better and better. And that's when mental training is important as a solution. It's still amazing to me how many players don't do it. It's just retraining the brain. I'm doing a lot of mindfulness work to make those players really be present, in the here and now. You can't go back and change what happened so you have to let it go, or you're going to waste too much energy on that. It's something you have to practice all the time, also to change the coping mechanisms in stressful times and in non stressful times."

And it's a very long term work, states Aliotta: "I guess Djokovic had to start working a year in advance, basically from his last loss in the final: they've started to deprogram in order to be able, little by little, to program again. If I have lost three times there and didn't do anything to deprogram them, it's stress multiplied by 100. It never happens overnight... Those negative flashbacks that would come are what I'd talk about as mini trauma. Yet the effects of the flashbacks should disappear through the mental preparation work. The memory remains but doesn't have a negative emotional impact." Thierry Van Cleemput, who is more the "action, action, action" type of person has a really good way to sum this up: "If you're going to be scared, you stay at home. It's forceps time, time to influence things. It's also very hard for the great champions."

As I'm waiting for Darren Cahill, he's having a chat with Lleyton Hewitt in a corridor of the Australian Open. When you start delving into tennis champions' actions and brains, you try to go and talk to the Australian former player, now regarded as one of the most famous and respected coaches in the game, having brought his compatriot Hewitt to the World N°1 in 2001, then having done the same with the all time Great Andre Agassi in 2003, before working with the likes of Andy Murray, Fernando Verdasco, Ana Ivanovic and the Romanian star Simona Halep. For years, he has also been sought after for his analysis and has become a respected tennis commentator for television. He's the straightforward type: he doesn't put on gloves to send the message. So when he told me that the way Novak handled that 2015 French Open final loss against Wawrinka had made Djokovic stronger for the next year and so able to move past the scar tissue, it's not to play cute. He really meant it.

Actually I had the sense that he might have discovered a new side to the Serb that day, to his own surprise. "I think beating Nadal the year previous and then losing to Stan in the final showed that he's human and that great things don't come easily to anybody, no matter how good they are. I think he made more fans in that loss to Stan than he's ever made in his career, by the way he handled it, the way that he spoke after that final. You couldn't help but feel bad for him even though he got beaten by a better player. I think the way he handled himself in that loss made him stronger for the next year."

That was also the power of the Djokovic quest in Paris: it was bringing everybody along. Everyone in the tennis business but also the fans and even the general public cared about it somehow. In the week after Novak won, you'd pop into some cafés in Paris and here really any kind of people talking would burst out: "Wait, who won Roland-Garros?", "Djokovic," "He did? Finally!" and then move on to gossip and whine about the cost of things in the city. This "Finally!" was also my dentist's reaction during the usual "so what's new with your job lately?" conversation. In 2015, I had been welcomed at the Starbucks near my flat by one of the baristas who knew my job telling me, totally definitively in such a very French way: "He's never gonna make it here. Crazy no? What's wrong with him?"! Novak Djokovic's chase in Paris had become everybody's business. With that degree of scrutiny and expectation, it would have been easy for that whole story to have created what one would call an obsession from Novak towards the French Open.

So what if that second set against Roberto Bautista Agut had been one of the most important sets of Novak Djokovic's career? What if, on his second set point at 5-4, RBA on serve, that absolute genius of a lob, when Novak was sent out wide defending on his backhand, was going to be one of his most important shots ever? Maybe. It stayed in the limits of the court, hitting the line of the alley, then it was back to the boxing match from the baseline, until Novak decided to take the ball on top of the bounce on two successive forehands, finishing off RBA on a crossed backhand. No gesture of joy, no fist right away in the air. Head down, finally locked in and also surely aware that the suffering was far from over. He just ran to his chair and set his head firmly under a towel: do not disturb. He kept all his frustration and maybe anger as well inside and just kept fighting.

Novak had been asked time and time again if at this point Roland-Garros had for him become an obsession. And his answer had never varied: no, absolutely not. "I don't like the word 'obsession' because it doesn't come from the right emotion," he had to explain again that year in Monte-Carlo. "It is a wish, a goal like anything else is and was, and that's what it's going to stay. Of course I'll try to get a step further in Paris than what I've done in the past but I'm not the only one who wants to win that title. But sure Roland-Garros being the only Grand Slam I never won gives me even more incentive to give my best there. Being the slowest and physically most demanding surface, it demands a lot of patience." You wouldn't succeed getting him beyond that statement. He wouldn't open the door now to what were the consequences of this missing piece in his mind.

But if indeed he didn't feel obsessed by this unfinished business, how had he done that? With all the scars, with his ambition: how was it possible for such an athlete not to be slightly obsessed by this French Open? His great rival Andy Murray gave some food for thought right before their final in Paris in his column: "Chasing a Grand Slam title or final for years can be frustrating obviously when you don't get it. But it can also be motivating, as well. If you really want to keep doing it or believe that you can keep doing it, then, providing you learn from the mistakes or maybe find some of the reasons for why you may have not got there in the past, then there's no reason why you can't keep getting a little bit closer all of the time."

He himself knew that feeling of chasing a Grand Slam title very well, so he wouldn't totally deny that obsession never gets in the way: "I've now played five finals in Melbourne without winning and Novak will play his fourth here in Paris, still chasing the title, so can it become an obsession at some point? I guess it can be. I wouldn't say that's necessarily a feeling I have had towards the Australian Open because I still have great memories from there. I don't see it as being all negative. Whereas it is possible that Wimbledon for me was actually kind of more an obsession and something that I thought about a lot and put a lot of pressure and sort of stress on myself at that event more than in Australia."

Novak himself admitted that he'd been thinking about Paris for a year, since he lost against Wawrinka in the 2015 final. So how wouldn't it become an obsession? "Well first of all, everybody needs to have goals. Then, you need to play it all down, as it's mandatory not to be focused on the event itself," explained Aliotta. "You have to stay focused on your abilities and competences. Also, Roland-Garros mustn't be seen as a whole: one plays one match after another match. If you don't do that, it's way too scary. Matches are like steps you climb one after the other. Players are used to it, used to breaking a task into several stages, and also to adding intermediate steps in order to avoid being overwhelmed by what's at stake. The player needs to distance himself from the challenge, so he can anchor the priorities. That's a way to consolidate motivation and to reinforce confidence."

It's easy to tie this to the meditation work Djokovic has been doing for years, to the visualizations and this mindfulness approach he mentioned this year in Monaco. For him it had become as much a tool for his tennis success and a daily work as, now, a lifestyle. Mindfulness, or being in the here and now as you hear more and more players saying all season long, is a pretty efficient way to not get obsessed or stressed out during a tournament or a match. If Novak was able to come back one more time in Paris and was now back in this match against Bautista Agut despite everything playing against him, it was also because he was trying hard not to think about all of this, and he had started this work months and months ago.

That's the thing with him: if he's not obsessed by Paris, it's surely because he spent months consciously getting this out of his mind. "Being in the here and now is a crucial work in stress management, because it keeps the brain from going afield," said Aliotta. When Novak all season long tells the press "I focus on what I can influence: I can't do anything about the past, and I can't guess the future, so I focus on the present moment," that's the work being done backstage. How many times has someone wondered how those champions dealt with such huge levels of pressure so well? The answer is surely for most of them: they don't. They learn how to cope so at the end they close the door to it most of the time. That's what Aliotta specified: "With meditation, I'm cutting myself off from the outside and I stay in my perceptions or I focus on a thought. But this can be also triggered during a match, by listening to my body, by the breathing: 'I think when I inhale, I think when I exhale and I'm only focused on the sensations it's bringing to me.' When I'm in the here and now, I don't think about what's to come so I'm not afraid. Stress starts as soon as I have the feeling that I don't have the abilities to face some situation. So if I keep anticipating what's going to happen, I'm stressed out."

What about Djokovic then, who was asked since January about the French Open? "If people start talking to me about Roland-Garros six months before and I'm like 'whoah,' then for sure I'll never get there because I won't ever feel able enough," explained Aliotta. "But it's different if I stay in the here and now and keep asking myself: 'How was this match? How do I feel after this win? How do I feel regarding my motivation? How does my body feel?' If he's in this all the time, then there's no mental anticipation."

Coach Marian Vajda confirmed that the here and now techniques had indeed been the only way for Novak to cope in Paris that year. "I think he pretty much knows that the worst moment has to come just before Paris. Too many ideas, it's not very effective later. Novak is very creative so whenever he came to the place, he felt to be in the present, to deal with the present moment, and he wanted to forget about the past. He came each time with this new fresh breath. I've never forgotten what Jan Kodes[9] told me: 'You have to come to the venue as if it's a completely new story'. You're starting all over again. Everything comes new." And when all of this wasn't working anymore, Vajda had an other method that could be summed up by four words: just let him vent. Because at some point, this 2016 French Open quest was too much and Novak would be close to imploding. "There were all those flashbacks... We would talk about it, he would let all the negativity go out, would tell me and the team everything so it just gets out. And we are there to listen... No, not to listen: to filter! (Laughs) That was very important and also to encourage him all the time. You are a kind of mentalist as well, you are always with him, loyal to him and you believe it can happen. But you can't tell him 'if it doesn't happen, that doesn't really matter,' that's bla bla bla."

But everyone had apparently decided to play the motivational coach with Djokovic that time in Paris and so it wasn't always easy for him to stay in this relaxing here and now. Nor to feel better after ranting to his team. A mindset that would again this year often push him to stay in the intimacy of the locker rooms, and not mix with everybody else in the players' lounge. It's not a coincidence if many top players have one goal in Grand Slams: spend the least possible time in these lounges. It's better than having to play the mean one and refuse all interactions and solicitations by the people having access there. No signing for the cousin of one, or posing for a selfie with the girlfriend of another.

---

9. Former Czech tennis player who won the French Open in 1970 and 1971, and Wimbledon in 1973.

Not having also to lunch two chairs away from your biggest rivals nor to chat with other players to be polite. Some players told me their secret when they have to walk around those places is to watch the ground: "If I look up and cross someone's look, I'm done," one prominent player explained to me.

So in Paris I rarely crossed Novak in the players' lounge or restaurant, but often saw a member of his team getting the pasta bowls. Staying in the here and now, saving energy, keeping focus: that doesn't go well with the social life. Yet, in a great initiative, by those of course who were not the athletes trying to manage their own stress levels, the French tournament organization decided to make a "Legends" videos saga. They found a way to have Novak reading Andre Agassi's words about Roland-Garros, the tournament in which he played and lost the final in 1990 against Andres Gomez, and kept missing in order to complete his career slam before finally clinching the title in 1999 in dramatic fashion after he was two sets down to Andrei Medvedev.

Paris, hopes, trauma: does that ring a Serbian bell? In an even bigger "soulmates moment," Agassi said this: "everything happens for a reason." After seasons of covering tennis and so Novak Djokovic, I lost count of how many times he'd utter that line. Here are the words of Agassi put in Novak's voice: "Me and Roland-Garros was a long, long road but ironically it's almost the first Grand Slam that I should have won, as it was the first one where I had decent results. And then everything came unstuck. I had to wait a long, long time, so much it ended up being the one big title that I was missing. I think that everything happens for a reason. If I didn't win Roland-Garros when I was young, it's because something was missing, and I needed to search inside myself for the answers." Novak's face when he finished reading looked emotional. There's this pause, straight look and quick jaw move: the parallel is too close for him not to be a bit shaken. It's only for a few seconds but it says everything. The everything that isn't closely and daily monitored by the mindfulness work.

But soon enough, the control was back and he could comment. "He was one of the very few players that won all four Grand Slams and that's what I'm trying to do. At the beginning of my Grand Slam career, I had the most decent results in Roland-Garros. Actually I grew up in Serbia playing the most on that surface." Then he smiled at an obviously not so funny statement for him: "Unfortunately the title hasn't arrived yet in my career, but I can definitely be inspired by these words. Andre Agassi is a great example, somebody that never stopped trying. He did it with persistence and self-belief, so if he can do it, I believe I can do it too. I'll just keep on trying."

Darren Cahill would give an interesting take on the Agassi - Djokovic parallel in Paris, as someone who spent enough time with the American to know how much it had meant to him to finally win the French Open, even if the Australian started to coach him some years after. It was obviously still a recurring topic. "Andre's life was a bit of a rollercoaster with what was happening on the court but also with what was happening off the court. So for him to win that final piece of the puzzle in Paris... In his words he said while he loved it and it was a great feeling he felt a little angry because the feeling he got meant so much to him that he was a little bit offended that it did mean that much. Why does it feel so special, Why does it mean this much? Nothing in the world should be that important. But it was. For Novak I'm sure he went through the same thing. I'm sure he spent every day and every night, every time he stepped onto the court thinking of that moment of finally winning the French Open. It's a lifelong dream for these players who are good enough to be able to do it. For Novak to finally accomplish it, one can only guess how much goodness it brought to his life, but I think it's also part of the reason why we saw a little bit of a letdown for the rest of the year because it did mean that much. When you're thinking about something, dreaming about something, eating for something, practicing for something, when everything is going into a particular moment and you accomplish it, there has to be some sort of a letdown."

And that's why when Novak said he'd keep on trying, it's not that hard to understand he meant he was going to manage every tiny detail to make sure nothing was left to chance. Tennis players have digested the fact they should only focus on what they can control, and not get worried by the rest. With an already somewhat control-freak personality, it's easy to guess that with Djokovic the proportion of the things on the "to put under control" list can be massive. Anyone who has read Novak's book, Serve to Win[10], knows that very few things escape his control from the food he eats and when he eats it, to the amount of time dedicated to yoga, type of fitness training, on court practice, etc. There's discipline and there's Novak Djokovic discipline, which is really as thorough as one would think, confirms Guy Forget, Roland-Garros director and former top player. He had been around Novak long enough to know it, between his BNP Paribas Masters - the Parisian Masters 1000 - director's job, his TV commentator's role, not to forget that his Davis Cup captaincy had him lose against Serbia in the 2010 Belgrade final.

"Novak is a very meticulous person in his approach. Nothing is left to chance, each minute matters. There's an omnipresent care for details," he told me. And this had apparently reached a peak this time in Paris. "I talked to Marian Vajda at the players' restaurant after the final, Forget would add, and he told me: 'You have no idea how tough this fortnight has been, because Novak wanted to win so much and was so demanding with himself that he couldn't stand missing a single ball, and thus was so very demanding with us too. If he was making 20 great backhands in a row but was then missing one...' For Vajda it was a relief at the end too because they must have all been pretty tight and feeling a huge amount of pressure. So when apotheosis comes, there's joy of course but beyond that, also a kind of pressure that is released and that is beautiful too."

When asked about Novak's attention to detail, Thibault Venturino who played the sparring partner for the Serb, smiled knowingly and gave a good example. "I couldn't stay until the final so Novak's team was searching for someone to replace me. I saw that Guillaume Rufin was still around, and he's been a Top 100 player so...Nevertheless Novak still enquired to see exactly who he was, checked all of Rufin's results before deciding that yes he could be trusted so it was fine."

For the French player, there's no doubt that Djokovic is all about control, but for him it's a trait shared by all those monsters of the game. "That's where you see he's an out of this world champion. Another

---

10. "Serve to Win: The 14-Day Gluten-Free Plan for Physical and Mental Excellence", by Novak Djokovic.

example: last year he beat Gilles Simon in Bercy but his serve stats that day were just terrible. He was going nuts about this. At the same time, I'm practicing with Federer and after that I'm scheduled to hit with Nadal. Except that someone jumped in and told me Novak needed me to work on something. I was like 'he has just finished his match...' But the person insisted, so here I am running on court 1 and there he was, just wanting to work on his serve for 15 or 20 minutes. That's the impressive thing: he felt that at his level he had no right to get out of a match with his serve in this state. It's just for his confidence, like after this is dealt with, I can go and sleep well."

Thierry Van Cleemput has shared the practice court enough with David Goffin and Novak to know exactly what it's about. The experienced Belgian coach doesn't actually see any other choice for Djokovic than being ruthless with the details and so with himself and his own game. "Because if you take his accuracy out, you take nearly everything out," he told me in the winter of 2016 near Nice where Goffin was practicing at Patrick Mouratoglou's academy. I was also to discover some time after that the Belgian would practice with Novak there the day after. "That's how I translate the fact that he's so demanding: he just can't afford not to hit exactly where he wants to. But that's also probably why those guys are so much stronger than the rest: they know the value of the point, know that it's also how they're going to make the difference."

And David Goffin, who's been hitting more and more with Novak the past couple of years, hadn't seen anything that different while he practiced with Djokovic before and through that 2016 French Open. "I found him focused, already well into his tournament, in what he had to do. He was feeling the ball really well, his clay game was already in place. He was really ready. I wasn't thinking about the stake of that Roland-Garros for him when we were hitting, I was seeing this as any other practice session. Maybe for Novak it was more an obsession to want to win this one and I guessed he'd do everything to get it this time, but I didn't notice a big difference. He was as usual very friendly and nice."

Boris Becker had been witnessing the Djokovic mindset from the first row since 2014. He knew perfectly well that enormous concern for details. He knew it by heart: "He's a perfectionist, always. I wouldn't say Paris was any different than Melbourne. He's like that. He wants to not miss a ball, period. We could talk after and he'd say 'that's impossible but I still want to try.'" Marian Vajda, who had a decade of having to cope with Novak's demanding personality, would insist that in Paris that year it had little to do with tennis, but much more with the Serbian's mindset. "Technically all was great, even if he had a couple issues on the backhand, but mainly it was all mental. You want it or not but it all comes back to you, all this negativity. Everything was perfect but he needed to be reassured, and also he had to find a way to release himself."

All the team was on the same page, as Gebhard Gritsch also saw this as a crucial part: "It's 15 years of daily work on the court, being focused, and trying to fine-tune your movement and your strokes. And it is still a mission to come into the match feeling 'I have the control over the ball.' You hear everybody often say 'I couldn't feel the ball'. And Novak is very game smart, mentally very strong and physically fit: it's been proven many times that it's crucial for him to feel that everything is working. And when it's the case it's very tough to beat him because he has no flaws. If the opponent realizes this, then often he's not really motivated."

Patrick Mouratoglou is among the coaches who get it as he's been working with the female version of that mindset. "Serena is exactly the same. She's going to serve two double faults and tell you it's not professional. There's an extreme demand towards themselves, and expectations in everything they do. They reject the idea of being average. Rafa is also one of a kind in that department. But that's also the mark of the Greats. People who are fine with average generally aren't those who are going to catch the moon. I find it rather nice to work with those kind of demanding people, because if not you feel as if you'd have to carry them all the time. If I'd have to do it, I would but it's nicer to work with someone who just wants to do the job as well as possible."

That's also Darren Cahill's opinion and he has shared enough years with all time great players to know: "Those great champions are such perfectionists. They'd hit a bad shot and throw their racquet on the ground in disgust. It's what makes them so good: they're never satisfied, they're always pushing to be a little bit better. But also, yeah, sometimes stubbornness can get in the way of the results on the court as well, because if you keep pushing for that perfection, sometimes you're not playing the game plan that would allow you to beat that particular opponent. It can be a great strength but it can also be a curse, so you have to find that balance."

Djokovic doesn't deny at all this side of him, as he also considered it his personal engine: "Because we are all trying to be better and perfect ourselves, it happens that sometimes you're not satisfied and want to do better. But on the positive side: I think it's good that there's something you want to work on which motivates you. Of course sometimes it can get too much in your mind, but one of the things that constantly keeps me going is the fact that I still see things in my game that can improve. If I've played good yesterday, it doesn't mean that I will today too. It's a matter of constantly trying to get better and evolve with life." After his match against Darcis, he would give what for him were the consequences of any lapse in this quest for fixing details. "Top players' teams nowadays look like Formula One teams: they are fighting against each other with guys already close to perfection. It's a fight for a so thin margin, and it's a fight under pressure. Anything amiss, any detail, can have dramatic consequences. And by dramatic, I mean losses and / or injuries."

It's actually this trait of Novak's personality, this professionalism, that got Fabrice Santoro caring about the Serb when he was only a teenager: "I've always liked Novak. And sometimes I feel like I've seen his birth! He arrived on Tour at 16 or 17 years old and right away I was astonished by that guy who was already so professional, who would spend hours on the court, who would be the last one to leave the gym in the evening. He would always be stretching, doing abs, weight training. All the time. He was already really mature and professional, so you just knew he wanted to go all the way to the top. And this drive, you've got it or you don't." That's not being obsessed, that's being determined.

Marian Vajda agreed on the general principle, but he's been stubborn in preventing Novak from getting lost in this perfection quest. He was pretty animated when telling me about this, and that made me want to be a fly on the wall when the Slovakian was trying to explain to the Djoker that it was fine not to be perfect all the time. "He's a perfectionist and it's an unbelievable plus, but it can also bring you down. I just want him to understand that it can happen, he's a human being, he cannot punish himself for that: 'come on! What is this?!' Stay focused, and anyway the mistake is already in the past. Just go point by point. Not being a kind of robot, but you really need to get that frustration out."

Boris Becker was the least traumatized of the team by the French Open but it didn't take him long to understand how Paris was a different animal, nor how the guy he was coaching was a different one too. "It was a different Grand Slam because he had never won Roland-Garros. So it put a lot of attention, a lot of focus on succeeding in Paris. But Novak kept coming back despite everything that happened here. He has an incredible determination. It's very rare for people or professional athletes to have so much drive for so long, and to fall short every time. He'd been winning everything else a number of times, and Roland-Garros was the last hurdle against Nadal but also against Stan. I think that was a painful loss but he said 'ok I'll try again next time.' I think that mindset is very unique." For the former n°1, there was never any feeling of being cursed here: "No, I don't think like that. And he never felt like this either. Novak is different: I felt that as long as he was giving himself the right chance (preparation, tournaments before), there was no reason he shouldn't win the French Open. After all he learnt tennis on clay: that was his first surface."

All over the stadium, umbrellas were swirling but on the court there was nothing above Djokovic and Bautista Agut's heads as they were fighting for each point. Novak had saved a break point on his first service game in this third set, and then after many efforts he had broken to now be up 3-1, just to find himself now down 15-40. You could feel he was a bundle of many emotions at this time, seeing the finish line for that third set but having to endure absolutely dreadful conditions of play and an opponent who would still bring a millions balls back. Boxing rounds in the mud. O Joy. No doubt he was reaching the limits of his composure. As he had to again save a break point, he went for it on a superb rally, hitting each ball at 200% and ending it on a "zero margin" inside out forehand. Both arms up in the air in the pure enraged relief of the one who gave everything not to fall off the edge of the cliff.

The crowd erupted. At this point, Djokovic was yelling his lungs out, leaving few doubts to the frozen but passionate people watching on court about how much he was struggling or how badly he needed every game. They might have also been helped by his now regular talks to that sky that wouldn't stop raining. Bautista Agut wasn't that fresh either, calling the trainer for blisters on his right foot. No wonder with all the running he was doing!

At 4-1 for Djokovic and after two hours of play, the supervisor would take pity on both players and spectators, sending everybody back inside. Presumably under blankets and close to warm drinks. It was 4:55 at the end of a gloomy and rainy afternoon, and no one that day would set a foot again on the court Philippe Chatrier. There would be no long analyzing work among the Djokovic team, no crisis center opened. "We just talked in the locker room about what he should do better, some little tactical things," said Vajda. "But then he went to his house with his wife, their son Stefan and all the family, and he was pretty much relaxed there. He was going through this himself." That's how it goes in the team: they give Djokovic his space, that's the best option. "He has to have his time alone," Vajda explained. "Because too much talking brings you too much, too much technique talk, too much theory: he has to have energy. I do my job, he knows what he wants to, we do the tactics: finished. He has to have a room for himself, it's very important." So Novak would go to sleep in a dreamland between "the dream is still alive" and "all is lost, again".

CHAPTER FOUR

The Red Holds The Key

On that Tuesday, May 31st, when Novak Djokovic was stuck in this battle against Roberta Bautista Agut, every missed shot could have sent him a bit further from not only the title in Paris, but from tennis history. Every racquet swing he took at Porte d'Auteuil in 2016 was with the goal of entering legendary status, so his personal demons were screaming even louder with each line asking to be written in the history books. Djokovic wasn't asked to rise and shine on his beloved Rod Laver Arena, but on a court he had never tamed before. History was demanding that he accomplish something he had never done in a place that was summoning all his doubts and fears. Why make it easy? In order of difficulty, Novak had to: win his first French Open, achieve the Career Grand Slam and then he would become the first player since Rod Laver in 1969, 47 years ago, to win four Majors in a row.

The only way Novak knew to face this tennis ordeal, was to find a silver lining, whatever it might be, and he had to be the sole member of his team to still find a way to smile while remembering that match! "All in all those kinds of circumstances actually help you, I guess challenge you, to become aware of the situation that you're in. It makes you concentrate and give even more of your effort and energy than you would normally do. I didn't expect to win Roland-Garros without losing a set under perfect weather or whatever (laughs): it's very hard to expect that. I was thinking really one day at a time and really making myself believe that the present moment is the only thing that I could influence, that I could be a part of with 100% of my energy."

But in this suspended time between losing and winning, when he was trying to find some recovery sleep and to forget about Roberto

Bautista Agut trying to spoil his quest, he probably also had to remember and repeat to himself that he was, after all, playing on his turf. That this red dirt was as much in his DNA as it was in his Spanish rival's. That he was actually the best clay court specialist on that court. Contrary to Boris Becker, his head coach at the time, or to his idol Pete Sampras, Djokovic is a natural friend of the clay. Thanks to Serbia.

"I grew up on clay," Novak again told me, stating the obvious he may feel some are always forgetting. Truth being that unless you're Spanish or South American not a lot of people assume you've grown up playing on that surface. But Novak insisted it was his reality: "All my childhood I played on clay. Clay for me is a natural surface. I feel comfortable playing on clay courts. Even though results-wise my career on hard courts is the most successful. Still I didn't have too bad of a career on clay courts." He smiled as he knew perfectly well it was an understatement. And indeed he absolutely could slide his way through the dirt, could enjoy the drop shots, could thrive in his element in this chess and geometry game you need to play to outfox your rivals on the red as there were very few chances to just blast them off the court. Unless you were Thomas Muster or Rafael Nadal.

For Christopher Clarey, American sports columnist and writer for the New York Times, there was really zero surprise in the fact that Djokovic was a great clay court player right from the get go. "His childhood coach Jelena Gencic always had a really long view of things and had him play on everything very early. Also he's got a really good vision of the game; he's very flexible so he can handle the sliding and the movements to the corners, and that's part of his game on every surface, crazily enough. He slides on all surfaces, and he also created the reality of that as well: the shoemakers of sporting goods companies have actually followed up that style of play by creating products. I remember lots of guys in the 90's who were trying to slide on other surfaces, trying to figure it out but Novak took it to another art. What amazes me, still, is how he's able to anticipate and move and cover angles that used to be defensive and make them offensive. Rafa did it too, but more on the forehand side, Novak did it on both sides." Clay demands patience, accuracy, great footwork, endurance and a strong tennis IQ: there was then indeed no reason at all why it wouldn't be a perfectly suited surface for Novak Djokovic.

Nadal's reign has made every other achievement on clay look negligible to the general public, but in Novak's case, it could easily be argued that he was already one of the best clay court specialists even before this 2016 French Open. Right from his first seasons on the Tour, he proved he could shine there. In July 2006, at 19 years old, it was on clay that he won the first title of his career, defeating Chilean Nicolas Massu (7-6(5), 6-4), a known clay specialist, in Amersfoort.

For his former coach Niki Pilic, there was never a single doubt that Novak could shine on that surface all the way to winning Roland-Garros. "I thought he could have won there earlier, and of course in 2013, but then he went to touch that net against Nadal at 4-3 in the fifth set... Then in 2015 too, but he played that semi-final in two days against Murray and I was sure after the second set against Wawrinka that he didn't stand a chance because he was simply tired and slow. Roland-Garros is the toughest one because you need to run more than anywhere else. But on clay you have to be both mentally and physically very strong and Novak is like that."

Only a few weeks before this first title in Amersfoort, "Nole" had reached the first Grand Slam quarter final of his career in Roland-Garros, barely turning 19 during that tournament. He made waves in Paris beating Fernando Gonzalez, ranked 9th at this time, in five sets, then Tommy Haas in straight sets, and Gaël Monfils in three sets too, before falling to Rafael Nadal, retiring with a lower back injury after losing the first two sets (6-4, 6-4, ab.) He was 63rd in the world when he entered the draw that year. Since that 2006 campaign, Novak would lose only once before the quarter finals in Paris (2009, third round), and not a single time before the semi-finals since 2011.

If it was a quiz, it would make a nice question: do you know where Novak Djokovic won his first match in a Grand Slam? You guessed right: Roland-Garros. He was only two days past his 18th birthday when, after getting out of the qualifications, he beat Robby Ginepri in the first round of the main draw (6-0, 6-0, 6-3) in 2005. And that same kid, ranked 128th at the time, would go on to take a set from Guillermo Coria, Argentina's 2004 finalist, before retiring (6-4, 2-6, 2-3) due to breathing issues. Nowadays Novak Djokovic is known and renowned for being a ruthless and dominant hardcourt player, but it's on clay and in Paris that he first appeared to the tennis world as a potential star of the game.

More than a decade later, Darren Cahill can still go on about how the young Djokovic piqued his interest at that time. The Australian never doubted Djokovic's potential and was reinforced in his intuition after this 2006 French Open. "I knew he was going to be good," he told me in Melbourne during the 2017 Australian Open. "Anybody could see from his junior days and when he first came on the Tour, that he was somebody very special so we were watching him with great interest. Also when he played the quarter finals of the French Open in 2006 and lost to Rafa, retired after the first two sets, and then came off the court making some remarks he felt fairly comfortable even though the scoreline didn't suggest that: you knew that this is a kid that felt like he belonged on the big stage."

I can still remember the utter shock mixed with disbelief within the tennis world, media included, after that press conference. They couldn't decide if it was pure teenage bragging, utter lack of respect or proof of an ego that was borderline insane. Down two sets to Nadal, struggling with his back, Djokovic had given up on the court, but not off the court as he'd affirm that he was the better one that day. "At the start he was not that comfortable, I saw that," Novak would say[11]. "I think I had the control of the match. I just didn't finish it in the right way when I needed to. For sure, he's the best on this surface, but he's not unbeatable. I think I could win today. He didn't know how to play against me, because he never played against me, so it was a difficult position for him as well."

Could you hear it? It was the sound of jaws dropping to the floor, Rafa's included as he would be told that later on. This bravado didn't go well with most of the tennis world that day, as I think I was the only one around laughing when told that story as at the time I wasn't on site. Cahill hadn't been shocked or upset about it: he saw it as a promising sign.

A week after that, he'd cross the path of the teenager at Stoke Park where Novak was playing an exhibition match on grass against Andre Agassi before Wimbledon. And Cahill would definitely decide there

---

11. "Djokovic quits as Nadal marches on", CNN, June 7, 2006, (*http://edition.cnn.com/2006/SPORT/06/07/tennis.nadal/*).

that the kid, who ended up winning 6-3, 6-4, had what it took to make it big. "We got to see first hand how easy he made the game look, how well he was able to move and that not only did he have a defensive game that could retrieve a lot of balls, but also he could turn defense into offense very quickly, with one strike, and that's rare. You can do one or the other extremely well but he could do both extremely well. He had the eye of the tiger as well: you could see in his eyes that he was desperate to be among the best players in the world. He felt like he belonged there, a bit similar to Lleyton Hewitt really, with the look he gave you when he shook your hand. Since, he's been able to turn himself into one of the all time Greats."

Cahill told the other part of that Stoke Park story in 2013 while doing commentary for the Hopman Cup, as reported by "The Australian" newspaper[12]. In true "young and bold Djokovic" fashion, Novak also made an impression on Agassi by explaining to him what he should do to beat Nadal, who had won their previous meeting, on the way back from this match when they were sharing a car. Agassi would still lose to Rafa in that 2006 Wimbledon but there was a 19 year old Serbian convinced he knew how to beat the Spaniard.

Days after having retired against him in Paris, he wouldn't let go. It is also tough not to smile at this mental image of a 19 year old Djokovic telling the legend that was Agassi how to win a tennis match. Right out of his first Grand Slam quarter final, the Djoker thought he had it in himself and he was right to, as his natural abilities to shine on clay would be worked on again and again until made perfect. Until they brought him his first win against "Rafa" on this surface and then the Paris trophy. Had he accepted Rafa's superiority right away without arguing in 2006, who knows if he would have ended winning that much on clay through his career? Because Nadal was the last code to crack, and Djokovic had been working on it right from the start.

---

12. "Andre Agassi formed the view in 2006 that Novak Djokovic would become a great", The Australian, January 26, 2013, (*http://www.theaustralian.com.au/sport/tennis/ andre-agassi-formed-the-view-in-2006-that-novak-djokovic-would-become-a- great/news-story/36168ede6410dc126652cc0911e28f23*).

One of his former coaches, Riccardo Piatti, said back in 2006 during that French Open that Novak was already spending a lot of time watching Nadal play during every tournament, and that as he was smart he already understood a lot of things about the Spaniard's game. The target on Rafa's back had been drawn a long time ago. For ten years Djokovic would indeed know no rest until turning himself into one hell of a fantastic clay court player, getting better and better by the season until totally mastering it. "You don't win Roland-Garros if you're not physically a monster," said Fabrice Santoro. "And Novak is one. Then you need to have an iron-made mental strength: he owns one. Then beyond those two facts, he also found the key to stand eye to eye against Rafa on clay." So, really, in the 2016 plan there was not a single line about Roberto Bautista Agut messing this up.

Novak Djokovic had become a favorite every time he set foot on a court, whatever the surface. Something that happened for very few players through the history of the game. It's one thing to be also good on clay, but it's totally another to become a clay master in an era when Rafael Nadal reigned supreme on the red. When Roger Federer himself hadn't found a way through the Spaniard in Paris despite being hailed by many as the Greatest Of All Time. When all the so-called clay specialists were eaten alive in every tournament by Rafa. Alone with his thoughts that night, if Djokovic was searching for a last extra confidence boost before letting the comforting darkness of sleep take over, he could always turn to Rafa. His biggest Roland-Garros and overall clay tormentor was also the biggest proof of his own worth: if you've found a way into Nadal's head and game on clay, if you've become one of the greatest on this surface too, surely you can handle being in a tango with Bautista Agut.

"I think the only curse that Novak had in Roland-Garros was the same that everybody had: Rafa Nadal, the greatest clay court player that has ever lived," said Darren Cahill. "To come up against him in his prime, to beat that guy over best of five sets at the French Open... I'm not sure there's a bigger test in tennis. Novak's been able to do it on other surfaces; he worked on the game plan and it's been efficient and successful, but to do it on clay where your footing isn't so sure makes it that much more difficult. But he finally did it."

Nowadays some may have forgotten the tremor that shook the tennis world in 2011 when the Djoker beat Nadal (7-5, 6-4) in the final of Madrid's Masters 1000, then confirming it the week after in the Rome final (6-4, 6-4). But that's when Djokovic became a favorite for Paris every year, and not just a natural outsider below Nadal. Gustavo Kuerten, the Beloved Brazilian who won Roland-Garros three times (1997, 2000, 2001) and has close ties to Djokovic, always believed Novak could make it big on clay: "He has always been a very talented player. The toughest for him was to get going on clay where he has to generate power and where his forehand has to hit winners."

People have endlessly dissected why Rafael Nadal's game was the best ever on that surface, how he could crush any opponent's style on the red. How there was something beautifully inevitable in the way he just dismembered everyone. The spins on his forehand have made their way into tennis history. But in the meantime, it led to most of the people not noticing the obvious about Novak Djokovic and, of course, Roger Federer: they too were terrific clay players for totally different reasons. "We underestimate everybody on clay because of Rafa's separation between him and the field on all clay courts," agreed Cahill.

The great Rod Laver pointed out exactly the same thing to me: "Novak has the clay court game, used to playing on it as he's European. But well, he was losing to Nadal and it's almost unfair the way Nadal plays on the clay courts (laughs). It's just unbelievable to be a 9 time Grand Slam champion at the French." And for Djokovic it led to many not giving his game enough credit when the red was coming.

More than Federer, he was the one contesting the Nadal supremacy with success. The Swiss had never beaten Nadal in Roland-Garros, but the Serb did. Federer never left the impression that he had solved the Nadal-on-clay equation with his two wins against him on the dirt in Hamburg 2007 and Madrid 2009. Djokovic did. To everybody's astonishment, and Nadal's own disbelief, he ended mastering the clay by also mastering its King. Something that had been deemed impossible.

At the end of the 2016 season, Novak had won 13 titles on clay, including 8 Masters 1000. Sure, it's far from Rafael Nadal's 49 trophies on the dirt, but it's better than Roger Federer (11), Andre Agassi (7), Pete Sampras (4), Boris Becker (1), John McEnroe (5), Andy Murray (3) or Stefan Edberg (6), and equal to Jimmy Connors. Not only has he finally clinched that French Open title, played three semi-finals there (2007, 2008, 2013) and contested three finals (2012, 2014, 2015) before winning in Paris, but he has also won every clay Masters 1000: Monte-Carlo (2013, 2015), Madrid (2011, 2016) and Rome (2008, 2011, 2014, 2015). Among the champions of recent history, Djokovic is really high on the short list. So how did he achieve all of that? How, confronting Nadal at his prime, has he made the impossible possible, building his way to clay titles?

The context of his era certainly explains a part of his success on clay. Gone indeed are the days where as soon as the Tour would see red, you'd see a bunch of super specialists getting out, all topspin and forehand raging, to trust the finals. "We're far away from the 80's or the 90's," said Thierry Van Cleemput, David Goffin's coach. "In this time, yes we had real clay specialists, but that also meant that it was useless to talk to them about grass or hardcourt. Nowadays, every player can play well and win on every surface, as far as the top of the ranking is concerned. Tennis has been standardized, so one has to be strong on every surface even if when you get away from the top you still find guys who are more specialists of a surface. But at the top, they're good everywhere: there's this consistency, this timing, this ability to adjust and to slide. If you take Novak, he has what it takes to adjust to every surface."

But exactly what does he have that other great champions didn't? What turned him into an answer to Nadal's hegemony? What made people think he was cursed in Paris as he should have already won there despite falling most of the time against Nadal, deemed the unbeatable?

For Paul Quétin, it all starts with outstanding physical abilities. The French fitness trainer knows what he is talking about: he's been heading the French Federation physical training department for years, has spent more than a decade working with Richard Gasquet, and is now supervising the French female players as well as also some male juniors. Season after season he's been trying to prepare these athletes for the clay season, and he has in the process seen what the others were doing too. He's been crossing paths with Djokovic for so long that he can't even remember when the first time was, but has vivid memories of some hard fought football matches he saw the Serbian play on the grass of Indian Wells. "He just loves sports, any sport, and what an athlete..."

We met in the brand new national training center in Paris, right near Roland-Garros. Here he actually saw Novak coming, among others, during the 2016 edition of the French Open. For Quétin, it was no wonder that Djokovic had won so much on clay and finally succeeded in winning in Paris because we were talking about someone whose extraordinary physical abilities helped him to basically dance on the dirt. "He's playing on clay nearly as he is playing on every other surface, by using athletic abilities that surely are different from a player like Rafael Nadal who is the clay reference. Novak is all about flexibility, elasticity, looseness. He's great on clay for the same reasons he's great anywhere else... His speed on the footwork, his absolutely extraordinary timing on both wings, and the fact that he's not spending that much energy to play his game. He has a huge technical quality that helps him save energy and that's a massive help in five set matches. And his flexibility turns him into the absolute reference in this area, as he has pushed it to something quite exceptional: he can slide like nobody else, and even when he's in an extreme position he can still hit the ball in a balanced way. Not a lot of players can do that. The way he covers his ground is fantastic."

Van Cleemput is also amazed by what Djokovic displays on clay: "The huge abilities that in my opinion no one is talking about enough are his physical ones: he has the outstanding looseness that allows him to be powerful without getting tired. And it's not for everyone. Being lose and accurate on the footwork is an art and a difficult balance to find." That's surely why Novak has been the first player to defeat Nadal in straight sets at the French Open (2014), or the only one to beat him in every clay Masters 1000 tournament, starting with that earthquake in Madrid 2011. When Djokovic won in Madrid that year, he broke an incredible streak of 37 consecutive wins on clay by Nadal, and clinched his first victory over him on clay in ten attempts. It would push an astonished Carlos Moya, nowadays Rafael Nadal's second coach alongside Toni Nadal, to say[13] "it's the first time I've seen him beaten

---

13. Source: L'Equipe, May 9, 2011.

on clay despite being 100% physically. It wasn't the case two years ago here against Federer nor in Roland-Garros against Söderling..."

It was also Novak in 2013 who put an end to eight consecutive years of domination from Rafa in Monte-Carlo, regularly finding a way to counter the power of the Spaniard's heavy topspin, lifted by his amazing backhand that was setting up deep into Nadal's head and game. "One shouldn't confuse muscle volume and muscle quality," explained Quétin. "Djokovic is less massive than other players, displays less power than someone like Nadal or Wawrinka but his muscle quality is very real. He's very lean but owns strong explosiveness and a real quality of arm speed."

Also like Rafa, Djokovic doesn't really have to adjust for the clay: he's a natural. "He's been playing on clay since childhood and moves on it like he moves on hardcourt: he never had to adjust his footwork massively," said the French trainer. "It all comes naturally to him and that's a huge advantage as nowadays players don't have a lot of time for preparation: you come back from the Miami Masters 1000 and it's already clay season basically."

Inside the Djokovic team, there's no doubt as to how Novak's footwork explains why he's turned out to be that good on clay. "It's his movements," answered Marian Vajda right away when I asked him why Novak was so good on the red. "His movements are so flexible. He can slide fantastically. And this is the secret: sliding. Because most of the guys recently they have different movements, they run instead of sliding. But on clay if you are fine you slide, because if not you are out of reach on every ball. And then you also leave an open court and it's finished. Novak can cover the court in an excellent way, and then always come back into position."

Gebhard Gritsch, whose job has also been to take care and improve those movements, of course agreed. "Novak is one of the best mover if not the best mover in tennis, and he's very explosive." But the Austrian also pointed out that to make it look that natural it had also taken some work as, strangely, Djokovic's strengths could also be an issue. "Sometimes I feel he's too explosive for the clay court because he has sometimes trouble to really get the power into the ground, and his running style with sliding doesn't always help him on that surface either. So we were working quite intensively on some adjustments:

take smaller steps, set up properly, don't slide off. It's a fine line: like him, if you're too strong... When he's sprinting he's sliding four meters and there's nothing you can control anymore. Once you slide, you slide: good bye! (Laughs)."

For anyone who has been lucky enough to be court-side when Rafa plays on clay, his virtuosity on the surface is mind-blowing. Often I would just focus on watching his feet and it'd be a show in itself: the accuracy, the speed, the perfect mix of power and subtlety. And the noise that the ball makes when he hits a forehand! Until 2011, it was impossible to imagine anyone repeatedly beating him on his turf: how could you beat perfection?

By offering another kind of perfection, that's how we could sum up what the Djokovic answer had been. "Novak has the perfect game to play well on clay," stated Patrick Mouratoglou who often sees the Serb coming to practice at his academy. "He commits very few unforced errors, he covers his ground in an outstanding way, can play a lot of inside out forehands, has huge endurance and can take the ball early so he constantly takes time away from you. Sure, he doesn't have Nadal's power but he has a better ability to take the ball on the rise and to speed up the ball that way. And he can go from defense to offense in some amazing ways."

Cahill added that the key for Djokovic was to "transform a hardcourt game onto clay extremely well." Yes, Novak grew up on clay but he did it with his own set of rules: he didn't adjust to the surface as much as he made the surface suit his game. As much as he made every turf be his turf. The closest tennis version of a chameleon. And his maestria on the drops shots and lob, that makes him an even more unpredictable nightmare on clay, had always been there: "Regarding the touch, growing up in Serbia we played a lot of mini tennis, a lot of different games in the service box, and I think that helped," he said in Paris that year. "And over the course of my career, I tried to always keep that, you know, routine, especially in the practice, preparation parts of the year where I get to do that with other players that I practiced with. It's nice. It helps on clay, especially."

Djokovic's game, where the talent in his hands and eyes isn't praised enough, has never been thought nor made to be one-sided, and

115

at the end it totally reflects his personality: Novak fits everywhere, can decipher and learn the social codes of any world, always has another trick waiting for you, loves to be the star of the show, and loves to play and compete. There was then not going to be a single part of the tennis tour that he wasn't going to try to rule. Others may have decided to leave Nadal's red land alone, but not Novak Djokovic. If it's out there for anyone to win it, you could count on him to plant his flag there somehow.

Tournament director Guy Forget couldn't recall one moment in particular where he'd been in awe of Djokovic that year in Paris. No, not one special game, set or match stood out... Simply because Novak astonished him all the time: "It's on sequences that he impresses me. There's such speed in the way he moves, such accuracy in his shots, such variety too. When you're on the side of the court and you see him play it looks so simple but it's in fact so hard to do. Even more at this speed! The backhand I could hit at 80 km/h, he's going to hit at 160 km/h, and while moving his legs like a sprinter. And it goes on and on. It's prodigious to watch."

To be that prodigious on the court, you also have to be prodigious off the court. Talking about Djokovic's abilities on clay or elsewhere always brings you back to one word that has tennis people's eyes wide open: his flexibility. It's not just that he moves and defends amazingly well, it's that he does it by putting his body in positions never seen before on a tennis court, and that he can be aggressive while doing it. There is no safe zone on a court in front of him, not a single area where one can breathe a sigh of relief thinking the ball won't come back, and come back with a vengeance. There is just no stop to the pressure he puts the others under.

When I reminded Paul Quétin of that day we watched Novak stretching after his practice in Wimbledon in 2015, he had the same smile as before. A "You cannot be serious" smile that would end by him saying back at Aorangi Park that "the only person I see stretching like this on a daily basis has to be my daughter...who is a ballet dancer. It's so rare for a male tennis player." When an experienced fitness trainer who has seen generations of guys couldn't stop watching Djokovic being stretched in all possible positions by his physiotherapist, you knew there was something uncommon going on.

And it was the same for Novak's rivals. Most of them are now used to it, but someone like Thibault Venturino still couldn't wrap his head around what he often witnessed on the practice court with the Serbian. "That flexibility, it's just out of this world. If I would try this, like just when he puts a leg on his physio's shoulder, I would break my hip in four places and land in hospital for three months! It's absolutely scary. The first time I witnessed this, I froze. I just couldn't look away. I'm lucky he didn't see me! (Laughs) I thought it was a joke. It looked plainly impossible."

The Djokovic warm up is famous for that: just looking at how Novak can bend and twist under the care of Amanovic hands! I've seen people court side closing their eyes in terror as if they were getting ready to hear him scream in pain or something. The only thing they'd hear would be Novak chatting with his team and even laughing through what looked like torture. "He has a very surprising elasticity," said Quétin. "An outstanding laxity... And he works on it, clearly. It's his muscle quality range, even if it's pretty atypical for a tennis player. Players are elastic, but Novak is like rubber-made. It's an advantage that could also produce some issues for his body but he and his team deal with it really well. They establish all the motor-skills work around it regarding his muscles but also his footwork and his techniques. And nowadays you see someone like Andy Murray working a lot on his flexibility too, especially since his back issues. That's where those guys are impressive: they never stop working despite all their success."

The impressive thing in this incredible ability of Djokovic is that it is Novak himself who figured it all out, as Gritsch would tell me: "Novak is an intelligent person. He felt in the early days of his career, even when he was a junior as he was never the strongest, what he needed to do to catch up and to change things to his advantage. And I think the flexibility, especially in the time where he was with Niki Pilic, he realized it was so important for his game. He was only 14 years old. And at that time none of the coaches insisted that you needed to go stretch every day. But he himself did. And from that time on he did it basically every day."

Something Amanovic was also stunned with: "He started this when he was so young. He was taking all the things around him seriously you know, starting with two or three more t shirts, socks. Everything related to body was the same: he was stretching on daily basis, massages. As a young player, he had a huge support from his family as his parents did a lot to organize the stuff around him so he didn't suffer. That was the best possible decision and everything paid off, so he continues to apply all of this. That has become an automatism. So stretching, yes, is a big advantage: he's reaching balls you think it'd be impossible to defend, and he's still hasn't faced any big injury related to over stretched, pulling hamstrings or adductors. "

As others have stated, Novak plays on clay like he plays elsewhere, with an out of this world timing and an astonishing ability to take the ball early. Novak doesn't dictate on clay because he's the most powerful, he does so because he pushes every match to become a PlayStation demo. And even on clay, his return does wonders, as recalled Thibault Venturino, whose practice sessions with Djokovic tended to make the round inside the French circle. "Often I'd serve to him being like two meters inside the court and each time it impressed people. One time I had friends in the crowd taking pictures, so I ended tagged on Facebook and then the sports director of my club was like 'Ventu, tell me that he doesn't return when you're set up like that!' The thing is that Novak is maybe going to miss one ball every ten years... and he's also going to be super accurate. I was not telling him where I was going to serve but he was going to decide to always return down the line inside 10 square centimeters, and he was going to make it. My friend was like 'Can't be possible!' But it is! Just unreal. I have no idea how he does that. Even if, sure, you can improve the eye. Still, at this point, I don't know how it's possible. For me, it's pure genius."

For Quétin, you couldn't develop such skills overall if you hadn't been taught them as a kid. For Djokovic, it had to have been worked on probably since the first times he took a racquet with his first coach and mentor Jelena Gencic. "It's taken years and years, hours and hours to reach the level of perfection that it is now," he said. Players and coaches always praise the Djokovic timing, the way he takes the ball so early all season long, and Quétin saw first hand how the Serb works on it. "I've watched him training with French players a lot of times and he's mainly focusing on one this: his timing. And his timing is about playing inside the court or on the baseline but never ever to step back.

For years he's been pushing himself to read the game and organize himself quickly, to be super fast on his legs. As soon as the warm up starts, he's into this. Eyes and legs have been trained to play at this rhythm: Novak demands that and people around him always have and still do too. He's nearly always inside the court, even if that means playing a half volley. When you practice with that in mind, when you never go away from what has become a rule, you sharpen the eye and the motor ability in outstanding fashion. It's really hard to do all the time, both mentally and physically, but when you succeed in staying on this baseline then you're going to save so much energy... Your rival is running, you're not."

For this aspect of his game, Djokovic praised his early years of training: "To be close to the line, that's how I grew up. I always had coaches who made me be closer to the baseline and be aggressive with my shots, including the return. It gave me a lot of confidence, and it paid off."

The technician that is Darren Cahill could only admire the overall result that was now Djokovic on clay: "He doesn't get pushed back too far, he's able to take the ball on the rise, which on clay you don't need to do as much but if you have that ability, you take a lot of time away from your opponent. But to be able to do that, your hand-eye coordination must be incredible because the bounce on a clay court isn't a perfect bounce. But he has the ability to adjust really effectively. He's got a complete game: his transition game over the last two or three years has improved a lot; he's coming to the net a lot more now to finish the points to preserve his body a little bit more but also to add a different weapon to his game. I think Boris Becker helped him a lot with that. His serve improved incredibly over the last four years. His second serve mostly. He's a smart tennis player, he's doing problem solving extremely well."

"Smart" has to be the word that has come back the most when talking all things Djokovic for this book, as people would praise his game as much as his intellect. There's a highly functioning brain under that big bunch of dark hair, and that's a huge part of his success. By constantly chasing Nadal when the clay was coming, Djokovic raised his own bar every year a little more, and pushed his focus, game and determination to levels he probably never thought he could. He had no choice if he wanted to win in Paris someday, as he thought the Spaniard would probably always be in his way, as he was in 2006, as he was three times in the semi-finals (2007, 2008, 2013) and twice in the finals (2012, 2014).

He neither saw the French Open nor Nadal as some kind of personal curses, never feared them enough to not dare making them surrender. He saw them as he's seen everything since he decided as a kid that he would one day be the best player in the world: problems needing to be solved. Confronted with them, he put his whole being into it as again there are very few players out there who could put a goal as a red cross in their mind and never ever deviate from it, whatever the sacrifices and the odds.

Nadal and Roland-Garros were between him and glory and so needed to get out of his way. The key to Nadal was found, but the French Open remained. So now Roberto Bautista Agut really needed to go. I hardly doubt the fact that between leaving the court up 4-1 in the third on Tuesday and coming back to it on Wednesday, Djokovic had mentally reviewed every possible scenario, every solution to every disaster that might come, every trap he could put under RBA's feet, every hole he could burn into the Spaniard's shots, every game he could play with his mind. Bautista Agut was dancing in his brain and Novak was just trying to pick the best way to pin him against the red wall.

It was all written on his face when they resumed this match: he hadn't gone through so much since he lost against Wawrinka last year for good old Bautista Agut to ruin his plans. Boris Becker never doubted that Djokovic would win that match after all this drama: "I knew it would be fine the next day. I felt it when he was able to switch his mindset, even if he couldn't finish and that was upsetting. But he was on the winning streak. I just hoped the next day he was not going to play for too long because on the following day there was another match. My motto is always: if you can get the job done, don't wait on it." It had never been an enviable situation to be Rafael Nadal's prey on clay, and over the years it also became a terrifying prospect to be left in Djokovic's claws there too. If we were in the jungle, Bautista Agut might have started to run, even more as he knew quite well what Novak in full gear could turn into as months later during the Shanghai Rolex Masters he would say "the first time I played him I thought he was from another planet." And he also knew very well that the 2016 version of the Djoker was way scarier than this 2013 one when they first crossed paths in Dubai.

CHAPTER FIVE

Mister Resilience

On the evening of this May 31st, there was a fabulously glam party in Paris set up by the ITF to honor its champions. In the very chic and intimate Pavillon Cambon Capucines, the International Tennis Federation was having its annual dinner and trophies ceremony for its world champions. Guess what? Many of us would not set foot near the Place Vendôme for this event, thanks to rain, delayed matches and crying deadlines. And when Novak was announced as the men's champion, guess what? He didn't show up either. The only Djokovic in a black tuxedo that came to receive the trophy was his uncle Goran.

There would be no fancy evening for his nephew that day as he was off to treatments, stretching, eating and trying to forget that his 2016 French Open campaign was not exactly taking the easy road. Still, he could find comfort in knowing that at least he'd come back at 4-1 up in this third set against Roberto Bautista Agut. Another comfort would come early on June 1st: at 11am Serena Williams, who was able to attend the ITF dinner, trashed her Ukrainian opponent Elina Svitolina (6-1, 6-1) in the fourth round and so Novak was going to resume his match quickly. It was still raining that morning, then a stubborn drizzle remained and slowly but surely the conditions became playable again.

But the sun was still sulking and it was winter-cold in Paris. Marian Vajda had a good feeling about that second part of the thriller, as the Serbian he met again in the morning wasn't the one he had left the last evening. "We went back to what he should change tactically, to play Bautista Agut more on the backhand. We tried to lift him up, but the next day he was completely different." Miljan Amanovic wasn't extra worried either about how Novak would physically adjust to that match over two days played in very tough conditions: he knew he was ready for a battle. "We didn't do anything special. We have our own routine that is already so well organized and prepared that, yes there are surprises, but not that match in two days. Yes, heavy balls, heavy conditions, heavy legs so he was spending more energy but he was healthy. And as Novak is somebody who is recovering more than well and who is doing everything right, my job is easy (smile). There are still things we have to do and that's it. But also, it's the goal here, so the adrenaline does its part, the expectations too so you're pushing yourself because maybe it's the one. And yes, as you play for the Four In A Row the pressure on the body is here too, not only on the brain. That make things different. But in every tournament we arrive well prepared, dealing with minor things as with every player at this level, hitching here and there, but if it's just hitching it's not a problem."

Bautista Agut was one, and he hadn't changed a thing from the day before: same white shorts, same red and white T-shirt. But Novak had decided to really write a fresh page: the red t shirt was still on from the third set the day before, but white shorts with red lines on the sides had replaced the black ones. And if RBA won the first two points of this second day of that match, Djokovic then played flawlessly to clinch the third set, 6-1. Great depth, fantastic work and accuracy on the angles and a slight but efficient tactical change as he was now fixing his opponent way more on the backhand, trying to give the Spaniard very few forehands to hit.

The Serbian, who was now totally dictating the game, looked in the zone, his rival out of it. But as Vajda was giving Novak one more encouraging clap, his charge was now... down 4-2 in the fourth set, because it was said that this match would be a test of mental fortitude until the end. As it was said that: Novak, seeing the light at the end of the tunnel, would always find a way in Paris to take another and longer road. It is not Djokovic playing at the French Open if at some point there isn't a missed overhead on a very important point.

That year it came at 2-3 40A in that fourth set: right into the net. Followed by a backhand flying long. The calm and ease of the new day was long gone, and the pressure cooker was back. One more time, Novak was pretty close to seeing his 2016 campaign go awry. But he had been through so much worse in his career and his life that this day again he succeeded in summoning his best weapon: his resilience. Head down, jaw clenched, all his guts out there on the court, he suffered and suffered until the pain was rewarded. "He's an unreal warrior," Mouratoglou would say. "It's one of his greatest abilities. He's someone who's never going to give up. He shares this trait with very few others, like Rafa or Roger."

It's funny to notice that Djokovic fits both the mental and physical definition of resilience. A resilient person is someone able to endure, to recover quickly from adversity. Applied to a thing, resilience means the ability to resume its original shape or position after being bent, stretched or compressed. Resilience is elasticity. How suited to a guy that fellow player Gilles Simon calls "Mister Gum" and that I've been regularly guilty of comparing to a cat as much for the amazing flexibility as for the number of lives he seemed to have in a match, season, career. There's a "born this way" feeling with Novak, and with other champions that have through the years paved the way for the tennis legend.

More often than not you'd find a personal story that mirrors that tennis mindset trait, and Djokovic doesn't of course deny that what he went through at an early age shaped his whole persona, his tennis one included. "It's something written in my DNA code a little bit, because of the culture of the Serb and Balkan areas, considering the history and what we've been through. People in the region developed a kind of character feature, and also an existential need for battle. And then obviously the circumstances that I had in my childhood...they did help me, when I look back now, to get tougher and to know what I want and to appreciate what I have. This kind of past made me hungrier for everything, including success."

He might now be enjoying a great quality of life, comfortably set up in Monte-Carlo, where we were when he pronounced those words in April 2016, launching businesses and knowing that money won't ever be an issue ever again, but that's not the Novak he would connect to when on court. That's not the one he again needed that day against Bautista Agut. The only side of himself mattering in those moments is the determined warrior one, the one that would say, defiantly: "You won't down me. Throw whatever you want at me, I won't bow down. Been worse than there, done tougher than that." Glued with a "you have it or you don't" kind of ambition, it had pushed him from a wonder kid to a ruthless king.

Something those who crossed his path early on had already noted, like Thierry Van Cleemput. If he's now known as David Goffin's coach, back in the day he was the coach of the Belgian Davis Cup team, and he has never forgotten the first time he met the Djoker. It was at the end of April 2005 in Belgrade for a tie. "Novak was around the Top 200 in the ranking. But here came a kid with such poise and unbelievable self-confidence. He stepped on this court as if he was the World n°1 and that was very impressive. We weren't taking him seriously at all, until the matches started and he found a way to make everybody struggle! Yet when I came back to Belgium right after, some people in charge of the training told me 'no, you're wrong, that kid doesn't even have a backhand!' Now we can see how ridiculous it was, sorry for them... Because this confidence, that's the mark of the all time greats, of those who end writing the history of their sport." Novak at this time was 17 years old, and he would lose in five sets against Olivier Rochus and in four against Kristof Vliegen in the decisive match. Right after he would go through the French Open's qualification, win his first main draw match in a Grand Slam and take a set from Coria.

Djokovic is the kind of champion built on adversity, so finding himself back to the wall and in a tennis version of do-or-die is actually the most familiar territory for him. "Those circumstances of my childhood have shaped me as a person, have brought a lot of lessons to my life from which I could learn. Because I was forced as a very young boy to already face some circumstances that adults were facing, that's why I think I had to develop and grow up faster in my mind. And mature quicker."

He also had to grow a thick skin much quicker than many of his future rivals, which would explain years later why casting him in the villain's role would only make him stronger. Why, chosen as a target by the entire US Open stadium against Roddick in their quarter final of 2008 or again in New York against Federer from the first point to the last of their 2015 final, he would thrive rather than crash. Adversity, antagonistic behavior, it was known territory for the Serbian since the first time he started to travel the world running after a yellow ball. "As a Serbian after the war, it was not easy to travel the world. When you would say you're from Serbia, people would take a step back and really observe you in a very strange way. They would think that you're aggressive, that you are a terrorist, that you're going to do something wrong. So it was very awkward for myself and my family, especially my father who was traveling with me throughout the junior events. We had to make a double effort to impress people."

There is nowadays no sense of resentment at all from Djokovic towards this time or even towards those hostile reactions from some tennis crowds: "Not at all. Honestly, I don't feel this emotion at all. I am proud to share my celebration and my success with the people in a very positive way. I'm going to share this joy with you, thank you for the support that you gave me and let's enjoy this moment together. Rather than 'hey I did it: in your face!' I don't have these kind of revenge moments. I don't think it comes from a good place in the heart. Why would I do that? It doesn't make me feel good, nor the other person. Of course I'm very proud with all the team of what we have achieved, and with the family and everybody who's been with me from day 1, but we're coming from a positive place."

All of this has actually become one of his best triggers, finding also its root in a natural confidence that has long banished any ill-fated augurs. There's never been the need to turn him into a bigger and tougher competitor. Never been the need to make him understand what suffering and sacrificing meant, that beyond the emotional or muscle pain there would be success, or to remind him that without hard work he wouldn't go anywhere. Tennis was the love and the chance of a lifetime for Djokovic: he understood it quickly and never let it go however high the obstacles in his way.

Holding to an amazingly strong belief in his self-worth, helped by years of learning how to master his own brain and pushed by months of success, Djokovic in 2016 was totally ready to make Roland-Garros surrender. So down 4-2 in that match that didn't want to go his way long enough for him to move on, he offered a masterclass of his best tendencies: the resilient champion. He broke back, 4-3, by being relentless and pushing Bautista Agut to miss. "We saw he was in trouble, but we felt his form was good enough to come out on top at the end," Gritsch would say. "He had a very efficient forehand in this tournament; he was dominating and had the confidence to hit through, so for me it was just a matter of 'can he release himself, can he get to the point where he can play freely?' and there would be no problem anymore." And that's exactly what happened: Novak took the upper hand by getting over his nerves and being bold again.

It's also part of his resilience: he doesn't play small to dig out of those matches; he finds an uncanny ability to enter a "go big or go home" zone, to also set aside all his doubts. That would be a laser-like crossed backhand, or a remarkably touched drop shot that was as much daring as crazy to try at this moment. The "Edberg-esque" drop shot backhand volley that he basically picked off his shoe-laces to come back to 30A at 5-5 on RBA's serve was a perfect example of those moments of grace he could create under pressure.

The survival instinct again now put the Djoker at 6-5 serving for the match, Boris Becker on his feet in the box. Faced with that will power, Bautista Agut bowed down, finally, after still saving a match point. When you had thrown everything you had at someone, when you had used every trick up your sleeve, but you still got choked by an iron hand, you would drop to your knees on the ground, exhausted and defeated.

Taking his Paris destiny in his own hands, Novak moved forward on a great forehand before having a firm hand on a forehand volley. A simple fist pump to his box would come to salute the end of a very nerve wracking couple of days. And a smile followed by a hug would welcome Bautista Agut at the net: there's the kiss of death, and there's the Djokovic "I've killed your hopes again, sorry but not sorry" hug.

He was as calm by the end of this rollercoaster as he was nervous and tight for a huge part of it, and it was surely the result and success of this inner negotiation he had all along with himself. "I kept really talking to myself and believing this is the right way to approach things, and then the next day was better," he would explain to me. "And it kept going in the positive direction." It was tough, but once again he emerged from this as a winner and that match, in retrospect, maybe changed everything. Something Vajda was convinced about when he told me that "after that match Novak just overcame everything. He needed to overcome that match mentally and after he did it he really felt good on the court, finally found himself."

On that day he also clinched another tennis record, as he became the first player to earn 100 million dollars in prize money. Not too shabby. Yet it wasn't something Novak wanted to emphasize, as he told Serbian reporters[14] that day: "Money does not mean a thing to me. I do not look upon tennis as a profession and at my life through the eyes of money. It is a means that increases the quality of my life and lifestyle, but no more than that... Money comes as a consequence, a positive one, of course, of dedication, love, passion for the sport and a consequence of your success. Can you imagine me speaking about money right now, while the average salary in Serbia is 200-300 €? What would that be like? That is all I have to say. I am not trying to present myself as something I am not, being too modest or something like that... I do not pay much attention to that and I don't like it when prize money discussions take over. The media put me in a very unpleasant position when they want me to talk about the amounts that I've won during my career... That is the number one issue and the society of today insists on that – success is being presented and explained through money and power and that shouldn't be the unit of measure. I am 100% against it and I have completely different views and values."

Tennis and the money it brought had socially helped Djokovic and his family, but that part of the story was a done deal, not a motor anymore. "Money can't be the basic and most important inspiration for a young athlete. It just can't, that will only put him and his parents under more pressure, if you play only for the money and the fame. If your inspiration is true love for the sport and if that's your primary emotion, then the rest will come, life will fix it for you."

He was looking as regal as ever when he came to meet the press that 1st of June after escaping Bautista Agut. Immaculate white jacket, perfectly set red cap with his logo on the front, still discretely chewing on something through the first answer. The boss had to work hard,

---

14. "Novak on 100 million: 'Sport nowdays is a machine for making money'", Saša Ozmo (*http://www.twitlonger.com/show/n_1soob6i*).

the boss had been shaken, but the boss was still alive. And rather than dwelling on what went wrong, he was looking at the bright side despite the gloomy days he'd been through. "I'm in the quarterfinals, and, you know, I dropped one set. So things are going the right way. Of course I know that I can play better and I have a couple more gears. That excites me, actually, motivates me to work and get myself into that maximum speed hopefully for the next match and see where it takes me."

You could see no trace of the internal battle he went through for two days nor of the doubts and fears he maybe had to face, even if in the on court interview he said that it felt like he had played three matches against Bautista Agut. But Novak was fully embracing one of his other mantras: "Pressure is a privilege." It goes directly in the Djokovic dictionary with: "Everything happens for a reason," "I can't act on the past nor influence or guess the future," "I have a holistic approach towards life" and "I allowed my opponent to come back into the match, and all credit to him for taking his opportunities," among others.

And behind some of them, you could often track or guess what kind of mental work had been done to get there and why. So what about this privilege of being confronted daily with expectations, goals and stress? Catherine Aliotta nodded with a smile, as the more we talked the more I had the feeling that Novak was a textbook case of the efficiency of mental preparation work. "It's a way to give a positive reading to something that's negative. Without that, it's tough to face it. If I decide that pressure goes with the privilege of my status, it just testifies to my competence so it's positive and I have nothing to fear from it. It's part of the job, and it's even something to hope for. Then of course they're not all able to deal with it. And that doesn't mean that at some point he can't get overwhelmed by it."

And in a Grand Slam, pressure was everywhere every day. If the Big 4 made it look easy to go through those two weeks four times a year, those who discovered going deep in them felt the heat. David Goffin played the first Grand Slam quarter final of his career in Roland-Garros in 2016, having lost four times in the fourth round before that, and his coach Thierry Van Cleemput testified as to how draining those events were. "I can easily imagine that for the guy who wins, it's exhausting. But for everybody, a Grand Slam tournament costs a huge amount of energy. And it starts with the preparation, with the whole atmosphere in the place. You are suffocated by the event, and the further you get, the more time and energy you lose. You don't get out intact from those tournaments."

The Swedish coach Magnus Norman, who helped Stan Wawrinka win three Grand Slam titles, and Robin Söderling reach two Roland-Garros finals (2009, 2010), confirmed it, explaining how the US Open 2016 title had basically killed the Swiss at the end of season. "It takes a lot of effort to win a Grand Slam, it's mentally very tough to come back after something like that. If you look at Rafa, Roger, Andy, Novak... The more I'm involved in tennis, the more impressed I am with those four guys because they just keep going. For Stan, it's tough: it takes a lot of mental energy, and after you're empty. I am empty as a coach and I'm sure he's also empty as a player. It's tough to recharge."

But Djokovic kept finding a way and a hunger to do this season after season. And after years of battles, he had also finally made a nest for himself at the top of the game, despite the two giants of the sport that many said would always come to doom his career. But by pushing his resilience to the extreme for years, Nadal and Federer had also made it possible for Djokovic to have the last word over his demons in Paris. If he was now in Paris at the peak of all his abilities, it was because they gave him no other choice.

Being ranked above Federer and Nadal, chasing their Grand Slam titles numbers among other records, or leading at this time in the head to head against both of them didn't mean that their influence and threat had died for Djokovic. Even less as their star power kept being thrown at him week in week out throughout the year. He was surely not stressed out over Roger for this 2016 French Open, having seen how his nemesis was far from his best, having also beaten him in Melbourne and most of all knowing that nowadays on clay he had the upper hand against him. So his absence didn't change his grand scheme of things.

It would be a different affair when Nadal would withdraw from the tournament the day before his third round match against his compatriot Marcel Granollers. In this "where were you when" game, I totally remember where I was when the news struck. It was close to

5pm and I was seated in the main interview room listening to Andy Murray who had won his third round match that day against Ivo Karlovic. Suddenly someone from the French Federation, behind me, whispered in my ears that Rafa would come to press right after Andy. I nearly broke my neck turning back to face the news. No need to ask what was going on as a player coming to press like this when he's scheduled to play the day after had only one possible reason: to explain why his tournament was over.

I would always remember how Andy was looking at all the people suddenly entering the room with complete confusion. He was finishing things with the written press and was up now to do radio, so usually at this time the place should have started to empty out. But here it was packed. His face was still as confused when he had to make his way to the door as more and more people were coming in. We were May 27th and a shock wave would rock all the corners of Roland-Garros. Even the one where Novak was, as his sparring partner Thibault Venturino remembered. "You could feel the pressure after Nadal withdrew because maybe Novak started to tell himself 'if this is not now, that won't ever happen....'"

Roger Federer has never hidden that when Nadal, who had been his nightmare in Paris, lost against Söderling at the 2009 French Open he felt all the pressure of the world falling on his shoulders. Rafa out, that's the chance to take. And if not, it could be regret for ever. Added to the fact that suddenly everybody was telling you that it was your year. Djokovic had been in a similar situation in 2015 but it was maybe even worse for him that year as he had beaten Rafa in the Roland-Garros quarter finals. We all know how it ended. So there he was going again with a draw opened up by Rafa's withdrawal but with a sudden rush of pressure.

"There's been nothing worse for Serena in this 2015 US Open than having to face Roberta Vinci in the semi-finals, while trying to do the Slam," explained Patrick Mouratoglou. "All the expectations suddenly raised. It's plain awful. Suddenly, you don't have a single right to lose, and all the pressure is rising. That was just terrible news on the emotional level. Everybody around you is like 'fine, done deal!' It's like Federer in 2009: yes, he had one chance only and knew it, and that's why he's been exceptional. Same for Marion Bartoli in

Wimbledon. Being able to take the sole chance you're going to get, that's massive."

Djokovic had just played Nadal in Rome, had all the trouble in the world winning that one (7-5, 7-6(4)): he obviously thought that if both had made it to the semi-finals in Paris it would have been another episode of their Gladiators' saga. Novak might have been as astonished as everybody else when he heard Rafa was out. Catherine Aliotta adds another layer to explain why suddenly the pressure seemed to mount on Djokovic's shoulders, because "yes it can be a 'now or never feeling,'" she told me, "but it can also be a 'Shit, my rival gets injured! It's scary because it means I can get injured too.' It's like a mirror. Lots of things can get combined, so one needs to rationalize but also to work on the emotional side as it's working together. There's such a quest for performance with those athletes that it also creates weaknesses."

Novak had watched his arch rival announcing his left wrist was now too damaged to go on as it would be too risky to go on playing on injections. He had seen how the tears were coming to Rafa's eyes at what was one of the lowest moments of his career. "It was sad seeing him in the press conference," he'd say the next day after his match against Bedene. "You could feel his pain, definitely. If he retired from the tournament, then it's something really serious because he's one of the greatest competitors that the game has ever known. It's sad not to have him in the tournament, but we keep on going and I'm still in and hoping it's going to go well for me." But was it creating extra pressure, Novak? "No. I feel empathy for him, because as an athlete who was also injured before, I know this particular feeling when you need to pull out. I mean, I can only imagine as here this is his favorite Grand Slam. That's all I can say. I wasn't thinking really too much about anything else." A "really?" crossed many minds.

His coach Marian Vajda didn't dwell on this at the time and told me he didn't feel that the pressure, which was already high, got worse for Novak after that. Yet he wasn't fully sure that somewhere in Nole's mind it hadn't still played a little part. "I didn't think like that... Maybe Novak thought about it... But obviously Rafa was the biggest contender, and it's always a relief mentally a little bit that Novak doesn't need to meet him. But overall I think the strength was Novak thought 'I am ready.' Obviously it influences a little bit when such a contender is out, it always affects your senses but in the long run he always has to focus on what he is doing."

I was in the players' lounge trying to get some words from Toni Nadal when I saw Rafa going back to the locker room. You could read all the anger and sadness of the world on his face. "Taking the decision to withdraw, to retire from a competition such as this one, which is the most important in my career, to reach that decision you can imagine how tough it was," he had said to the press earlier. His uncle was a bit less destroyed but still at a loss for words: "It's a bit a desolation for us not to be able to play here, but that's how it is. It's easy to be strong when everything goes well, but it's now that it's tough that one really needs to be strong."

When Rafa withdrew from the event, it felt like a veil of sadness had spread over the stadium. And that day showed again how much Roland-Garros was attached to Rafa. "It is a tournament that I love so much," Nadal had also said. "I feel the love of the people not only in the crowd, I feel that the crowd is supporting me a lot, but at the same time during the whole tournament, no? The organization, all the people who work in the tournament, we always had a great relationship. I have a close relationship with a lot of people that work here. So, for me, it is a very tough moment because you expect and you wait for these two weeks for the whole year, and having to retire today is very bad news for me."

As he would later go to say goodbye to the people of the organization: he would receive a huge ovation, something that moved Rafa very much but also his whole team. I crossed his publicist Benito Perez Barbadillo at Roland-Garros during the second week, and the emotion was still there as he told me they had never seen that in all Rafa's career and that tears had been flowing. Months later during one press conference in Melbourne, Nadal would come back to this moment. "Last year was tough. When you feel that you are playing very well and you have to go from Roland Garros without going on court, I remember myself crying in the car coming back to the hotel, no? That was a tough moment."

It had been a shock all around and an event that would have consequences for both Djokovic and Murray. They were the last of the Big 4 standing; they were the heavy favorites for the title even more than 24 hours ago. "I think for everyone it's obviously a good opportunity," Andy would comment in his column. "Mainly for the guys who were in his section of the draw. For me it would only be relevant if I was to reach the final." But for Novak, it was already pretty relevant.

Novak Djokovic would have probably won Roland-Garros three or four times if Rafael Nadal hadn't been around. And his status as one of the greatest ever would have been clearer sooner if, added to Nadal, Roger Federer hasn't been that good for so long. But it works both ways, and no one can be sure Novak would have become the Djoker without those two legends of the game. As much as Rafa pushed Roger to evolve in order to survive in tennis, and as Federer built Nadal's game in return in order to take over, there is no real doubt that those two guys have created the monster that Djokovic would become.

Stuck behind them, Novak had no choice but to take his game, body and brain to new heights as it had never been his plan to remain the gifted number 3. Novak totally acknowledged that they were and still are a part of his success: "I said a million times before and I will say it again: The rivalries with all three of the guys - Rafa, Roger and Andy as well - have definitely, in a big part and big margin, helped me to become a better player and helped me achieve all these things. The rivalries that we have are important for the sport, and in one way or another you try to compare yourself to them and what they have achieved before. Nadal and Federer were so dominant in the sport when Andy and myself came in the mix."

When many observers were giving him the "for ever the outsider" sentence, he was enduring and plotting his takeover. Yet, this n°3 wall nearly happened between 2009 and 2010, when for the first time of his career, Novak was really doubting if he'd make it. That is adding Grand Slam titles to his lone 2008 Australian Open and becoming the World n°1. In 2009, Nadal had sent the first huge blow by saving three match points during their Madrid semi-final. It was Djokovic's fifth loss in a row against Nadal whereas things looked to be better set up in 2007 and 2008. There suddenly in this tunnel, Novak thought it was too much to bear, especially as he had just lost Monte-Carlo and Rome's final against the Spaniard. Glory was around the corner but Rafa just wouldn't move.

So missing three match points against him on clay was pushing him into despair. "It's happened too often. It's very disappointing to play as well as I have and still lose the match. I played one of my best matches ever. I was a couple of points from the victory. I even played a few points above my limits and I still didn't win," he said[15] at the time. He would get the next three wins against Nadal that year, would win Basel against Federer, and then the Bercy title. Still it wouldn't calm for long his frustration as he'd stay the n°3 and was not winning the Majors, having been beaten by the Swiss in the US Open semi-final.

Worse, it even looked as if he was going backward when he lost against Tsonga in the Australian Open quarter finals and had just one final and title to enjoy (Dubai) on his way to Roland-Garros 2010. And there came the blow that would be a defining moment for Djokovic: losing that quarter final against Melzer despite having the first two sets in pocket. The collapse.

"This period was very challenging for me mentally," he told me in Monte-Carlo in April when the 2016 clay campaign was starting. "Because I won my first Grand Slam title in 2008 and then there was two and a half years where I was really struggling to win big matches. I was very good and cannot say I was disappointed because I was number 3 in the world, which is a huge success. But I knew what I wanted and I wasn't satisfied with that, it wasn't enough and I knew that I could reach more. So I did go through my doubtful moments because most of the big matches against Rafa and Roger I was losing."

He'd also dwell on this time right before the French Open as he would tell the Herald Sun[16] right before Roland-Garros 2016: "I just couldn't break into that No. 1 or No. 2 spot — Federer and Nadal were just too dominant, winning all the Grand Slams. I was there and consistent but I just couldn't challenge them. I hit bottom mentally

---

15. "Nadal Defeats Djokovic in Classic", BBC Sports, May 16, 2009 (*http://news.bbc. co.uk/sport2/hi/tennis/8053901.stm*).

16. "Tennis champ Novak Djokovic chats to Hamish McLachlan about Belgrade bombings, family, fatherhood and more", Herald Sun, May 21, 2016.

and I thought about stopping tennis — that's how far it went. I was just so consumed by the pressure, stress, expectations, speculations and so forth. I expected too much from myself and I didn't meet the expectations. I wanted to reach my lifetime goals of winning Wimbledon and being No. 1 in the world, and I wasn't managing to get there, and I didn't think I was close."

There he could have given up and decided to enjoy being a top player even if not the greatest. Others had done so. But he rejected the idea and pushed even harder on the door. Marian Vajda had fought hard at this time to make Novak keep the belief in himself, and he had been quite stunned to witness doubt taking over for the first time, as he recalled during our chat: "At one stage he lost the belief that he could do it. In 2010, he was like 'I'm not doing it, Marian. I can't do it, I can't overtake these guys, it's finished.' I said: 'Come on, what are you talking about?! Come on, stand up and deliver! What's the problem? You did so much, you can do it. Be patient.' He was, so he did it.'"

Again, Vajda was there to be the shoulder he could lean on, to pick him up, to show absolute belief. The discrete Slovakian has really been crucial in Novak's career along the years. In 2010, also crucial would be that win over Federer in the US Open semi-final, even if he'd lose the final against Nadal. Then would come the second big event that would put Djokovic on track to reach the sky: the victory in the Davis Cup final in front of his home crowd. Those two events really had a huge impact on him mentally, as he confirmed to me back in April in Monaco: "There were a few turning points. One of them was this match against Roger, and the other one was winning Davis Cup, cause this kind of sensation on the court I never felt before. It was so special because I could share it with all the others, and also being at home: it was just so fulfilling and joyful that it brought a huge wave of positive energy, reinforcement and encouragement."

At the end, losing so often against Nadal and Federer had pushed him to salvation in the form of his first big crisis and so his first bounce back. He refused to become a footnote on the tennis history page. "Those kind of matches made me understand what I had to go through in the thought process, in my mental approach, in my character growth. Also after doing more technical stuff on the court on my game and so forth. All of this in order to get where I wanted to be and that is the number 1 in the world, winning against those two guys and breaking their dominance. It was a big task, but I managed to do it, make that quick and crucial transition from being in self doubt self-belief and confidence."

From that moment on, Djokovic has been looking both his nemeses directly in the eyes, accumulating titles and his own records. While still chasing theirs. Unapologetic, as he'd say in Rome in 2011 after beating Nadal for the second time in two weeks in a clay final: "I don't know how much good it brings to tennis, but it's good that someone else is able to win other than just Federer and Nadal. It makes it more interesting."

Neither the Swiss nor the Spaniard ever made the mistake believing Djokovic would just stay put, watching from below. They were right from the start very aware of the threat he represented. But probably didn't expect that it would turn into such a domination. 2011 brought all the nightmares to reality for Nadal, and in 2014 then 2015 it was Federer's turn as he'd lose three Grand Slam finals to the Serbian (Wimbledon twice and the US Open 2015).

Those three are now at the top of the history of the game and kept pushing each other to new heights. As a result, Djokovic is now involved in two of the biggest rivalries ever. Indeed, the Djokovic - Nadal one and the Djokovic - Federer one have created the most battles in all tennis history. The first one with 49 encounters, the other one with 46! Way above the 37 of Ivan Lendl and John McEnroe. And all three are still active players so the count is bound to grow bigger. For now, it's the Serb who leads both head to head, as a last proof of his rise to power. "Each match we now play against each other is engraved in my memory forever as something important," Federer would say. "Because they've accomplished so much in their careers, and same for me: the amount of records and everything among us three is just unbelievable so each match obviously remains special."

Roger and Rafa were Djokovic's biggest career hurdles. It took him years, doubting moments and many crushing losses but he found a way. And when he stood on the French Open podium on this last Sunday, holding the trophy close to his heart, he had just done something few people would have thought possible a few years ago:

he achieved a historical feat both Rafa and Roger failed to. "But they were both not a match but a couple of sets away from doing that a few times in their careers," Novak was quick to specify. This 2016 Roland-Garros would still actually come to highlight one of Novak's greatest achievements: crashing the well thought scenario and narrative that insisted Nadal and Federer be forever front and center. Born to tennis greatness in the "Fedal" era, Nole looked at this with frustration, then respect for finally embracing with the sole aim of reducing it to ashes.

In Paris for this 2016 edition, his walk to triumph was as much a testimony for the road accomplished as the achievement of a career. Even more as he went through a period in his career where he doubted his time would ever come. As he didn't always appreciate being on the opposite side of Rafa and Roger, he will admit it easily: "At the beginning I was not glad to be part of their era," he laughed when talking about them to the press after his triumph in Paris, before explaining how he ended up finding the bright side of the situation.

"Later on I realized that in life everything happens for a reason. You're put in this position with a purpose, a purpose to learn and to grow and to evolve. Fortunately for me I realized that I needed to get stronger and that I needed to accept the fact that I'm competing with these two tremendous champions and that, you know, then everything was uphill from that moment on." Vajda confirmed that in the end Novak took decisive strength from this rivalry, even if it sometimes prevented him from getting all the recognition he deserved: "The dominance of Federer and Nadal was big and they brought a lot of fans with them. I don't know if Novak wasn't enough valued in front of the media, that Novak was maybe a little bit too behind. That was the good part because he had always the motivation to get there."

For Rod Laver, it was actually the only way for Djokovic to behave regarding this Big 4 situation: "He must feel good about being linked with those three. Someone like Novak had to think that way, and I'm sure now he feels he's part of the Four Musketeers. All great champions are all a little different. I'd think today's players, this group of 4 people, are all individually very talented, and it's highly unusual to see so much talent at one time. Yes it was Lewis Hoad, Ken Rosewall, myself and Roy Emerson but generally never four."

Patrick Mouratoglou still puts hands over his head out of astonishment when he recalled what's been for him one of Djokovic's biggest strengths towards Nadal and Federer, visible as soon as 2007. "Rafa and Roger were winning all the Grand Slam titles. Surreal! Everybody was saying they were unplayable, even guys inside the Top 10. Not in public, but in private. And there comes this 19 year old guy, playing Roger in Melbourne's fourth round in 2007, who during an interview said that Federer "was going down[17]." And everyone is going nuts, like 'Who does he think he is, that little brat?' Everybody. But he wasn't bragging, he really believed he could win. Ok he lost (6-2, 7-5, 6-3) but he kept on believing and he became World n°1 when both of them were still at their peak. They weren't declining at all: he took their place up there and started to win Grand Slam titles. And this is extraordinary. I feel he doesn't get enough credit for that. What he did was tremendous. Whereas there wasn't a single other guy who believed he could win one when they were still here. But Novak? He goes and takes their place and keeps on winning those titles."

For Djokovic, this kind of defiance right from the start was indeed mandatory, and years later he totally owned up to it: "In order to get in the mix between these two guys that are great champions and were so dominant when I was starting to play, self-belief was key. A confident approach, mental strength and, you know, importance in relying on my abilities and really believing that I could one day reach No. 1 and start winning against these top guys and winning Grand Slams. So certainly it has been one of the key parts psychologically: looking to have that kind of self-belief and strength. Something that was necessary, because these two guys were and still are such complete players and personalities that it was the only way to break through."

Marian Vajda still has a vivid memory of that 2007 turning point of a season. He still smiled like a proud dad when he told me about the moment that had probably connected them for good. "When I took

---

17. "Roger Federer pays Nadal ultimate compliment", The Telegraph, September 2, 2007 (*http://www.telegraph.co.uk/sport/tennis/usopen/2320308/Roger-Federer-pays-Nadal-ultimate-compliment.html*).

Novak, ok there were predictions by all those experts that he'd be Top 10... But I always had my daily routine that I have to work on a daily basis: I see him being an excellent athlete, that I have to make him improve on the technical part, serving, forehand, all of this. My role as a coach is to make him improve to get there. But I had quite an easy job (smile), because he came to me in 2007 saying 'Marian, sit down with me' and I'm like 'ok, what's happening?' and he said 'Marian, I tell you something, I feel inside of me that I can be n°1 in the world.' Ok, Novak... Good job! Let's do it!'" (laughs). So it was quite easy. Even though we went through all these years with many changes but all the time I had this belief, he felt it and we stuck together. We are very connected, also on what we want to achieve, and there's trust. So that's why I stayed with him for so long, for this decade."

Christopher Clarey agreed that, stuck with those two very popular giants, the Djoker had to take a bolder approach, also because social codes had decided it a bit for him anyway. "In terms of rivalry, if I had to pick one to watch... Maybe Roger and Rafa on grass, but otherwise I'd pick Novak against Roger. Also because Roger had the thing: he loves no controversy, he loves to be the magnanimous one in front of the crowd, loves to kind of control all his environment. Novak rocked his world a little bit. And Nadal was so respectful, smooth, played the game with Roger just the way he could handle it. The manner counts a lot for Roger and I don't think the manner of Novak felt the way he wanted to be beaten. But Novak needed that edge. Rafa and Roger both come from upper middle class families, have very different vibrations. Novak came up from nothing through a difficult period: he knew the odds. Roger and Rafa were sort of anointed from a very early age. Roger was always the chosen one, and Rafa won his first match on Tour at 15 or 16 and was a French Open favorite from the start. Very different psychological make up. And I think maybe Andy and Novak have more in common."

One would still be curious as to why it would require such a battle for Djokovic just to get his own fully deserved spot. Clarey, by crossing the eras and generations, advances a very interesting theory about that. "It's very complex and goes back to a lot of things. It probably goes back to where he's from and where the whole story started in Serbia. It's also the style of play: less accessible and less flashy. But I think that if Novak hadn't had Rafa and Roger to play after and just emerged in a kind of mediocre era, he would have been even less known and less appreciated. Nothing better than coming along and beating those mega stars, play after them. There's some similarity between Lendl at his peak and Novak at his peak: Ivan had to beat the McEnroes and the Borgs. I started to care about Lendl because he ruined McEnroe's dream at the French Open: that was my entry mentally into Lendl. And then his frustration at the US Open until he finally won got my attention. Novak, I'm sure for kids of the age that I was then, it might have been 'Oh he beat Roger', 'god, he beat Rafa', like in this crazy 2012 Australian Open final if you're a Spanish kid. Maybe you get to not like Novak, but at least you care. And I think he's smart enough to understand that. I was in Miami and Novak had won against Rafa. I asked Nadal 'are you happy that you have the chance to be in the same era as Novak' and Rafa said 'to be honest, no.' And I asked the same question to Novak about Nadal and Federer, and he said 'I am happy because they made me reach a higher place.'"

In Paris that year, Novak had the perfect opportunity to step out big time out of Nadal and Federer's shadows. That's how it looked from outside, but not totally how Djokovic thought about it. And he had a long time to think about it, he who was already n°3 in the world in July 2007, had to wait until February 2010 to become the n°2, then stayed between n°2 and n°3, having to wait until July 2011 to finally enjoy the throne of the ATP World Tour. Four years trying to grab the sun, but he insisted it was a tennis sun that he wanted, and wouldn't start dwelling on the rest as far as getting out of their whole shadows (tennis, business, image, popularity) was concerned: "Well, I don't think it's for me to judge that. In some ways I was comparing myself to them in terms of game and what I needed to do to learn to get the best out of my abilities and try to overcome the challenge of winning against them and trying to break their dominance. I'm not comparing myself to them, you know, as people, as persons. We are all different. We're all unique in our own ways, and I have great respect for both of them: who they are, first of all, and what they have achieved in their lives. They mean a lot to the sport. They are great champions on and off the court, and because of the time they spent on the tour, they have lots of fans around the world and lots of support. It's wonderful to see. I'm just glad to be competing with them. That's all. I obviously am trying to focus and direct my attention to what I do and to who I am and what I bring to the life and to the sport. So I think all of us contribute something different."

But down 1-3 in the Roland-Garros final after losing 10 of the last 11 points, back turned to the back of the court and eyes closed while muttering to himself, Djokovic for once couldn't have cared less at being ahead of Nadal and Federer in their head to head. He couldn't have cared less about getting out of their shadow. He couldn't have cared less of any of them to be honest. Freed from both again in Paris like in 2015, he was still failing to take advantage of the situation. Why? Because on the other side of the net, someone named Andy Murray was now fist pumping to his own box after hitting an ace that meant he was now up 4-1 in that first set.

Good old Andy had decided to be the one that would this time crash his Paris party. One more backhand in the net from Novak would soon give "Muzz" the first set, 6-3. Djokovic, three time French Open finalist, was looking rattled. It was his never ending "Final Of Roland-Garros" story going on again. Nadal out of his way wasn't changing anything in this last step: Novak was as tight as he had often been in Paris when the trophy was in reach. It felt like each breath Novak took demanded a maximum effort, that he was fighting twice as much as usual to stay in the rallies, to hit the right shots. Nothing was flowing, everything was a struggle. The contrast was then striking with the steely determination of Murray who was crushing the ball and making the right choices at the best moments. He was the one playing that Grand Slam final being fearless, which hadn't always been the case with him.

Novak might have thought that after Wawrinka played the match of his life in the 2015 final, he was of course having to face Murray who had picked that year to become a full clay threat. How many tricks up the Universe's sleeve? But the Djoker still had one thing going for him: he knew that over the course of his career he had many times dug pretty deep holes under himself through matches but that more often than not he had found a way to get out of them. He knew that in that tournament itself he had found a solution to get out of Bautista Agut and the weather's claws. He knew that for many months he'd been the one always pulling the last trigger. He was an expert at pulling that trigger. There was still hope.

As it was possible to track down nearly twenty matches that had scarred Djokovic in Roland-Garros, it was indeed also possible to track down many matches that had put Novak's confidence high up in the sky in Grand Slams in past years. High enough for him to finally pull through in Paris. His defeat against Wawrinka in Roland-Garros excepted, Novak had become the definition of clutch, especially in finals, and he had also earned through the years the reputation of a player who could always come back from the most dire situations.

Knowing that you've been able in the past to come back from two sets down and from match points down in Grand Slam events remains that little voice in the head saying that no matter what happens you still have a chance until the last point. And even in Paris, the mother of all trauma, Djokovic could rely on those memories. The year 2012 alone had been a masterclass in the matter. He was also playing for the "Novak Slam" that year in Paris, surfing on his amazing 2011 season and that epic 2012 Australian Open final he had won against Nadal. He hadn't dominated the Tour in between as much as in 2015 or 2016 but he was definitely the favorite for the title with the Spaniard. The pressure was high but for the first three rounds he demolished the competition. Then came two matches that would contribute to his legend at la porte d'Auteuil.

Everything could have stopped that year in the fourth round when the Italian Andreas Seppi found himself up two sets to none against the Serbian on that 3rd of June. Novak was a mess, had a combined 34 unforced errors in two sets, and couldn't find anything working in his game. But still, by fighting and accepting this "winning ugly[18]" situation, he climbed back and won in five sets (4-6, 6-7(5), 6-3, 7-5, 6-3). No one was sure that day how he had pulled this out, what kind of magic spell he had cast on Seppi. But he did. The most vivid image

---

18. A well known reference in the tennis world about a player winning despite playing far from his best, as the theory developed by the coach Brad Gilbert in his book "Winning Ugly".

I still have from that day is Novak's face during the press conference: utterly annoyed at himself. He'd state that the only good thing coming from that match had been a win clinched thanks to his fighting spirit, but that now the only solution was to just forget all about this match. As you do with what you feel has been a disgrace to your talent, and not really a good sign for your overall Paris ambitions. Little did he know then that his next match would be an even bigger tennis miracle.

In what remains a classic at Roland-Garros, Djokovic would save four match points in his quarter final against Jo-Wilfried Tsonga on June 5th. Four. And not because the Frenchman would crumble, but because each time Novak would just raise the bar and play fearless shots, be it at the net or from the baseline. This match quality had put everything else to the side that day, as even outside of the Lenglen, you could see people packed in front of the giant screen. Yelling, cheering, sighing through the points. Years later, I'm still not sure how Novak escaped that day: he was tight, Tsonga was on fire even from the backhand side, the whole Chatrier was pushing for the Frenchman. That should have been it. Actually when he lost the third set to be now down two sets to one, he really looked on the way to the exit. For the second set in a row he had cracked in money time. Surely, his mind had enough no? No.

With a determination and a mental strength that you just can't learn, he'd find a way back. And he'd find a way to raise his tennis level a notch, at least. I advise you to watch or watch again the match point saved at 4-5 15-40 in that fourth set: he touched two lines, one with an overhead, and had the guess of his life on the Tsonga passing shot. Unreal. Saving match points here and there, fighting for each service game, taking all the risks, going through every attack of nerves: Djokovic did all of this that day, as he died and resuscitated half a dozen times. All of this to end in a deafening roar in the fifth set when a backhand down the line gave him the victory (6-1, 5-7, 5-7, 7-6(6), 6-1). A masterpiece.

So he could do it even at Roland-Garros: he could save himself when everything looked lost. And the examples through the years and the tournaments are way too many to all be given here. Semi-finals of 2010 and 2011 US Open against Federer, anyone? Match points down, sets down, back against the wall, crowd against him: pick as you please.

But, from recent memory, what about this fourth round against Kevin Anderson in Wimbledon 2015 too? He was two sets down on grass against a big server. Had lost the second set tie-break from 5-2 up on that court 1. Came back to two sets all before seeing the match being interrupted. And still won (6-7(6), 6-7 (6), 6-1, 6-4, 7-5). His only issue was that until 2016 he hadn't been able to let the Djoker out of his box during the French Open finals. He knew that of course when things started badly against Murray.

Still, he did pull the trigger on Andy many times in his career, like those Australian Open finals or, more useful here, during their 2015 French Open semi-finals played over two days (6-3, 6-3, 5-7, 5-7, 6-1). A bittersweet victory, surely, when he looked back on it because had he won in straight sets as it looked possible that day, maybe he would have had a different answer to the Wawrinka state of grace in the final. But as far as finals were concerned since then, he was on a streak that could be named "The Clutch Masterclass."

The way he got his hands on the trophies in Wimbledon and the US Open against Roger Federer in 2015 had been amazing, especially in New York where after hours of delay due to the rain, he also had to face a raunchy crowd ready to do anything to get the win for the Swiss. It was both amazing and shocking. And many would say they had never seen anything like that in a Grand Slam final.

But Novak didn't bat an eyebrow, didn't get mad a single time, saved all the break points of the world and won (6-4, 5-7, 6-4, 6-4). As he had done a few weeks before against the same Federer in London's final (7-6(1), 6-7(10), 6-4, 6-3). When you're able to turn the tables on Federer during a Wimbledon final, that engraves even more confidence in your tennis DNA. Even more as Novak had done it twice in a row as he also had the last word in 2014, after another huge battle (6-7(7), 6-4, 7-6(4), 5-7, 6-4), where he had found himself in the fifth set despite leading 5-2 in the fourth. Back on this French Open centre court in 2016, down to Murray, "Nole" still knew he had that in him against anyone despite what the scoreboard said.

And actually, without being masochistic, Gebhard Gritsch kind of preferred seeing Novak fighting his way back in a match: "I personally prefer him being down at the beginning and working his way up, overtaking and staying on top than to come out firing like crazy, winning 6-1, and then asking himself 'what's happening to me? Can I continue like this?' (laughs). I think it's more his personality also: to analyse things, to see where he is, to find a way through and then once he's found it, he's going for it and keeping it up. I like this scenario much better." That's called knowing your Djokovic book. Still, I'm sure Gritsch would have gladly avoided some of his boss's thrillers!

Through his career, Novak has regularly shown this habit of going from being on the brink of defeat to enjoying triumph so no one could nowadays say he was lucky or that it was all a big coincidence. There are reasons why he keeps escaping. "As every great champion, he has exceptional mental strength," Fabrice Santoro would tell me. "An amazing ability to bounce back from one match to another but also inside of the same match sometimes." There were tennis reasons for that of course, as Rod Laver pointed out: "He keeps a player guessing all the time. He won't just stay with the same game. I think his greatest asset is being able to mix it up all the time. I do like to watch him play."

The opponents would never feel relaxed, would never feel they figured him out, never have the comfort of looking at the other side of the net thinking he had no more options. So when the moment to finish off would come, there would be this extra pressure, stress, doubt that would come and make them either hesitate, miss or take the wrong road. And that's all it would take for Djokovic to come back. Everybody knew it, so the legend would feed itself too. But this ability he had to go and take the win, despite matches where all was against him, wasn't only due to his game. "There's also resilience at work here. How to transcend something that is hurting me," Catherine Aliotta said. And I think it's something that you have or don't but can't really learn.

Something my Serbian colleague Vuk Brajovic agreed on, and about which he was still amazed, despite having witnessed it time and time again. "His resilience? It's an incredible trait," he would state. "We're used to seeing him turn around matches. People are getting used to something that is very much unnatural." And he has one telling recollection that for him said it all, during the 2012 Australian Open match Novak played against the legendary Australian warrior Lleyton Hewitt. "At a certain point Novak came to his box saying 'I'm dying.' In the middle of the match! Like, 'I'm out of breath.' I'm like: 'what?!' But he goes back, he steps in and he wins. Same thing happened against

Murray. He sorted it out." I still remember that match whose score (6-1, 6-3, 4-6, 6-3) doesn't reflect the street fight it was, with I don't know how many incredibly long and physically taxing rallies.

Djokovic is able to endure, to suffer and to go through everything to get a win, be it in the first round of an ATP 500, the quarter of a Masters 1000 or the final of a Grand Slam. He just rejects being the loser at the end. Never ever be the loser. Something that shouldn't be taken for granted nor underestimated. "It takes so much out of you to reach the semi-finals and finals of Roland-Garros, to come back and do well so really that was impressive," Christopher Clarey from the New York Times told me. "But Novak has been so consistent at his peak... The level of investment he has, all of this was one of the biggest stories in tennis."

And as Novak was struggling against Murray in this final that was starting to look like his French Open finals nightmare, he wasn't only up a tennis challenge in Paris in 2016. No, he was up against Mother Nature and the chaos coming from its temper as well. He was now standing on the Chatrier for that final, but it came after a long and bumpy road in that second week, after lots of mental energy spent on keeping himself together. Of being one racquet thrown in anger away from being prevented from going on in his quest. And so after all of this, he now had to confront his demons that were in full show time on the court Philippe Chatrier, as their heads had started to pop out in the open for a while already, warning him louder and louder. In 2016, it would be amidst pure chaos that Novak Djokovic would be asked to shine.

CHAPTER SIX

Master Of Order Shining Amid Chaos

Sure, Djokovic had arrived in front of Murray without losing a set in either his quarter final or semi-final. But he had still spent a lot of mental energy into not losing it during this French Open. He had spent a lot of work on containing the nerves and the demons. And he had received very little help from above while doing so. All around him, it was just a mess: every train had derailed and he was there in the heart of the hurricane, trying to make sense of it all. Or even to forget about it and to embrace this French Open which was like riding dangerously close to a cliff. Miljan Amanovic summed the whole thing in a huge sigh before going on: "The weather was bad, matches were cancelled... We had to practice at the national tennis centre. But questions kept being: when to practice, when to play... You didn't know when the match would start, when to prepare... All of a sudden you are playing or all of a sudden you're not playing."

All the players love their routines. They are more or less tied to them, and they all have some. It's their comfort zone, the virtual blanket or pacifier of their childhood. It's what they come back to when everything else is going crazy around them: it's the safe house. When you're in a Grand Slam tournament and the stress is all around you every day, you need a safe house to get through it. You will have a day off between two matches and the locker rooms and players' lounge will become easier to live in as the tournament progresses. You will find quiet times to mentally regroup, to keep your focus sharp and to lower the pressure.

Then Roland-Garros 2016 came and wiped out all of the safe houses, with an even harder blow at the top of the draw where Djokovic

149

was standing. From the start of his fourth round to his qualification for the final, the Serb saw the weather wreaking havoc with routines, schedules, conditions of play, matches, and even semi-finals tradition when he had to play his on the Lenglen instead of the Chatrier. He wouldn't get a single day off between the match against Bautista Agut until the Saturday before the final. Of course top players are as used to adjusting to new situations as they are to unknown opponents, but there's adjusting to a few things punctually, and there's seeing your whole environment turned upside down every day.

For the top of the draw, that Roland-Garros was like a simulation: "Let's say all things that could possibly go wrong, went wrong." Take a pause and spare a thought for what this scenario meant for someone like Djokovic who is far more the Master-Of-Order type than the let's-go-with-the-flow-and-improvise type. Now that it's all in the past and the adventure has known a happy ending, Vajda is laughing that it's actually that 2016 Roland-Garros that Novak finally clinched. "Always like this with him... If it was the best conditions and everything, no he lost. And that year when it was the worse conditions, really, well that's when he won! He is unbelievable."

There was actually a hint of the chaos to come right from the start for Novak. The tournament had a Sunday start, and he should have played his first match on Monday the 23rd. But, that wouldn't happen as rain washed out the Sunday start, with only 10 matches being played out of the 32 scheduled. There was no way to add any more matches on that Monday that would also see Murray interrupted in the evening, two sets to one down against Stepanek but up 4-2 in the fourth. Djokovic would start his campaign only on Day 3 of the tournament, with all the time in the world to feel the pressure mounting as Becker called this "a tightrope."

Novak, as many top players, loves to know what to expect and when. He wants his days leading to such an event to be set up perfectly, but he couldn't go mad over the weather, not as if it was someone messing with him, or something he could correct. So it made it a bit easier to accept, as he'd say: "It doesn't throw you off too much, but it does influence your preparations for each day because as you are coming closer to the initial stages of the tournament, the first round, you're obviously strategically approaching your practice sessions differently... maybe working on certain specific things one or two days before the match. So, yes, we aimed to play on Monday, but it didn't happen. It wasn't a big deal, something that could radically influence us. Weather conditions were not going in favor of the tournament: it's been raining a lot so the courts were a bit heavier and the conditions quite different. But this wasn't the first time. It happened quite often in Paris."

Still, right away that 2016 French Open sent a warning to Djokovic: forget all the plans you have made, we're in for a ride. "That weather was unbelievable!" lamented Becker even eight months later. "I've never seen more rain in the first week of a Grand Slam. It really beat Wimbledon! So the pressure and mentality of waiting and waiting... Novak played second so he was always a bit behind. But we always found a window of dry weather in the off days. He was able to win his matches quickly before the rain came so I think instinctively he knew there was no time to waste: it was now or never."

And that delayed start had at least one good side as he exited the Rome Masters 1000 in search of freshness. And as what happened from the day of his Bautista Agut match to the end of that against Thiem, it was going to be just one big nerve-wrecking mess. He really needed any recovery time possible before that tunnel. Thierry Van Cleemput, the experienced coach of David Goffin, readily confirmed this outdoor tennis version of 'all hell breaks loose': "It was just hectic. The worst Roland-Garros of my career. It was very hard to deal with and was eating our energy. We went to practice indoors so many times at Rueil-Malmaison (a Parisian neighborhood close to Roland-Garros where players found a tennis club to give them facilities). It was on hardcourt but we didn't have a choice; it was mandatory to hit that ball a bit still. This weather disrupted all the rhythm and had us playing in really tough conditions: rain, wind, heavy ground. But the organizers did a really great job through all of this and the fact that they even succeeded finishing the tournament was tremendous."

So players had plans, and Mother Nature laughed in their faces. A laugh with a wink sometimes in Djokovic's case. He was, for example, made to believe on Saturday the 28th that he'd play his third round against Bedene on the Chatrier after the Serena Williams - Kristina Mladenovic match. But thunder roared, matches were interrupted for three hours and the question went from: would all the day's matches be completed to would we even start the last rotations? Hence the reason Novak and Aljaz were moved to Lenglen, and scheduled to take court when Venus Williams and Alizé Cornet would be finished, as announced through the rain delay.

Men made plans, and women laughed... as they played three sets. Tsonga surely saved Djokovic that day, as his French Open would come to an abrupt end. It was the very first game of the match: one slide, two slides. The second was too much, as on it the Frenchman felt a pain he knew too well as it was this one that had prevented him from playing in Rome. During practice before the start of the event, he injured the adductor of his left leg, and so there it came back again that day in Paris. "I continued but it was becoming more and more painful. At 4-2 I made an effort and again I felt like being stabbed in that leg. I knew it was over," Tsonga would say.

Yet he did all he could to hold his serve at 4-2, letting his power talk, putting pressure on Gulbis. He fought and fought until that 5-2 score appeared on the screens. Then the trainer came in, and Tsonga left the court. When he reappeared, everybody knew what was to come next. It was all written on his face and through his teary eyes: game over. The Frenchman would keep it together long enough to shake hands with Gulbis but would then disappear under a towel, leaving the court in tears.

Needless to say that for the tournament, that day was turning into a nightmare. The day after Nadal had withdrawn, bad luck would just not go away. Overall, it was turning just terrible: no game would be played until 5.30pm, and there would be a power outage in the whole television compound that would then make it impossible to air the end of the Williams - Mladenovic match. It was absolute and general carnage. From the tournament people to the television people to the players, coaches, media, and of course spectators: no one had a clue how to deal with the situation. I'd walk out of the media centre and would basically have to walk on people to make my way to the players' areas.

When it rains in Roland-Garros, the truth appears: there's no real shelter for the crowd, except the tunnel under the court Chatrier. So again that day everybody was packed in there. You had to feel for the public who had paid tickets to see tennis and were instead trying to find a spot on the concrete away from the rain.

So to try to finish that day and, if possible, on a good note for the crowd, the organization decided to move Djokovic back on Chatrier. Novak would stay there until being tempted to ask for candles, in a version of "tennis in the dark" that Roland-Garros has shown a soft spot for through the years. "I played very well, 6-2, 5-1, 30-Love, and a couple of long games where I didn't use my opportunities," Djokovic would say. "But, you know, I closed out two sets pretty well. Started the third great. And then... Then the night show started!"

He was smiling when he said that last sentence, then while remembering how many times the umpire Pascal Maria would get down from his chair to check the marks and how it all turned into a kind of mess: "I dropped my serve, the games were very long, Pascal was on fire. He was coming down from his chair. Yeah, and we went deep into night. I think we played to the maximum extent of time we could. I'm just glad I managed to finish."

That he would go through that day undamaged and finish with a smile was the first big proof that he was really mentally ready to suffer and go through everything in Paris that year. He had both his shiny green eyes firmly set on the prize. In true Djokovic fashion, he even later found a way to make it less chaotic than it was when asked about the tough conditions right after his win against Roberto Bautista Agut. A match that should have happened on Monday but the whole day was washed out, a first in Paris since 2000. "I remember early in my career I played a match against Nicolas Kiefer in Wimbledon for five days. That was the longest I have played one match. The match was interrupted twice, and of course it wasn't easy coming into the facilities here at 9am and leaving at 7.30 or 8pm, but it's not the first and probably not the last time I'm going to have to face these particular circumstances."

Through this match against the Spaniard, Novak was at the peak of this Roland-Garros chaos, having to basically play in the mud, under a light rain, with all of his demons from the past having a party inside of his brain. Mother Nature had been on his case since the start, but was now really throwing everything possible his way on that day. And actually, when the match got cancelled for the day, "Nole" decided to see it more as a blessing than a curse. He just couldn't take it anymore, as he explained to me very honestly, still sounding as if he was back to that day and could still feel the turmoil he was in. "It was help from above a little bit to have that delay so I could continue the next day, because it didn't feel that great," he laughed. "When I was waiting the whole day to play against Bautista and it got cancelled and everything: at the end of the day I just said 'ok it happened and it had to happen this way, and there is a reason for that and I'm just grateful to finish the day, still being in the tournament and having another opportunity tomorrow.'" Those were the thoughts that also stayed with him to ease his mind when he would allow his body to rest before the fight resumed the next day.

All the people I talked to about that Parisian weather during the French Open told me how much of a nightmare it had been, even coming from experienced players, coaches, fitness trainers, journalists. "I never saw that in my whole life!" Patrick Mouratoglou still looked stunned when telling me that. One more sigh I'd collect when uttering the words "Roland-Garros 2016 weather". The trauma.

So when one tries to step into Novak's shoes, it becomes easier to understand the suffering that must have existed for him through that Bautista saga, even if as a professional tennis player, he's in some way used to it. "I don't know if it adds this much stress," wondered the French coach when asked about those interruptions. "Because when you're not feeling that great, when you don't really want to go on court to play that match, one can sometimes be happy to buy some time. I know many players that are sometimes really glad to see their match postponed to the next day: 'Phew, no more stress for today! I won a day!' Because that stress before the match is really uncomfortable, dreadful, even painful when one isn't in a good state of mind."

So amid the chaos that was raging, Djokovic, as he himself said, was happy to hit the pause button and have a chance to reset, to work on his brain more than on his body actually. From the moment he left the court up 4-1 in the third set to that when he came back the next day, Novak just focused on one thing: keeping the chaos from reaching his mind. He built a bubble of calm around himself so he could face the opponent and those damn elements.

"Conditions and weather are things you can't influence, are the same for both players, so you go out there and you try to make the best out of yourself," he told me. "Usually in these kinds of circumstances, the calmer player, the more composed one, is going to have a little edge. Because you can easily lose your mind in these kind of conditions: balls are wet, there's rain, it's slippery. You warm up and then you feel cold again like after five minutes being out there. So you can always come up with something to disturb you. And that's why it's the biggest work that one person can do and have: the internal work. By far the biggest. Especially for a professional athlete, and a tennis player on the court: you go through moments of doubt, confidence, moments of that balance 'in the zone' time. Then you have to balance all of these emotions and try to channel them in the right way. Also it's best of five sets and on clay, the slowest surface in the sport, so you need to be able to preserve energy in the right way, but also keep the right intensity. It's tough." Catherine Aliotta called it "being mentally wired" to deal with the rain and the interruptions and stated that without that work, without being mentally that strong, there was just no way to get over it.

"Of course it was more stressful. Of course," confided Vajda who, in February 2017, was still nowhere near forgetting those two French weeks spent in the rain and the cold. "You knew that in every match you'd have a battle, because it was 25 shot rallies all the time. Physically and mentally you had to deal with bad bounces, weather, big balls, wind that comes, play that went off... One of the toughest Grand Slams ever."

Yet, succeeding in creating order amid that mess was so very Djokovic. His fitness trainer would say it was one more thing, sure, but they could deal with it, even more as they felt the draw would help. "Novak partly grew up in the mountains," said Gritsch. "I grew up in the mountains, and Marian is not made out of sugar so I think overall it wasn't a problem. We knew that Novak could deal with this, that he didn't even think about those things, that it wasn't disturbing him at all. Only extreme wind could but that wasn't the case. And also after so many years as the draw was, I'd say, good, so maybe when he saw the draw he thought 'maybe now it's finally changing to my side!'"

Someone like Van Cleemput wasn't at all surprised that the Serbian would be the one to come out of this on top. "You're so much into what you're doing that I can't say it made the stress worse. But there were new things to handle, that's for sure. And also you were afraid of so many things because of that: getting sick, sliding and falling, etc. You were scared of everything but there's no choice so you adjust. But with how demanding Novak is in general with himself and the rest, I'm not surprised he adjusted that well."

Darren Cahill even hinted that in a situation where pressure was all around, players also tended to feel better on court even if the conditions are rougher than outside of it with all those external influences chasing them. "It's normal for tennis players. You expect variations, you expect to have curves thrown at you during the course of a Grand Slam event: injuries, not waking up feeling as well, having an argument with someone in your team. There are a thousand things that could go wrong. You expect to have to make adjustments. And a lot of players they feel like once they've stepped out on the tennis court it's their safe zone, their home, so whatever is happening in the other parts of the world, the news stories, they don't care, they just focus on the one person on the other side of the net. It's a simplistic way to look at it but it works with a lot of players."

Gritsch agreed as he felt that having no days off actually helped Novak to cope with everything. Keeping him in the tennis court bubble, preventing his mind from wandering. "Yes, I think it was better. We found out that the worst is when you have two days off (as happened in 2011). It doesn't help you at all. People think you can recover better but mentally it is so challenging, so difficult to focus again, to be back in this super focus you need in big matches. So that was good. Also he was never over challenged physically so he didn't have, like in many other Grand Slams, one or two very tough matches. Physically he was good, and recovery wasn't an issue."

It wasn't, because they also took good care of making sure that Novak's body could handle that weather. When even knowing when to eat and when to warm up could turn into a headache. "You need to be even more careful than usual about the quality of the warm up and recovery time," explained Paul Quétin. "And also on what we call the invisible practice, everything that's done off court. With weather like this, you need to take even more care of your body."

The French physical trainer remembered what Djokovic did while coming to use the facilities of the French national tennis centre near Roland-Garros. "Novak came here at the national center to do cryotherapy at -110°C so maybe he wasn't that cold on the court! (Laughs) The cold is a recovery tool, but playing in it is totally something else. Here we have had iced baths for some time now, but the cryotherapy, that's different: it's -110°C for three minutes so the impact isn't the same. In any case, it helps the recovery, and maybe also the sleeping quality. And it's not like you put only the legs in or the torso: from the moment you put the vital organs at those temperatures, especially the head, there are different physiological adjustments being made. So here players would enter a room set at -60°C for twenty seconds so they could adjust, and then it's -110°C for three minutes."

With this whole "playing in the rain" situation of course came the controversies. Players were furious to have been sent on court, like Simona Halep, Agnieszka Radwanska, Ernests Gulbis or David Ferrer and found choice words to describe the level of the organization. There was still also no roof at Roland-Garros in case you were wondering, so it brought back the astonishment of the tennis world about what the hell was going on in Paris. It even pushed the usually cautious Richard Gasquet to state that Roland-Garros wouldn't be at the level of the other three Grand Slam events as long as there wasn't at least a roof there. Tournament director Guy Forget didn't hide his anger at the situation as well and kept saying people were right to be upset and that it had to now move forward as soon as possible.

At the time, the tournament, the neighbors and the city were entangled in a dispute that was spending way too much time in court. Hands were tied all around. When it's a mess and everybody is going nuts, journalists are asked to write about it of course and to search out prominent opinions. So it was no wonder when Djokovic started spending his press conferences being asked to discuss the pros and cons, even more as he was directly concerned too: with that rain, the schedule was all over the place, especially at the top of the draw, and he faced some upsetting possibilities.

"Conditions were definitely on the edge. But once you accept the circumstances and the decision is such that you play, then you have to go with it" he would say while admitting that he had already talked to some official representatives to see what was possibly going to happen to his schedule. He had even reached out regularly to understand what was going on with that "no roof, no lights" situation: "Well, I have heard one of the biggest reasons why they still don't have even lights at this tournament, or roof as well, is they are facing a lot of difficulty with surrounding residential buildings. If you take in consideration the locations of all four Grand Slams, I think Paris has the most challenging position in terms of dealing with surrounding residents. It's definitely not easy. I'm sure that they have already heard it a million times that we need a roof, that we need lights. Not only for us players but it was also difficult for the crowd coming and paying tickets to watch the matches. You know, you could see a lot of improvement with facilities this year with Jean Bouin and the National Tennis Center which is amazing. They are trying to do whatever they can do within the regulations, and I'm just hoping that for sake of this tournament and all the players that we are going to have that roof at least on the main court as soon as possible. But I also understand the other part, because I talked with some people and I understand that it's not just their decision whether or not they want to do it."

One thing that was sure to push his "sigh" button was how players would be told to go on playing in the mud despite insisting it was dangerous. "It's a very delicate subject. But priority should always be the health of the players, no doubt. I have had situations before, plenty of situations before where I thought that the courts were not good enough for us to perform at such a high level because it was quite dangerous on the edge to twist your ankle or, God forbid, something else. So I understand the frustrations that some players were going through. I went through the same, but sometimes you just have to deal with it. Of course sometimes the tournament referees and the grounds people, they were trying to do their best to evaluate the condition of the court. Sometimes it did appear that maybe they didn't because they didn't play, they didn't maybe understand what you went through with your movement and why it was so dangerous, you know. So that's why, for me, it's in one way both funny and unacceptable as well at the same time to have a chair umpire come in elegant shoes and try to slide and check whether or not the lines are slippery. I think it's important at least that they wear tennis shoes and check the conditions. I think it should be a decision of a group of people. It shouldn't be just players saying, 'Okay, I'm not going to play and I'm leaving the court' It's not fair I think towards the crowd and everything if the other player doesn't feel the same. So that's why it's always a conflict of interest and it's important that you have some neutral sides there to kind of try to find a mutual understanding and solution that is the best for everybody."

Novak mostly succeeded keeping his cool despite that chaos determined to spoil his quest for the title. But it was a huge mental effort, an every moment challenge to keep things under control. Yet it still cracked, but not only at the start and the end of the final, no. It cracked during his quarter final against Tomas Berdych. On that June 2nd, all could have stopped for Djokovic as he would be a few inches away from disqualification. I mean, try to picture that: the n°1 player in the world trying to get to a fourth final in Paris and achieve the non calendar Grand Slam disqualified in the quarter finals. Yes, those were goosebumps you could see on Novak's entire team.

Back in his red t-shirt and black shorts, "Nole" had been absolutely ruthless in the first set (6-3) against the Czech, one of his favorite victims on Tour as at the time he led 24-2 in their head to head. He had found his way out of a rough spot in the second set when, despite being up 3-0, he found himself at 4-4 and had to dig to get that second set 7-5. After those two days fighting Bautista Agut and the universe, with having again to play under light rain, Novak's nerves were now feeling the heat again. Djokovic also knew he'd have to play his semi-final the next day so each moment wasted that day on the court looked as if he was risking his chances.

But Berdych wasn't going away; here he was breaking in the first game of the third set. Heavy hitter and surely one of the cleanest hitting on Tour, the Czech refused to get dispatched that easily. In all the glory of that terrible zebra-like outfit that Adidas had put out that year. The only reason Berdych was by the way getting away with it was the same explanation of how he had gotten through those H&M outfits: being that pretty, with blondie curls and blue eyes included, helped a lot. And actually those blue eyes were suddenly wide open: not because Djokovic had sent a routine inside out forehand in the net at 30-40, wasting a break point, but because the Serb's racquet was flying in the direction of a line judge's head.

He held his breath, as did probably everybody in the stadium. Novak there would come close to utter and complete disaster. He had lost it. Missing that forehand on that break point had just driven him nuts, and that was it for that racquet. Go away, you useless and betraying tool. Except that, in what could have been terribly bad luck, he didn't just break it on the ground, no, it looked like the racquet slipped from his hand as he was trying to throw it on the ground, and he did it so violently that the racquet went flying behind him at high speed. Ending its course way too close for comfort to a line judge's face, lying all guilty on the red tarp at the back of the court. That's how you go from disqualification to a great escape in the space of a few seconds and inches. Djokovic would immediately apologize, saying "sorry, sorry, sorry." But everybody around was perfectly aware of what could have just happened. "If he had hit the guy, it would have been over," summed up Berdych.

After that, it was like nothing would matter anymore. Berdych could go into tantrum mode when the match got weirdly interrupted at 3-3, despite players being under the rain from the start. "This is an absolute circus, one big circus!" he would say on the court. Then later telling the press: "That was one of the worst calls that I ever had on the court. They're under pressure and so are making those kinds of decisions." No one would pay too much attention to that mess. Nor to the fact that Djokovic would win the next three games after the match resumed and so qualify for a new semi-final at the French Open, for the eighth time in his career. That he was now two matches away from that Novak Slam, from finally winning the French Open. Nope, his racquet would be the star of the day, the video of the incident being played and replayed over and over. The scrutiny it would cause wouldn't go well with Novak at all, who felt that he was receiving special treatment and not understanding at all the fuss made about it.

He was deep in his quest, focused on the prize so anything coming, aggressively as he felt it was, at him from outside provoked total revulsion. Hence why the press conference following that incident was one of the most tense I've witnessed with him in Paris over the years. Questions kept coming, asking him to reflect on an eventual disqualification, implying he had some kind of anger management issues. And that didn't please Djokovic at all. "It's obvious what I tried to do," he'd say. "I don't understand your question. I threw a racquet on the ground and it slipped and almost hit the line umpire. I was lucky there. That's all. I'm just not thinking about those kinds of situations. I'm trying not to worry about it at all. I am aware that I have been lucky, and I apologized to people that have been in this particular situation with me and that could have been hurt by my racquet. But it was never the intention. It was just some unfortunate bounce, but fortunate ending of that scenario. That's all I can say." Someone asked: "You're lucky he moved, weren't you?" Answer: "Yeah, I'm lucky. Great." If looks could kill....

Boris Becker didn't like the whole situation, from that flying racquet to the way Novak was treated by the media afterward. "He was on a tightrope, on the fence. It was really nerve-wracking. So in the spur of the moment, the racquet flew as it does with many other players but obviously everybody was just watching him. Tennis history was being written so everybody was watching him. So that's sometimes a bit unfair, but that's the price to pay when you're called Novak Djokovic, when you're the best. Also sometimes you need a little bit of luck...."

Marian Vajda didn't like this incident at all either, surely because it had already kind of happened in Rome when, again trying to bounce his racquet, Novak had seen it fly into the crowd. This bouncing trend needed to come to an end, and Novak to go back to his good old way of getting the frustration out: break that thing clean. "Some little things I'm not happy about, like throwing the racquet," would later say the coach who's been like a second father figure for Novak and knew when to give him a pass or when to sit him down.

"The pressure was very high and he threw the racquet but it wasn't a nice thing to see and I think he realized this later. But the guys in those moments they don't even realize that there's somebody there behind. There's too much anger. Pfff... I don't think he realized he could be defaulted...But for sure afterwards there was a big rush of blood! (Laughs) 'What did I do?' and then waiting if he was hearing any umpire's announcement... This is a temper, which you can't stop. So that was difficult... At the French Open, there's always something happening."

Vajda didn't lecture Djokovic about that racquet, also probably because an official already did it, and also because he sensed it wasn't necessary to annoy Novak any more. Two matches away from his dream, nerves were raw and had to be dealt with cautiously. He'd still be relieved after Thiem's match to see that coming so close to being disqualified had done Novak good: "There his emotions were very good: he could control it and I think this is the way to approach it. Because if not this could be really playing against him. Definitely I didn't like it. He realized immediately what he did. I'm sure."

I tried to find out who had lectured Djokovic after that racquet incident, as Vajda said it was someone from the ATP but then the ATP denied it, so I failed, yet the supervisor Stefan Fransson from the ITF told me it'd have been logical if someone of their ranks had done it. "I don't know. But if something like that happens, it's not unusual that we'd talk to him, sort of just remind players that they took a really big risk because if somebody gets hurt or injured, the match would be over. It could have been disqualification, yes."

One can easily imagine that both Fransson and the tournament were quite relieved not to have added Djokovic being expelled from the tournament to that weather nightmare. Stefan Fransson had a few close shots through that 2016 French Open and, even if he didn't want to give too many details, the supervisor would still admit that at some point it had been discussed changing the schedule substantially. "There were quite a few times when we've been thinking like a Monday final was looming, yeah. When you get two or three bad days and you see how many matches are behind, for sure you start looking at different options and plans. To be fair to the players, but also the tournament and the spectators. It was all a little bit stressful, as the weather just added one more thing."

As had the talks with the players, whose mood couldn't be that great in those circumstances. But Fransson maintained that they had been overall easy to deal with even in the depths of the Parisian chaos. "Nobody likes to play when it's not such nice weather. But at the same time we have to sort of try to find a line where it's acceptable even if it's not good. It's not great but it's acceptable. You don't get too many complaints because they realize you can't do anything about it: it's raining, it's raining. You do get discussions when you have this little rain and they want to know how long we're going to play under it. I think most of the guys understand that we have to try a little bit even if it's not perfect. Then with that kind of weather you often get delays and then you get in the darkness, and in Paris they don't have any lights so we have to finish when it gets dark. That's always a little bit of a contention as well: how long are we going to play, when is the right time to stop? And you want to try to be fair to both guys, but normally the player who is losing wants to stop first."

Guy Forget, who was inaugurating his director's hat that year at Roland-Garros, was on the same page, and was even grateful to the players for their understanding: "The players were great. They're the first to suffer from that, but they are sorry as well for us. They were saying 'Oh Guy it's the first for you, you're not very lucky, are you?' They took it really well." So well that Stan Wawrinka decided to give public support to the tournament at the end of his press conference after he lost to Andy Murray in the semi-finals: "I'd like to thank the organizers, the organization here at Roland Garros. We have heard many criticisms, but I'm a player, you know, and I think the organization team have done an incredible thing. You know, there are two things: there is the infrastructure on the one hand, that is the roof and this cannot be changed in a day. And then, unfortunately, the appalling weather conditions for two weeks and all the things they had to manage. I think they did a lot better than what we have seen in other Grand Slams, so I'd like to thank the organization team and Guy Forget, because it's his first year and he's had the worst-case scenario, I think."

Forget would actually have one last drama to deal with. The semi-finals would be played at the same time on Friday, meaning one match had to be sent on the Suzanne-Lenglen court. And he had decided it would be the Djokovic-Thiem one, provoking the anger of the Serbian's team. The Frenchman was now off to calm another storm, and cross fingers and toes for everything to finally fall back into place. As for Novak, it was the last step to get out of that tunnel of pure chaos he was stuck in. It was the last obstacle before being back to where he had sworn to come back to twelve months earlier. An Austrian was on his way, and a pretty talented one. And Novak wouldn't be strolling the Chatrier like the boss, no he would have to go on that Lenglen where he had had some tricky ones in the past. And where at the opposite extreme, Thiem had reigned supreme. His comfort zone was attacked from everywhere, and he could feel his nerves cringing.

His fifth match in a row was already going to be a tricky one, so he really hadn't needed Mother Nature to enter the mix. But Mother Nature again had crashed the party so Novak wouldn't set a foot on the Chatrier for his semi-final, as the n°1 player in the world had been sent to the Lenglen. A semi-final on the second main court of Roland-Garros? Yes, that's the decision Guy Forget and Stefan Fransson had to take in order to ensure a fair treatment for both finalists. "It's one of those cases where you try to be fair to both, want to give them a day off," confirmed the supervisor. Murray would face Wawrinka at 3pm on Chatrier, and Djokovic, for the thirtieth Grand Slam semi-final of his career, would do the same on Lenglen against Thiem at 3pm. Both matches played around the same time, same for the women, as Serena Williams was on the Chatrier at 1pm against Kiki Bertens, and Garbine Muguruza on Lenglen at the same moment against Samantha Stosur. History will remember that Lenglen would be the winners' court at the end.

"As the tournament director, I wanted both finalists to get a day off before the final," Guy Forget told me. "I didn't want to risk putting Novak on Chatrier after Wawrinka - Murray, that somehow it would rain again and then Novak would have had to play the rest of his semi-final on Saturday. Playing both semi-finals at the same time was giving the best chance to see two guys at their best on Sunday." So one more time this year in Paris, Novak would see his routine messed up, and this change of court didn't really go well inside the Djokovic team.

On the eve of that semi-final, Guy Forget found himself trying to calm another crisis as Marian Vajda wasn't happy at all with his decision to send Novak on Lenglen. "Novak isn't among the players who ask a lot. But when I told Marian Vajda that I was going to make Novak play on Lenglen out of general fairness, that led to a heated discussion. Sometimes it felt like there was a bit more tension inside his staff than coming from Novak himself. The whole team is here to protect him, to make sure everything goes well, I understand that."

Forget kept the situation from escalating thanks to his good relationship with Vajda and also the intervention of Novak's agent Edoardo Artaldi. "They are all very smart and we've been working together for a long time. At some point Edoardo tried to convince Marian, telling him 'Listen, it's still good for him, even if he's the n°1 in the world. We're not going to have him play after Murray on centre court...' I knew the risk for them was that the smaller court could be less an advantage for the champion who had his habits on the centre court. But, luckily, Marian is a friend, we've known each other since we're 14 years old."

Forget held no grudge at all; he knew too well how that worked and how big the pressure could be. "There were a lot of expectations, everyone wants to do everything perfectly, that's normal. But honestly, Novak has never been tough to deal with. Maybe he was a bit upset when he discovered the schedule but he didn't show it that much as he was already so focused on the match he had to play. That shows that if sometimes players can be demanding and difficult, they also can be easier to handle than their entourage. But I really have a good relationship with his staff: they're all very professional so you can always work it out. And it's not like that with everybody... With some others it can really be an issue: it's normal to defend one's interests but sometimes they act as if they're the only people that matter."

If Forget took every player's requests into consideration, he owned the fact that at the end, he was going to be the one deciding. "Sometimes it feels like, for them, it's a pure disaster. And also lots of superstition is coming into this. Richard Gasquet loves playing on Lenglen but now he understood he could also play very well on Chatrier. Serena Williams used to refuse to go on Lenglen but she played one great match there and now it's fine, but before that it used to be tough. That's part of the job and I have no issue with it. I accept that sometimes they're not going to be happy with me."

Marian Vajda, months later and with the trophy secured, could laugh about it all, with this strong, joyful and infectious laugh of his. "I was fighting so much! So much..." the Slovakian coach told me while taking his face in his hands. "Oh my God. I had to do something in order to change it but ok...." Why was this change of court causing such anguish? Surely because the team was already way stressed enough and didn't need to now have to deal with novelty when they were two wins away from the title. That was undoubtedly taken as a new manifestation of their Parisian curse. Vajda could only see what could go wrong on Lenglen, nothing else than the fact that it was suiting better someone like Thiem than Novak: "It's a smaller court, a faster court, a court that suits the guys who really hit the ball, and it bounces so high! It's a completely different court! Completely different."

So on this Friday, June 3rd, the whole Djokovic team had settled on Lenglen for the morning warm up. A new big bunch of tickets had been put on sale to make sure the players on Lenglen wouldn't play to an empty court. Prices had been reduced, so it was a bargain: 24 euros, and the first spectators to arrive would get the best seats in the house. Consequence? Djokovic's morning practice ended being crowded and, feeling a crowd asking for entertainment, Novak answered and displayed his now notorious trick of catching a flying ball directly in his shorts' pocket. Spectators probably didn't notice anything, but that practice wasn't actually going that well. Sure, Novak finally looked at ease with his backhand, having fixed it since the warm up before the Berdych match. He was still discussing it with Vajda but on court it was working really well.

So what was the issue? Stress. Novak was now getting so close to his goal that nerves were starting to act up. Flashbacks of the past semi-finals and finals too maybe. He also knew Thiem was playing like in a dream this season, had this one handed backhand able to torture him and was a great clay player. The young Austrian was on the rise: the pressure would surely only be on Nole's shoulders. And he was not on Chatrier. The word 'danger' was dancing in bright bold letters in his brain.

For his last practice session with Novak, Thibault Venturino was feeling the heat. "Those guys, they have days where they're really stressed out, and you feel it right away. Novak, on that semi-final day, was very tight. And I wasn't exactly feeling comfortable out there... Especially as the Lenglen was packed, and despite the fact that usually I love when a lot of people are watching. Looking back on it, it was funny, but not at the moment. We were working on a sequence; I was following the coach's orders but Djokovic thought we were off to do something else, and then Becker would tell me to play something again different...That Vajda would say no to. And Novak wasn't in the mood for this that day so his frustration was rising and I didn't know where to hide. It lasted maybe thirty seconds but for me it was like this mess had been going on for two hours. Boris Becker came right away to tell me not to worry, that Novak was very stressed. But all I wanted to know was where to put the ball (laughs)."

Venturino hasn't forgotten that session, as it was the first time he saw emotions getting the better of Novak. "That's the only moment of the event where I saw him like that," he recalled. "The previous days you could feel the pressure a bit, but that day before playing Thiem, from the moment we started to work on specifics, you could feel the nerves. Not before, as he arrived pretty relaxed and chatty. We know each other a bit now so we talk in French and so on. When he's tight, he's not like yelling at people or anything like that, but he's suddenly going to go and change the racquet, or shoot a ball in the sky just because he can't stand it anymore, or he's going to talk with Vajda and Becker a lot. You just can feel that he needs to let the stress out."

Boris Becker actually saw reasons to be confident in this nervous state Djokovic was in, as he now had way enough experience with the Serbian to know when his tantrums were good or bad omens. "Thiem was the up and coming player so... But I tell you what: I've had much worse practices before finals or semi-finals than this one. Some of the practices before the Wimbledon final, I tell you: not so nice... So this one wasn't that bad actually. And yes, it's a good sign. I don't like if it's too smooth, too perfect and too nonchalant. I like if he's already mentally in the match."

He would indeed vent this stress in time to deliver a stellar performance against the Austrian. Something that now makes Vajda have a laugh attack. After all this stress and change of court crisis! "I was very worried about the semi-final and this was obviously tough but, hey, it was his best match! He played so well. That proved that he was already mentally much further, released." In the outfit that would also be the one of the final, red T-Shirt on black shorts, the Serb made a point to dictate the game right from the start that day, to make Thiem feel he was stuck in a corner and about to suffocate.

His accuracy was at its best, finding every corner and angle. Same for the depth of his shots and their variety. Thiem, wearing the now infamous zebra-like outfit, couldn't move into the court to attack, nor have enough time to launch his missiles: he could only defend and run.

With less patience than Novak, he was also bound to fail there. A strong fist pump after the break for 2-0 in the first set had also set the tone for Djokovic's mindset: he would show no mercy and was aiming for the jugular right away. He would behave like a matador. "This match was the moment where he played totally freely, and you could see what was actually the potential," said Gritsch.

Novak was pumped and decided to show who the boss was. A fist pump welcomed a break point saved at 4-2. Then at 40A he won the point after a succession of overheads, his least favorite shot and one that in Roland-Garros always brings back the memory of the missed one that probably killed his hopes against Nadal in that 2013 semi-final. So when the third one in a row gave him the last word, he threw his right arm and fist in the air towards the crowd. Another fist pump would come to greet the first set win (6-2), and I thought at the time that this fist had been used more in this set than in all his previous matches combined. The Austrian was the last obstacle between Novak and the final, and so he had to be put away quickly.

On the Chatrier, the battle was more intense between "Muzz" and "Stanimal" but the feeling was the same: there was one guy on a mission with a firm hand on his opponent's throat. All of this under the eyes of a common face in the Roland-Garros "celebrities rows": Leonardo DiCaprio, under a béret and behind sunglasses, but still "Leo!" That's part of the Grand Slam's glam: the celebrities watch. You even often get the list of who's coming and where they'll sit from the tournaments. People also make the show.

On Lenglen, Djokovic was now destroying Thiem, being up 6-2, 6-1 on a massive crossed backhand winner. His opponent looked helpless. But we were arriving at money time and the closer Novak got to the finish line, the more chance there was to see his nerves try to act up. And on this court Suzanne Lenglen, the memory of that 2010 quarter final against Jürgen Melzer wasn't that far. He had been two sets up that day too, and it had looked like he was comfortably on his way to the semi-finals. Then he collapsed and the Austrian took over. There was an Austrian again on the other side of the net in 2016, and he was super talented. So the nerves couldn't fully be at peace, and would maybe just need some stimulation to show up.

It happened right at the start of the third set, when Thiem started to play freely as he had his back against the wall, and when Djokovic took the foot off the gas a bit. A crossed forehand winner right in the corner gave a 2-0 lead to Günter Bresnik's pupil. A good hold and it was 3-0. But panic wouldn't enter Djokovic's brain cells: he would take the ball a bit earlier, would push more on the backhand to inflict maximum damage and would just not miss a ball anymore.

Soon enough he was back at 3-3, both feet settled on the baseline. It wasn't the moment to step back but to step up, so onwards he went at 30-15 on Thiem's serve. The Austrian threw everything he had at that point, all the tricks in his box but Novak was there all the time, defending, finding answers, cornering his rival again. Until he sent a wonder of a forehand down the line. Boom. He paused, out of breath but the right arm and fist in the air, silently asking for the crowd to declare him its winner. Gladiator mode, activated. And the crowd obeyed, in a frenzy.

His heart was starting to beat louder but Djokovic still broke then held to lead 5-3. He was now one game away from a fourth final at Roland-Garros with all that it meant. Twelve months after the heartbreak, he could see a new chance looming. At 30A on Thiem's serve, he had one foot across the finish line. But the second foot would need some convincing to join and it'd be painful. Thiem would hold his serve, refusing to bow down that easily, pushing Djokovic to serve for the match in a "If you want it that bad, brace yourself and go take it" way. A sliced backhand out of the limits put Novak at 30-15 on his own serve at 5-4. But the fist pump he had at this moment looked very emotional. It was a "please let me end it now" fist pump, a "please, please, I need those next two points" one. A nervous one.

So of course he then sent a crossed backhand in the alley and soon enough found himself down 30-40. A great first serve pushed Thiem to miss, and Novak to a huge roar. Second foot inches from crossing the finish line too but the leg was heavy. As was Novak's deep breath and the crowd's support. People, feeling Novak's stress, were doing their best to just push him through that damn finish line. The relief would come after a great defense and a Thiem's inside out backhand in the alley. Both arms in the air, Novak immediately turned to watch his coaching team and family in his box, who were on their feet to celebrate him. Novak didn't smile: he shot them a very intense look, and a right fist pump. Eyes straight in their own eyes in a "Here we go again: one more win" way.

Again in his bright red jacket and cap, with the dark D of his name's logo on the front of it, Djokovic in front of the press was enjoying not only the win but the way. With the final looming he was now feeling that everything in his game was exactly where it should be. "Best performance of the tournament. As I was hoping, after the long fourth round, that I'm going to start playing better as the tournament progresses, and that's what's happening now. I'm very pleased with the way things are going."

He waited twelve months for a new chance in Paris, and had succeeded in getting one. On that Friday, he held his nerves almost perfectly, but he knew the toughest was to come. And he felt again at 5-4 that familiar feeling of fear when it was closing out time. His biggest mental hurdle was lurking, as were his biggest demons. They were probably smiling in a corner, as it was show time again for them too. "He's a human being like everyone else, it's the end of the tournament and the stress is here. You could see it at the end of the match: he wasn't bragging out there nor feeling the fun," said Venturino.

But Novak could take so much confidence from a semi-final where he showed the very promising Thiem who was the boss. Where he found a way to right the ship at the best times throughout the whole match. And he did it in a packed stadium that celebrated him from the start to the end. He was ready for the last fight. He was ready and he was pumped: he wouldn't be denied this time. To show how good he was feeling, to thank a crowd that was giving him a standing ovation and to celebrate this come-back into the final, Djokovic put on a show on Lenglen. Making first a point to clap for Thiem on his way out, as he had made a point to give him a long hug and to whisper some comforting words in his ear at the net. He then called on six ball boys and girls to do the celebration he had started in Rome, hands on heart then to the crowd. They would do that on all four sides of the court, Novak leading the timing by counting in French "3, 2, 1..." Even celebrations had to be perfectly organized and in sync. You're a control freak or you're not!

170

In his box, his mother Dijana had a gigantic smile on. Her eldest was on his way to glory again and the place was celebrating him. Novak appreciated the amazing energy of that day: "Today it was a Davis Cup kind of atmosphere on the court. That's how it felt, you know. A lot of support for both players. Dominic as well deserved to have that support. The crowd recognized that he's a young player, that it's his debut in the semifinals of a Grand Slam. They wanted him to do well, and win today's match. On the other hand, I also had plenty of support throughout the tournament, not just today. It was just a lot of energy, a lot of emotions on the court from the very first point to the last. In a big match like this you always want to feel special on the court, because... you worked hard to get into that moment. It adds that extra special kind of weight to the match itself when the crowd is there, when it's a full, packed stadium, when they get involved and they stand behind and support both players. Those are the moments that you live in your mind when you're training every day. That's where you want to be. That's why you practice." By the way, the irony of that Friday was that playing on Lenglen had given him a little advantage at the end, as Muguruza was faster than Serena to qualify for the final, so Djokovic started his match on time, ahead of Murray, and also finished before the Scot. Guy Forget surely sported a grin on his face somewhere in the stadium.

Vajda was for sure smiling, eyes shining, when I saw him going through the door out of the court. I and another French colleague needed a few words from him and he readily obliged. The word that came back most was "perfect," as the Slovakian coach was over the moon with Novak's performance. Maybe even more as the stress had been close to its maximum for 48 hours. "It was almost perfect! Everything worked for Novak; he was the better player on court. He played fantastic today. I said that against Berdych it was one of his best matches, but today was even better. He was dominating all the way. He played tactically perfect, had answers for everything. Novak didn't mind when Dominic hit so hard: he was ready. Also he read the game really well. In the third set, he stayed there, very focused. If Novak continues like this, being more active, more in charge of the ball, it will be very good for the final. Six matches behind him, lots of confidence and he's finding his game at the end of the tournament."

The second semi-final wasn't over when we talked but Vajda had a clear wish in mind: "Whatever happens, it'll be the toughest opponent in the final... You cannot make a choice... But he has a better record against Andy so..." He smiled wildly and off he went. One more time, "Nole" was one win away from the trophy but he knew what had happened the previous times. He knew the taste of heartbreak. On this Friday afternoon, the final had already started. But Novak was actually looking at just one thing for now: "For a change, it's great to have a day off tomorrow!" he smiled. "I think it's going to serve me well to recover, to get that energy supply, and Sunday I'll give my all, as always."

Murray qualified for the final while Djokovic was in the press interview room, so the "who's the favorite for that final" game started. It was hard to find many people not having a single doubt about their pick, but Stan Wawrinka wasn't among those. Just defeated in four sets (6-4, 6-2, 4-6, 6-2) by Murray, he was still convinced it would be Djokovic's day. "Well, I think it'd be Novak, as always, even though their recent matches he's played were very tight. But when he's at his best he can beat anybody. I think he will win the match. Andy defeated him in Rome and it was really a tight score in Madrid. He's finding solutions now against Novak, but I have the impression that Novak is where he wants to be and he will be playing his final."

For this to happen, all the Djokovic team was focused on one thing as always: making sure nothing would be left to chance and that their boy would be ready to roar on the last Sunday. A team that had one leader but that's been extremely united behind him with a level of dedication that in Paris became an efficient shield. They were now all a win away from their common goal, from what was also a collective work. Thierry Van Cleemput could just admire how fluid this team was working under constant pressure.

"Novak is the boss and that's the ideal situation, because he's a guy who knows how to take care of himself. But now in his team you have pillars. His management: they are amazing professionals, everything is always perfectly organized. They're really good people: if I send a message for anything, I receive an answer very quickly. And then there's Marian Vajda who's been there for so long: he saw all the consultants come and go! Vajda is really gifted to take a step back in the tough periods and to avoid losing the head when everything works.

You put the victories in perspective and you built on the losses. It's always when things go wrong that you're working the most. Nobody talks a lot about him but his physio has been there for a while too, and 'the man with the cap' (Gritsch) looks to me like a very smart guy too. They all know to remain at their place, but it's a company. It's a big metropolis built around very clear goals. A war machine like the one you now can also see around Murray." Again, Djokovic and Murray had found a common point: one more in such an already long list.

CHAPTER SEVEN

Twins' Story In The Final

There was one player who actually could have benefited from this chaos and it was Andy Murray, who walked on the Chatrier that Sunday June 5th at 3pm for the final battle in his white T-shirt, his military-like shorts and his white cap stuck on his head. Followed by Novak Djokovic, head high in the bright red jacket over the now usual red T shirt with dark lines on shoulder and sides, and black shorts. Andy was fired up, as if inspired also by the minute of applause given before the start of the final in praise of Muhammad Ali's life as the legendary boxer had just died. Murray being a huge boxing fan, it was totally an image he could summon during that fight he was into against Novak. Placed at the bottom side of the draw, he was arriving nearly unscratched by Mother Nature and its rain-fest. He hadn't had to play every day like Djokovic in that second week.

In some way, the tougher the schedule for the other side, the better for "Muzz." As usual, he was honest enough not to deny it. "I haven't given it loads of thought," he would say after his quarter final. "Obviously, you know, your job is to take care of your own matches. Obviously the weather has been challenging the last few days for everyone involved. Especially the players in the top half: it's been tricky, for sure. But you have got to just try and concentrate on yourself. Right now, tennis players during these events have to be selfish and look at their own matches and try their best to get through them."

And it wasn't like everything had been easy for him, as his practices on days off had been washed out too. As all the players, he had to find ways to still hit some balls but also kill the time. "We hit off-site, indoors, which presents completely different conditions to obviously those we're playing outside. And then, yeah, you just hang around and wait. You've got to be ready. It's a Slam quarterfinals. You can't just sort of totally switch off, either. So just long days where you're thinking a lot about the match, and whether you're getting on or not. Not much you can do."

And even if the schedule at the time looked to be more in his favor, the Scotsman knew very well that his tank had been damaged early on in the tournament with those two matches played in five sets and even over two days for the first round one. Mentally and physically, it had also been pretty tough against Wawrinka so now that he was in the final, maybe he thought the conditions imposed on the top half of the draw (where Novak was) would even things out.

It's true that we were so used to seeing Andy nowadays being a monster physically that many had underestimated the fatigue he could feel. Five sets to beat Radek Stepanek and five more to beat Mathias Bourgue wasn't really the ideal script for a Grand Slam start. He had spent 17h50 on the courts through the final, for only 12h54 for Djokovic: that's a huge difference. The history books weren't really encouraging either, as only one man in the Open Era had won a Grand Slam title after coming back from 0-2 down in his first round match (Pat Rafter, US Open 1998). And only one man in this same Open Era had won Roland-Garros after playing his first two rounds in five sets (Gaston Gaudio, 2004).

Still, he was looking so good during his semi-final, ending a 3-match losing streak against Stan Wawrinka, and then the day before the final at practice. You could feel how badly he wanted that title, surely also to achieve something that he always enjoyed: proving people wrong. How many specialists and fans would have indeed said a few years ago that Andy Murray, becoming the first British man to reach the Roland Garros final since Bunny Austin in 1937, would be in a position to win the French Open? Very few, despite the three semi-finals he had already played in Paris in 2011, 2014 and 2015.

But here he was, stronger than ever before on that red dirt. Back issues solved, mind in the right place, top spin added where it needed to, forehand not shaking anymore, second serve greatly improved, footwork firing, endurance among the best ever. Having trained in Spain on clay during his teenage years, he had completed his puzzle.

Later than his Big 4 neighbors, but still. His whole game looked like a fortress. He was ready to change the momentum between him and his tennis twin, between someone he called "the biggest rival throughout my career" in Rome weeks before.

That final had to be special between two players that were basically reflections of a tennis mirror. They were both outstanding in defense, could both play at a huge tempo from the baseline, take the ball early, bring the game to some unreal speed of execution and this for hours. They were both praised for their backhands. Were both amazing with their footwork. They both had this nearly unmatched talent for counterpunching, this touch on the drop shots and lobs, this brain that could play chess on a tennis court. They were both determined to succeed and able to endure loads of hard work. They were ready for all the sacrifices. Even their personalities were a good match: great senses of humor, very smart individuals. Oh and of course: they were born a week apart! Andy being the elder by seven days (May 15 and 22, 1987). Like, too good to be true. But still totally real.

"Andy's problem was that he was a mirror image of Novak, and they've been friends for a long time and know each other, and that makes the psychological game even more complicated when you have those long standing relationships like that," Christopher Clarey would say. "Federer and Nadal never had that: not the same generation, different styles of play. That makes it more accessible to the public. For Novak and Andy it must be very strange to be in that match because you feel like you're playing yourself a little bit. They're both smart guys, so maybe the game doesn't look always so sexy when they play it, but you know the internal dialogue - and in Andy's case the external dialogue - has to be answering."

Some people in the tennis world complain when those two face each other in finals, arguing that they're so similar that it makes it boring, mostly because the match would be deadlocked. Yet, I don't see how it's possible to call that much talent, boring. Sure their matches were often deadlocked, but they were so because those two guys were just too good at the same game! You can't blame them for that. And if one can't recognize and appreciate talent when one sees it...

That Sunday, they would be the closest Grand Slam finalists by age, beating the gap of 16 days between Guillermo Vilas and Jimmy Connors at the 1977 US Open. And for now, in this twin story, Andy wasn't the Chosen One, and he intended to change that narrative. Even more since he lost his fourth Australian Open final, his fifth overall, against Novak that year. Victories over the Djoker in the finals of the 2012 US Open and 2013 Wimbledon were now far in the past. "Muzz" was stuck right behind his Serbian rival again, having lost 12 of his last 14 matches against "Nole." Being down 23-10 in their head to head. Andy was Novak's best victim in Grand Slams (7 losses) after Federer (9 losses).

But this time he had reasons to forget that he was also down 4-2 in the Grand Slam finals against "Nole" and hope that he could do it. You could read on his face that he was convinced this last Sunday in Paris could be another historical moment for him. Two Grand Slam titles to his name already at the time he was playing his Grand Slam final n°10, didn't seem enough for his talent. Also, no British player since Fred Perry (1935) and Sue Barker (1976) had ever won in Paris.

That looked like a good thing to add to his résumé which was already looking legendary for British tennis. "It's obviously a very big match for both of us," Andy would say after winning his semi-final. "I mean, Novak trying to win the Career Slam: it's obviously a huge match for him, and me trying to win my first French Open, as well. You know, neither of us know how many more chances we'll have to win here. It obviously took Roger a long time to win this one. And Novak, too. It's a very tough event to win. There's a lot riding on the match for both of us."

Murray had surely never been more confident that he could win Roland-Garros than the past couple of years. A button had obviously been switched on. "This is my forth semi-final at the French Open, but does this one feel any different?" he wondered through his daily column in Le Parisien, also posted on his website[19]. "I think last year and this year are similar. The two before that: I didn't feel that comfortable on the court, whereas now I feel more comfortable when I step on a

---

19. *www.andymurray.com*

clay court like just in terms of my moving and understanding of how I'm going to play the matches, how I'm going to win against the best players. Before, I never really had that, and wasn't ready at that stage to win those matches. I probably had the same ambition but maybe not the necessary belief. All of the players when they come here want to win, but it's not realistic for everyone. For me before maybe it wasn't realistic as my game wasn't ready, whereas the last two years here it's not been unrealistic to think I can win the tournament."

For now, Andy was the 4 in Big 4. And surely he must have wondered sometimes why his records were so far away from Novak's despite both of them being basically two sides of the same coin. How was he to avoid wondering about that? Even if he had wanted to, the tennis world was comparing them all the time. The most common explanations were that Novak was on court more naturally aggressive and could play a bit faster than Andy who tended to defend too much; that of the two, Novak's fighting spirit and cold blood in the big matches was superior, as was his endurance; that the Serbian hadn't been derailed in his progress by the internal battles and public tantrums that had sometimes slowed down the Scot. Others would just say that Djokovic had simply become a better player than Murray, polishing his side of the coin until it'd be the brightest, turning himself into a GOAT[20] candidate. Some would also add that Andy's ego and ambitions weren't maybe as sky high as Novak's, that the drive was different and that for now it made a big difference between two guys considered among the most gifted of all time.

Murray told me a few times that when he started on the Tour he was dreaming of entering the Top 100, then it was Top 50 and then little by little he allowed himself to think about winning Wimbledon, about being the best player in the world. His ambition grew progressively, whereas I tend to think that Novak's was burning inside of him from the get go. All those little pieces of the much bigger and more complex puzzle may have contributed to the fact that before that final in Paris, Djokovic was dominating the tennis world and fighting for a legend's

---

20. Means "Greatest Of All Time".

status. While Murray still had some doors to break. But he was on his way and Novak could feel it. Andy had worked like crazy on all those little factors, even on his flexibility, to close the gap, and was now as hungry and confident as anyone else at the top. If Djokovic always had Federer and Nadal to look up to and chase, Murray had those two but he also had Novak. The Djoker was his constant reminder: if Novak had made it, so could he. So off to work.

He could have easily lamented falling into this era of the Greats, but he didn't. Instead, he used those three targets as landmarks on his way. As lighthouses. "I guess if you're Real Madrid or Atletico Madrid when Barcelona are playing unbelievably, it's probably frustrating," he admitted during a talk at Indian Wells in 2016. "It's still great to compete against them but if they weren't there, it'd make things easier as well (laughs). But for me it has been a big positive in my career to get to play against some of the best players, maybe the three best players that have ever played the game. It has made me improve. There hasn't been a period where I haven't been looking to get better: if it wasn't trying to catch Roger, then it was catching up to Rafa and trying to catch up to Novak. I've always had someone above me. I've always had motivation to train hard and try to get better."

And he also had no issue admitting that, if despite working his ass off, he was still not upstaging them, it was maybe because they were too good and that's it, no need to depress oneself, even regarding that twin of his. There was no sense of "if he has this, I should too" with Murray towards Djokovic, as he'd tell me in the Californian desert: "The rivalries are not different for me: obviously when you're younger you do look at the age of the players around you and that's normal to say I want what that person has. But when you get older it's more about yourself and trying to achieve things for yourself. When I'll look back at my career, yeah I'd love to win 10-15 Slams but when I was 8 years old to 15 years old I would have never thought that I'd win 2, and the Olympics, and Davis Cup and been at the top of the game for a long time. It's human nature to always want more but you also have to remember that you can't have everything all the time. I've done ok, and I don't so much compare myself to Novak or Rafa or Roger." One has to smile at Murray saying he's done just "ok".

His mother Judy, who had been his first coach and remains a huge force in his life and career, has been a great witness of her second born and Djokovic's evolution side by side. And one of the nicest images of that French Open final would be seeing Novak's mother Dijana and Judy hugging and toasting Champagne after the match in the players' lounge. "I first watched them play each other when they were about 12," she told me[21] in Paris in November 2016, the day Murray became n°1 in the world for the first time. "So yeah I've watched them growing up, all the way through the juniors and then obviously on the Tour since 2005, 2006? It's a long time. The last few years I think a lot has been between the four of them. But obviously Djokovic and Andy being born in the same year, maybe you see that more of a rivalry because they're the same age. But they have huge respect for each other: they're good friends so it's a healthy rivalry."

It's noteworthy that these two, who are already pretty close, could have been even closer had Novak and his family accepted the offer of the British Federation made in 2006 to move to Britain and eventually switch nationality. Imagine that for a second. But Novak rejected the idea and never looked back, as he takes the biggest joy in being Serbia's pride and gem.

In this Paris match, the stakes were of course much higher on Novak's side, with this Career Slam and "the Four In A Row" on the line of his twentieth Grand Slam final. How could he feel in that moment, when he was one win away from basically everything he could dream of achieving at this time? I asked Patrick Mouratoglou about it as he was there with Serena Williams both when she did her second "Serena Slam" and when she was two US Open 2015 wins away from achieving the calendar one. She lost in the semi-finals at the general shock against the Italian Roberta Vinci (2-6, 6-4, 6-4). So the French coach knew how tough the situation was, even on outstanding competitors.

---

21. "Judy Murray : 'A reward for perseverance'", The Yellow Ball Corner, Carole Bouchard (*http://theyellowballcorner.blogspot.fr/2016/11/judy-murray-reward-for-perseverance.html*).

"When they arrive at the fourth Grand Slam event, they are both feeling great and not. Great because he's surfing on a confidence pushed to its maximum. But not great, because the pressure is also at its maximum. Everyday they're being told they can achieve one of the biggest thing in tennis... Then it becomes a question of balance between pressure and confidence. Coaches are here to lower that pressure, which isn't that easy to do. And no one gives them confidence just by saying 'you're so strong.' Worst is that if the confidence goes down just a little, then the pressure becomes unbearable. You can only deal with it if the confidence is a little above it. Issue being that even when they're perfectly balanced, at some point everybody is going to raise the pressure up a notch and it's not manageable anymore. It's the tennis world who does that, but also when you see your damn face on every bus around because suddenly you can write tennis history like no one else. Everything is multiplied."

In those circumstances, Marian Vajda felt it was sort of good news for Novak to see Murray on the other side of the net. "Novak likes to play Andy. He never likes to play Wawrinka. So this makes a huge difference coming into the final, playing the guy that you like to play. He knows he has the ability to beat him." Murray was known territory for Novak with mainly good memories, but the French Open final was also known territory for him with only bad memories.

So did Vajda think about changing his speech to him? Not really. The Slovakian took the option most of the team would take after a tournament that had already been rocky: don't risk panicking him by changing something. "Novak is good enough to see the big picture, so this is great. So I told him 'look what happened, you are frustrated, you are breaking racquets, you have to change and see the bigger picture.' But I don't like to emphasize too much, because too much is like a movie... Like I'm American Hollywood and I go 'Go for it!! Go for it!!' I don't like these kinds of words because he's a mature guy, and I am sure that I only have to give him management, that I am there to help him realize the things by himself. I don't like all these great speeches of coaches. Ok it gives you more of a lift, and this I like and I still do with him, mainly when he was young. But for this moment, I want to really find the things through him. But obviously with Boris, when we see Novak very down, we come and we tell him 'Listen Novak we are all supporting you, we are all behind you,' all these kind of things, like 'You really feel you need our support and look we are here. Whatever being said is between us. We want to lift you up.'"

Miljan Amanovic was on the same page: support, no change. And the physiotherapist didn't feel that much of a different feel in the days and hours leading to that final, compared to what they had already been through three times in Paris. "Ok you could feel something like 'Is it that day?', but the preparation and the feeling were exactly the same," he told me. "The routine was already there as he had already been there three times. He was not facing any trouble that we as a team and he as the main actor feel we should now do something different about. And even making something different (despite that, yes, you should be mentally strong and everything), could mean that the player wonders why the team changed something. It's a stress factor which in that moment might not look like a big deal but then if things go wrong and you are losing then you'd start questioning why we did this. So we didn't change anything. He spent the day with his family, the team stayed together, all the recovery was done."

And after what happened in 2015, he couldn't even want to start thinking it was better to face Murray than anyone else: "Against Andy, there have never been easy matches. So maybe it's better than Rafa but then he lost to Wawrinka so if he lost against Wawrinka he might lose to Andy. This is a normal question. But I didn't see any advantage or disadvantage of playing Andy or not: it was just about the fact that we did everything we could, we gave everything, all our soul and all our work. So if he's not winning, maybe it's not destined. Maybe."

Only Boris Becker felt he couldn't go on like the previous times. He was there for the 2014 and 2015 finals, and was convinced he needed to change something in his speech to Novak. That he couldn't let him go on court like the previous times. It was not an easy decision but, as he had done during the Bautista Agut struggle, the German star was determined that year to let down all his filters. "Yes, I changed my speech to him coming into that final. Obviously whatever we discuss in the locker room stays in the locker room. But I thought for 48 hours about what I wanted to tell him, because obviously I made a speech before the Nadal final and another one for the Wawrinka final so I had to do something different. (He paused) I said something that made him laugh a lot (smile), and we're talking ten minutes before the final. So whatever I said it must have really hit something."

Becker had also gone through that 2015 semi-final played over two days, so if he saw how Novak could roll on Andy here, he also witnessed how he could suddenly struggle. And in 2016, the clay season showed the whole team that "Muzz" was really ready to rumble. "The rivalry with Andy is much different than the ones Novak has with Roger and Rafa," he told me in Melbourne, in January 2017 when Murray was the n°1 seed above Novak for the first time ever in a Grand Slam event. "I think up until last fall we always felt we were better. With Roger and Rafa on their best days and on Novak's best days it was 50/50. And we felt that with Andy it's 51/49. But credit to Andy, he never stopped improving and him winning at the O2 (for the ATP Finals in November 2016) proved a point as well. And also to Novak. The mountain to climb now has to go over Andy Murray who holds the keys, and that's also something Novak now had to accept. Novak, Roger and Rafa, even though they play completely differently, have very similar attitudes. And I think Andy over the last two years became like that. He was not born like it but he worked his ass off and because of that he's like this now." Becker knew Murray could end being bad news for Djokovic.

Even more now that all the work Andy had done on himself had really started to pay off. Being a very emotional person didn't always help Murray at this level, and it gave him more homework to do in order to prevent this side of him from hampering his career. Acceptance had been the key, as he told me in California in 2016. "It's something I've always worked on, but that's also something I've kind of accepted, how I am on a tennis court. I don't particularly like it, because I'm not like that away from the court. But I've been playing this sport for a long time and I've been that way since I was extremely young. I spent a lot of time trying to improve that and it has gotten better. But that is who I am and that's how I've dealt with this whole stress and pressure, and that expectation you're meant to win every match that you play over a lot of years. Showing my emotions a lot, in some ways helps me. But in some other ways your opponent can see when you're frustrated and that's not ideal (laughs). I don't particularly like it, but that's who I am on the court and I've accepted it."

Many players are different persons on and off the court, but with Murray the gap always looked the biggest. He can be as calm and nice off court, and then mercurial and angry on it. But he has stopped finding it weird and worrying. "Until I started to learn more about the psychology and a little bit more about how the brain works, I found it very difficult away from the court to think 'I can't believe I did that on the court; I can't believe I behaved that way.' But when I started to actually understand, then it's a lot easier for me when I'm away from the court, it's like 'ok I understand why that's happening or when I reacted that way.' Because before it could happen that I got very angry on the court and then when I finished the match I was like so sad about it. Now it's like 'ok, it's fine.' I still don't want to do it but I understand better why and I'm a lot more forgiving I guess when I'm off the court."

On that Sunday and in this rivalry dynamic, maybe what also helped Djokovic in Paris was that he had lost that Rome final and also had to fight hard to win the Madrid one, as both times Andy unleashed hell on him. Clay wasn't safe land anymore and he had been warned. There would be no surprise on that Sunday, which was a good thing viewing the stress factor. Novak had also spent that clay season answering questions about how much Andy had improved on clay, so, yes, he was pretty much aware of what was coming. And most of all: he knew his Andy book.

"He's a fighter," he stated right after his semi-final win. "He has improved so much on the clay court over the years. Moving better and sliding better on the court. He is also more patient, constructs the point better, which is very important for clay. I'm sure that it's going to be a final with a lot of emotions and a lot of exchanges from the baseline because we have similar styles of game. I know his game; he knows mine. I'm sure we're both going to give it our all on Sunday. I think he's one of the most dedicated tennis players on the tour. He always seeks to improve his game and get better, which I do, too. It's another Grand Slam title up for grabs. One thing for sure is that I know what to expect when I get on the court with him. It's always going to be a very physical battle."

They've basically grown up together with a very similar game, but Novak Djokovic hadn't built his tennis game or his mindset to best

Andy Murray. Andy had never been his mental target. All of this now needed to change and maybe the situation was easier for Andy than for Novak, because "Muzz" had been watching this Serbian target for years. Novak was his tennis version of the big brother, the one he wanted to take the toys away from. And he'd now be relentless. For Christopher Clarey, there was no doubt this rivalry had influenced Murray's and Djokovic's games, but it was the Scotsman who had been the most advantaged by it. "I think Novak has done a lot more good in terms of the game and the way it progresses for Andy, than Andy has ever done for Novak. Novak probably owes his difficulties against Andy now to his own successes."

Yet, there is also a feeling that both of them are pretty proud of their tennis duet. "Looking at our history of the first time we played against each other and ever since we have met when we were 11 years old all the way until now, if we knew back then that we were going to fight for the biggest trophies in this sport, I think we would both sign the document. It's pretty nice that our rivalry has evolved over the years," Novak would say in Paris that year. Echoing what he said in Madrid a few weeks before: "We both thrived to be at the top, and we've known each other since for so long. I think you could see already in those junior days that both of us had serious intentions to conquer the tennis world and try to make a serious mark with our names in the tennis world. So I'm very pleased that I have developed a great rivalry with somebody that I've known over a very long time and somebody that I have a very good and friendly relationship with on and off the court." They both landed on the Tour as the new threats to the "Fedal" power, and no doubt being now 1 and 2 in the world was like their common achievement. For the record, they were now also together in the Players' Council of the ATP, Novak being President and Andy Vice-President. Inseparable.

I remember Novak once explaining that after both their careers were done, he'd hope to be able to sit down and have a beer with Andy just to talk about their achievements and so on. And both have often stated that nowadays they couldn't be as close as they were when teenagers just because the stakes were too high. They would still chat, talk about their families, be friendly but there would probably never be lunches or dinners shared, and the texting had probably slowed down too. Yet I remember Andy sharing that story of Novak sending him a picture of a Dunblane (Andy's hometown) signpost in 2012, when the Serbian had taken a few days off in Scotland with his at the time fiancée and now wife Jelena. Murray couldn't believe it and Djokovic had to swear it wasn't photoshopped.

Darren Cahill wasn't surprised they had both kept a good relationship inside of those rivalries, but he would also be quick to say that there had to be limits: "All those guys have a pretty good relationship off the court but I wouldn't go so far to say they're all great friends: it's impossible. You wouldn't expect it. And I don't think you'd see any of those four guys sitting down having dinner with each other. It's just not the way life works if you want to be one of the great players: you have to have some separation from your peers. It's very normal. Also Novak and Andy pushed each other to be better, so one day they'll look back on their careers at the end of it and see that it was a special rivalry." One that has already become a quite unique case in tennis history, and that would undoubtedly reach a new level that year. Something else was reaching a new level and it would come as a decisive part of that 2016 French Open final: the crowd's appreciation of Novak Djokovic.

CHAPTER EIGHT

France's Adopted Son Wins

A massive uproar. Descending from all the rows of the court. Interrupting the final. People were demanding that what they felt like justice would be given...to Djokovic. The umpire had just given the point, a service winner, to Murray after checking the mark on the T, and thus despite an out call when Novak was hitting his forehand return long. The point wouldn't be replayed. The public went wild. Novak went straight to the umpire to tell him what he thought about his decision. After the ovation the Serb received while he was walking on the centre court this Sunday, the reaction of the crowd was a new sign that Novak would be the crowd's warrior today.

To the surprise of many, they were ready to fight for Djokovic that day, and they made Murray feel it. We were at 5-3 for "Muzz" in the first set, and this stadium was making it clear that a Djokovic win was its only desired ending. Novak didn't rush to ask them to stop; he took it all in, making sure that Murray would too. Then after a while, as the umpire found no way to resume the game, Novak started to clap as a "thank you" to the crowd then asked them to calm down. It's Andy who ended winning that game and that first set (6-3), yelling a huge "Come On!" and pointing the right index finger to his head whereas Novak was hitting his left side in a frustrated sad way. But it was that unconditional and vocal support that started to help Djokovic fight back. "Today the crowd was very important," his coach Marian Vajda would confirm later. "They were fantastic! It really helped him. It was a big change."

And he needed it! In his first service game of the second set, Novak found a way to face a break point despite being up 40-15 and he was now watching Andy's warrior right fist up in the air after a winning forehand passing shot. But the crowd was still there, pushing. So yes he missed an inside out backhand and then had a double fault to waste those two game points, and yes it was now dire with this break point to save. Yet, there and now he could feel this safety net set up by the crowd, so he moved forward, hitting an inside out forehand and an overhead like a boss.

When he held after two big serves, the cheers of relief were those of parents watching their first born finally walking by himself without falling. The cheers from the crowd were of pure relief, surely echoing Novak's feelings at this moment. "I guess I needed some kind of long rally and situation like this where I saved a break point, where I win a big point and get that tension out," he told me. "And I felt like 'ouf, ok now the sweat is coming, you know, we're in the match, the engines have started.' Because up to that point I was still trying to find my comfort zone on the court, and Andy was doing what he does best: he was making me play, he was literally allowing me to self-destruct. So there was that turning point, crucial point at the beginning of the second set. I managed to re-establish my focus and my rhythm on the court, and all of a sudden I felt in the flow." After that point, everything had switched. Novak finally settled in that match, wheels stopped turning inside his brain.

Murray felt it too: "Yeah after that, obviously, he started to free up a little bit more and got the break immediately after. Probably started hitting the ball a little bit better. He did play extremely well. Gave me very few errors. Started hitting the ball a bit close to the lines, and I was sort of dropping a bit far back behind the baseline. Obviously if you're letting the best players control points, that's tough. I wasn't able to dictate enough points after the beginning of the match. But there are always changes in momentum and ups and downs throughout the best of five set matches. Unfortunately I couldn't capitalize on that chance. Maybe that would have changed things a little bit."

For Guy Forget that's one more proof of how special Djokovic is: "That's all the strength and mastery of those champions: to always be in control whatever the score says, whatever the weather is, etc. They find a way and they don't look back. That was unbelievable to see because Murray was playing amazing until that point, but he couldn't sustain the intensity or the quality of play."

From outside, it actually looked like a button had been switched back on inside the Djoker, and that's the feeling he leaves when saying he managed to reestablish his focus. "This is also one of his very good weapons," said Vajda. "That he can tell himself 'let's go!' Because you could see his quality of play was there. When you are in the final, you always believe, because there are so many times it can change. One set is nothing. I was just hoping that it wouldn't get to his mind and freeze him, like it did against Stan or Nadal. But this time he was able to free himself and say 'I go!' You can't run away from that match and by this I mean letting all those things come back to your mind and freeze you. But he was able to completely get out of it. He stayed in the moment, he stayed there and he started feeling good. That break point to save was the moment that really changed everything: you see, it's about one ball! And then after that he started to hit super clean and everything."

But that control over one's emotions surely isn't that easy, right? Some would even wonder how it's possible in this internal turmoil to suddenly see clearly again. The key is that no, it's not possible on a day... Unless you've spent months or even years finding a way to that switch inside yourself. "Changing one's emotional level through a match is totally possible and manageable through exercises," explains sophrologist Catherine Aliotta. "Novak was fine when he came on the court or he wouldn't have played the first game like that. So it means that at some point he may have thought: 'Wow I feel well, it's not a good sign.' In this awareness, there's the stake behind. At some point I told myself 'it's not good' and the doubt came. If the doubt came, then all my demons set up again. And suddenly I can't put the ball inside the court. It's all about the control of these demons, to keep them away. All the work goes towards recognizing what's happening, recognizing physically the emotion and so being able to stop it. Some of the exercises are about anchoring confidence in objects like the racquet or in motions. Or when they put the towels over their head to evacuate. It's about patterns that help to get the focus back, it's about clearing your thoughts. You combine emotion and motions so it becomes automatic."

In Darren Cahill's opinion, all of those emotional and intellectual abilities combine to make or break the champions, because the tennis world is more often than not owned by those who, in those close-to-the-cliff moments, can make career saving decisions. "You have to work it out yourself: the best players in the world are the best problem solvers. For what happened to Novak at the start of the match, one can only guess, but sometimes when everything is going too well, you expect things to implode. So maybe with Novak making such a good start, maybe he thought it was too good to be true and started over-thinking things a little bit. Then you get ahead of yourself and before you know it you've lost your game. And you lose the set, you sit down, you regather yourself, you loosen up the expectation a little bit and you just start playing for the moment. Maybe that's what happened for Novak. Maybe you expect too much when you walk onto the court and if it doesn't come immediately, then things get away from you pretty quickly. But Novak was good enough to stop it and turn it around."

And so Novak was indeed back on track, like in this first game of the match where everything was so fluid, where he said he was there and 100% ready. The flow came back. Djokovic was saved by himself of course, but also by all those people telling him one simple thing: "we're with you, you can make it!" This whole feeling was reinforced by the number of Serbian flags flying around the place. This year, it looked like the whole community had come here even stronger to help their best ambassador over the last hurdle. "This final was really in his favor," Vajda would say. "And at some point, everything had to come together! Somehow and finally! You couldn't write a better story. The crowd was almost the key, the people really lifted him up and he needed that!"

Novak was playing at home, to the big surprise of the Murray fans who were still trying to make themselves heard in the stadium. Andy might have wondered that day if he had missed something and somehow Novak had a double nationality. "That was obviously tough as well," he would say after the match. "But I handled it well and I'm happy with that. It was good for me to go through things like that: it toughens you up a little bit. I wasn't disappointed. I don't mind that. It obviously doesn't always make things easy but I handled it extremely well. It was not an issue for me. You know, what Novak achieved is something extremely special, and a lot of people would have wanted to have seen that and been a part of that. He deserved the support he got."

Still, some colleagues were stunned, borderline confused, as to why that centre court had turned into a Djokovic fanzone. Not even in Melbourne, where he had now won six titles, nor in Beijing and Shanghai where he was an absolute icon, would the stadium give Novak such unconditional support. So what were the French up to again? There's a narrative saying Djokovic is always facing hostile crowds, that he's the unloved one, and that even when he's not, his "lovemeter" can't ever reach that of Nadal's and Federer's. That for some reason people are always going to side for his opponents. A position they take so much as a truth that they would ask him regularly how it feels to always be the one-no-one-wants-to-see-winning.

I never saw Novak blinking at those questions. Always answering it's no news that crowds tend to take the underdog's side as they want to see a competitive match and that anyway he focuses on his own fans as he can hear their support too. That he of course knew how popular Rafa and Roger are but wasn't playing catch up and had no issue with it.

Novak's résumé was now playing catch up with those two monsters of the game, as he had built a strong case for a Djokovic era following the Roger one and the Rafa period. So maybe when searching for reasons not to treat him as their equal, there remained this so-called lack of popularity. Yet, people would pack his practices and matches, chase him for autographs and pictures all season long. Fans had made his bankable status rise so much through the years that, like Nadal and Federer you had to start negotiating from a million dollars minimum to get a chance to have him in your draw, and international brands had endorsed him. Television would request his matches to be at the best air times.

But no: if you come third after Federer and Nadal, that doesn't matter apparently. Narrative says you're the not-loved-enough golden child; so be it. Well, in 2016 in Paris you had to be deaf not to hear the obvious: France was pushing for Djokovic, loudly and proudly. He was their n°1 one choice. That first game of the second set would end being a turning point in this final, and the crowd had played its part. For Boris Becker it was an utter surprise: "What was unbelievable to me in that final was how many Serbians and French were here to cheer for him. For a moment I even felt a bit sorry for Andy because in a final of a Grand Slam it shouldn't be that one-sided, but on the other side I said: 'On this day, Goddammit, we'll take it. We'll take it!'" His contagious laugh then resonated around the players' restaurant garden in Melbourne where we were at that moment.

The fight back was then on for Novak, and this time instead of spreading salt on his open Parisian wounds, the Serbian would raise self belief above his doubts. The eyes weren't wandering around anymore, there was no more heavy breathing, no more panicked looks towards his box. "Novak started very slow, then he found his groove and domination on the court," said Vajda. "He found a great quality of shots and selection of those shots. He attacked more, came at the net, was very solid on the groundstrokes."

Djokovic was indeed settled in his own bubble and had closed the door to any negative thoughts. He was the one dictating, taking his responsibilities, not missing shots anymore. Andy was maybe still lamenting the chance missed in the previous game, a tiny blink that was enough to see his arch rival at his throat. The British player was now the one bowing down at the end of those huge rallies. Slowly, he went from the chaser to the chased and against Novak it's not an enviable position at all. You could again see it in Djokovic's eyes. As he was on the return waiting for Murray to serve in that second game of the second set, he was looking either as a hawk that had noticed a potential dinner from above, or any predator of your choice circling its prey, wondering which way to finish it off.

On the second break point, Murray hit a double fault: Novak was now up 2-0, soon 3-0 under huge cheers from the crowd. When he found himself up 4-1 and 40-15 on Andy's serve after a marvellous counter drop shot, he let it go totally, celebrating with a matador-like fist pump. Vajda and Becker, both wearing red jackets, were clapping in the box: their boy was back. The crowd erupted. Backhand down the line while moving forward: 5-1. Right fist in the air, Novak was playing with the public, now feeling serene and confident enough to handle its intensity. 6-1. He was now acting like the gladiator they were here to see.

To the great relief of Becker who knew this second set might prove crucial: "Novak started amazing in this match, breaking Andy at 0, but then Andy returned the favor and really played out of his mind for the next couple of games. But we felt that time was on Novak's side so he just had to get into the match and prolong the match. The longer the better, because Andy had played double the amount of time as Novak. We felt, if he can get into that second set, win it maybe, the longer the better because Andy just played too much. So when at the beginning of the second set he had a break point to save I was like 'Ok my friend, you'd better win this point!' (he smiled). He did and then he started to relax a little bit, did the first break, won the second set, then I felt: this is going to be good."

Looking back at it, Novak rejoiced at what he felt during those moments when the match started to turn in his favor: "It was one of those kinds of feelings where you feel like it doesn't matter how many players are across the net you can still win points. It feels so good! And I reached that optimum state of mind, in-the-zone-type of feel, from the middle of the second set all the way basically to the last couple games of the match."

Patrick Mouratoglou has been in this situation of fighting Roland-Garros demons and Four In A Row pressure with Serena Williams, both when she was trying to win Roland-Garros again (2013, 11 years after her first title here) and also when she was trying to achieve a second Serena Slam at Wimbledon in 2015. Adding that he now knows Djokovic really well, he knew even before the start of the match that the Serbian was in for an emotional ride that he could end mastering. "I did the preview of that match on Fox and I said that it would be mentally very tough on him at the start and at the end, because he knew what he was playing for and also there was no way he could close it out easily. It would also be a tactical battle as Murray had recently changed the way to play against Novak and it worked. Even more on that day as Novak was tight. Then it would also be a physical battle as one was fresh and the other not at all. And we saw it: Murray totally imploded. He made the terrible mistake to waste energy on the road where he shouldn't have. Novak is a really smart guy so I'm sure he knew before the match that time was on his side: the longer the match, the better chance he had to win it. I think it played to his abilities to stay in the match when it wasn't going his way at all. He got a grip on everything he could to stay in there. Had he felt that the opponent was in the shape of his life whereas he was in that state emotionally, I don't know if the result would have been the same. But for sure Novak was going to be in this state for the final: it was so heavy on his shoulders. I saw it with Serena... It's impossible to understand for people who haven't gone through it. There's nothing worse than not being allowed to miss, whereas it's mandatory to allow mistakes when you play or you can't swing freely. So here in this match all of a sudden, he's not allowed to miss anything at all. It's terrible."

So the Djoker fought all of this to turn this match around in that second set and then dictated the game and imposed his will and skills from that point, peaking in the third set on a 4-1 double break point with a backhand counter drop shot, sliding on this clay like a ballet dancer on an opera stage. Waving the right index to his box, he was like saying "I'm not going away this time. I'm going to make it my day." He had won ten of the last twelve games at that moment and didn't even flinch when he had to save two break points. A backhand down the line and a backhand volley later he'd be back at 40A, fist pumping.

Danger was still around the corner but as long as he was setting the bar that high, he was fine. On the other side of the net, it was obvious than Murray's legs were getting heavier and heavier. He had played two matches of five sets in the first two rounds and even if he had more time off than Djokovic through those two weeks, he had played a lot of tennis since January and had a more brutal semi-final on Friday. Sure he had immensely improved on clay but he was still less a natural on this surface than Novak. To beat him there, his absolute best was required.

Andy's emotion after beating Wawrinka was maybe also the sign that his tank was entering the red zone. Nevertheless, Muzz would give his all until the last point, and his will power remained a threat. A third break point indeed came, and an ace on the T to save it. Forehand down the line in the alley and a smile, still a fourth break point coming. Murray missed his backhand return, but Novak was not smiling anymore, instead vocally pushing himself. And the crowd agreed again and again, telling him it was not the moment to slow down or to show mercy.

Djokovic obeyed, and after a close to ten minutes game he held for 5-1. He would again have issues to close it out at 5-2 despite being up 40-0 but would eventually make it on a backhand out from Murray (6-2). At 40-30, the crowd came in again to ease his nerves right after a missed forehand had visibly frustrated him. They were on the watch to fill every confidence crack. As Novak showed a fist to his box, the stadium cheers grew louder: for the first time in Novak's career, he was a set away from the Roland-Garros title. And they were a set away from witnessing history being made by a player they adopted a long time ago. Novak's ties with the French are indeed way deeper than many thought, and through the years France's soft spot for that Serbian prodigy who came to challenge the legends kept growing. Even stronger as the feeling was mutual. So the intensity of the support on this last Sunday was actually the final click between Novak Djokovic and France.

The fourth set of this 2016 French Open final would be the crowning of Djokovic and the Parisian crowd relationship. As much as Novak's game and mental strength, the help he would receive from France in that set, the culmination of two weeks of support and actually a decade of mutual appreciation, would be the last decisive factor in his victory. The mercurial Serbian was at home in this also intense country: France had his back and had even put a safety net below him in case things would go awry. "It was a pleasant surprise," Serbian sports reporter Sasa Ozmo told me, "but I thought it could happen because it already did in the semis. It had a pretty large echo back in Serbia. People saying: 'Finally he got the crowd on his side!'"

At the start of that fourth set, all was now going according to plan: Djokovic was marching on the Chatrier as if it was the red carpet leading to his glory. How do you end toying with the n°2 player in the world? When you've decided this day was going to be yours this time, and when on the other side of the net legs were getting heavier by the minute and hopes were fading. Right from the get go in this fourth set, Djokovic showed Murray he had a next gear up his sleeve. Crisp crossed forehand, clean crossed backhand taken at the top of the bounce and a stellar backhand drop shot that forced Murray to kill his legs a bit more to try unsuccessfully to counter.

Out of frustration and helplessness, Andy shot that ball into the net. The crowd was also getting under his skin as someone again shouted something during his serving ball toss. Murray had enough, went to complain to the umpire, got booed in the process. The umpire told the crowd to keep quiet when players were serving, with surely little hope he could calm everybody for too long. Andy doesn't care about hostile crowds, as he usually takes it as an incentive and doesn't give a lot of importance to being the loved one or not. So here he was more venting to release his mounting frustration at this final that was getting away from him.

An unbelievable defense from Novak, an annoying spider cam over his head, and some deep returns would end pushing him over the edge. 1-0 break, Djokovic, who was now sprinting to the finish line, and nothing looked able to disturb him, not even that double break point missed at 3-1. His returns looked faster than Andy's serves, his accuracy was incredible as he would play only a few inches inside all the lines: there was no safe place on the court to hit against him. He would at some point be at 21 of 25 at the net. His resolve was total. Djokovic was in the zone as tennis players use to call this state of grace where you can try whatever you want to, it's going to work. You could see it on his face: each time Murray would look at the other side of the net, he'd see someone telling him "I see you, and you're done. So brace yourself."

When, pushed to try impossible shots, Murray landed a backhand down the line started from a bad position in the alley, Novak was up 4-2 and 40-0 on Andy's serve. His fist pumping as he could now nearly feel the trophy in his hands. The "Nole! Nole! Nole!" chants were dancing around the stadium. The next point was surreal: PlayStation mode, activated. Forehand down the line, backhand down the line, crossed forehand and another one down the line to finish Andy off. Both feet on the baseline, taking the ball so early you just had time to see it bounce. Novak couldn't hit more freely and loose than this. It was a masterpiece. 5-2. People were on their feet, celebrating what was surely to come: Novak Djokovic becoming a legend of the sport under their eyes.

So the Djoker smiled. Now sitting in his chair he looked at this crowd and smiled. Pure happiness. Crowd chanting louder, Novak enjoying the moment and zero doubts entering his mind. Yes, he was off to close it out. Yes, this communion with the public would soon have its golden finish after years and years of mutual understanding. "I think they were also feeling for him," Gebhard Gritsch would say with a grateful smile. "Especially after he cried the year before."

Djokovic first went to France when he was around 11 years old, and during one of young Novak's first trips there he discovered a place that would become a part of his professional career glory. He was crossing France by train to reach a junior event when it was one of the first things he saw while taking a break waiting for the next leg. His father was not far, and he was off for a short bit of sight-seeing. "I was passing through Paris: we would travel mostly by train, with the TGV, so we would stop at Gare de Lyon (editor's note: one of Paris' train stations) and walk in the area around there. I remember during one of my first visits to Paris I saw the Bercy arena as it was just outside of Gare de Lyon."

He recollects it with the smile of nostalgia, now knowing that he would go on and win, for now, four titles there. But his French Open memories wouldn't start before the junior Grand Slam he'd play there at age 16. Novak didn't need any adjustment time to feel comfortable in France. He decided it was a country worthy of his affection nearly right away, because people treated him normally here, would be nice to him and his family. That sounds overly simple but it wasn't for a kid getting out in the post-war Serbia world. "France was one of the first countries where we would actually felt welcomed, where we felt that warm friendship." And that's something he was hoping for as he already had a positive idea of what he would find in this land. "There is a long friendship between our two countries. We have a lot of French people living in Serbia so I got to meet some of them, and also I know many people in Serbia speak French. So we always had a positive opinion towards France even when I hadn't yet gone there. But when I went there, I experienced it. I liked it of course, and also I admire countries that have a long history and tradition, and France is definitely one of them."

Djokovic and France were a match even before he would turn professional, but now that Rafa and Roger were out of this

Roland-Garros, he was able to enjoy King-like status in Paris. He was like the little brother finally alone with the parents as the older siblings had left the house. All the focus and care turned towards him. From the ground staff to the tennis fans, you'd see them steal a few words here, get some stuff signed there, yell "This is your year, Novak!" in matches or practices. It was like the Djokovic quest had been embraced by the whole place, and so Novak would be strolling around for two weeks as if he owned it. And when the King rules, there's no denying him anything or complaining about his actions. Novak would be one hour late on Friday the 20th for his pre-tournament press conference: so what? Nothing. He'd arrive with a smile, sit on the chair behind the desk as if it were a throne and let the people know he was now ready to talk. He knows he's always late by the way and will swear each time that he's working on it.

A very nice proof of how he was The Ruler that year in Paris would come two days later, during the start of the first round, on Sunday the 22nd. It was his birthday and if some player ignored it before, not a single one would after that. The birthday tradition is a serious business at the French Open, but it usually takes on huge dimensions only when your name is Rafael Nadal. You'd arrive on site on June 3rd and one of the first questions would be: when and where do they set up the Rafa birthday party this year? And you would have to play the detective a bit as part of the game also seemed to be not to disclose that information too early or at all. I've seen numbers of colleagues surveying the corridor going to "Le Bar de la Presse" (the media café), at the top floor of the press centre on the Chatrier, to be sure not to miss the party, as it was usually set up there. The ceremony has changed a bit from past years and now the place-to-be is at the first floor players' lounge. And that's also where Novak now enjoyed his own birthday in Paris. When the tournament starts planning your birthday cake and what to pick as gifts, no doubt you've made it as a Special One in Paris.

So on this Sunday the 22nd of May, you could foresee it from the end-of-the-morning photographers queuing outside of the first floor players' lounge. That's also part of the ceremony: access to players' lounges during the season isn't granted to everybody, so they had to stay outside and wait. And to add to the fun, even when you have - as I do - access to the players' lounge, you can't take the stairs in the middle of this lounge to go upstairs. This area is really players only: a bit of a quiet land. Not going to lie: being at the bottom of those stairs and being told I had to actually leave to then access the first floor wasn't greeted with a big smile as it was raining outside and I knew the door wouldn't be open yet. I had been washed out in the morning arriving at the stadium and was finally dry after having to walk in socks for hours in the media centre while my shoes were drying or at least trying to.

But a deep sigh brought no pity from the security person so out I went. I readily admit that I like those birthday parties, and it's often a good place to spot the moods or to get to talk to people. Also, I'm curious. As are all my other colleagues who come while knowing that most of the time we're just going to get yelled at and elbowed by photographers and TV crews, not getting that much information. But that would always make a nice touch in the newspapers the day after or right away on websites and social media. You don't miss birthday parties.

Let's be clear: Novak's 2016 birthday party wouldn't be forgotten. Everybody was set, the photographers had stopped arguing about who was in front, who had a bad angle. The TV people not having the right clearances had stopped arguing with the tournament staff. The print press had stopped hoping they would have a nice spot to watch and settled in the back. As usual. Everybody was now gearing up for the "he arrives" moment, one where the "Novak, look over here! No, over there! Novaaaaak!" would start. That's a fun chaos, really.

And everybody knew there would be waiting. I mean we're talking Nadal or Djokovic here so one is going to wait a bit. We would actually wait 45 minutes, with tournament director Guy Forget looking out of the window, as if trying to conjure a famous bunch of dark hair showing up. With the cooks coming with the cake, starting a frenzy before quickly killing all hopes: no, it didn't mean Novak was on his way.

Actually I was set close to the cake table and so to some of the officials and when, after the first 15 minutes of waiting, I heard "Apparently, it could be that Novak still hasn't left his home." I laughed. I may have been the only one. And certainly not this TV news reporter on the phone explaining that he would maybe be unable to send his next feature on time for the mid-day editions, as he was still stuck waiting for Djokovic to blow out the candles. That's how a birthday party can bring down the house in an unexpected way.

But after a long and nervous wait, the Boss arrived, strolling in the middle of the photographers and TV cameras in his deep blue jacket and white shorts, smiling proudly while saying in French "Wow, there are a lot of people!" then going to hug Forget and have a look at the cake. "Wow, Fantastic." The cake looked like a clay court, with a racquet not far away. As the tournament had done in the past, and also for the birth of Novak's son, gifts were given, taken with a "Wow, merci!" Novak was in "wow" mood. The cake was of course gluten free and sugar free so after a nice speech, Novak started to cut some slices of it. He ate two bites. And I'm going to tell you also why we like these birthday parties: most of the time, staff and media are the ones eating the majority of the cakes! In 2015 around Indian Wells time, I remember there was a succession of celebrations with each time a big part of the cake landing in the media centre. No waste.

All in all it was a very nice and fun moment that ended taking way more time than we all thought it would but whatever. "Whatever": that wasn't the feeling I discovered while going downstairs after this little party. Yes, I took that forbidden staircase but come on people, I was already inside and up those stairs so surely going down them wasn't too much of a breach of conduct. Anyway, it was pure chaos on the ground level. Sure, the players' lounge in Paris is more often than not packed, as it's smaller, but here it wasn't packed: here it was people piling, trying to sneak into some micro-space to sit or even stand. There wasn't a spot left! And many eyes were actually pointed in my direction as I went down the stairs, as all those players were just waiting for one thing to happen: that birthday ceremony to be over.

It was now lunch time, thus rush hour, which was already bad enough. But it was also rainy and cold outside so no way players were going to enjoy the terrace. Everybody wanted in, but the whole first floor was closed as it was devoted to the King's birthday party. Yet, there was no riot, everyone was just simply hiding his misery and surely cursing Novak a bit in silence.

When I finally found a way out of there with "sorry, sorry...I'm going out, sorry..." I crossed one of the ATP staff, and sent a usual "Hi! Everything good?" With a nervous laugh, he answered: "Yes, all is absolutely fine! We have half of the players' lounge closed at lunch time on a rainy day at the start of the tournament when every player is here. It couldn't be better!" It was his "the world is coming to an end" laugh, and we both laughed a bit more. You know how you name hurricanes? Well, Roland-Garros may call birthday parties "Novak" for some time now. But the King was happy, so rejoice everybody while you try not to spill your pasta on someone basically sitting on your lap.

There had been even less doubt about the "Novak factor" through the kids' day the day before, on May 21st. Djokovic is involved in this day nearly every year, often ending up near the DJ on the Chatrier, making sure everybody is putting their arms up in the air. This year on that Saturday he participated in a fun doubles with several French Olympians among other tennis players also giving a hand on that day. The crowd was on its feet on Chatrier, finding it hilarious to see the Djoker with a French beret on and a mustache. Players played a "pétanque" game at some point, which held no secret for Djokovic as it's his end-of-practice ritual. No way he could have looked more French! And when the kids' day event came to an end around 3.45pm, when it would have been time for the crowd to go walk around and enjoy the rest of the stadium, barely anyone left: it was Djokovic's training time with his great friend Viktor Troicki.

The house remained packed, which wasn't something to ignore. Novak was soon to start his new campaign for the trophy in Paris and they were showing him they were here to support him right from the start. It was a collective "Let's go!" or as we say here, "Allez!" And Novak felt it as, right after his last practice ball, he went to give everything he could out of his bag to the fans: tennis balls, wristbands, T Shirts. He would sign and give it all to the kids who couldn't believe their eyes. Pictures were taken, high fives were flying around. And then while the staff was preparing the court for the next practice, Djokovic started to go around all four sides of the Philippe Chatrier to sign for as many people as possible. Like a round of honor. The connection was there and he felt it: that's the energy he would feed on through those two weeks. There wouldn't be any misunderstanding this time.

Novak had been visibly annoyed in 2015 when in the middle of a huge struggle against Andy in the semi-finals he felt the crowd pushing for the outsider. They wanted a longer show. He wanted support. One doesn't always go along with the other. Also, this has to be said right away: French tennis people are picky and sometimes tough to fully understand. They fall in and out of love without any clear criteria and for an unpredictable amount of time. They can boo you to no end on a day despite dearly loving you. In 2009, the same people that would cheer Rafael Nadal's mistakes and rejoice at every Robin Söderling winner were also those you'd cross a few hours after the match, lamenting that Rafa was out of the tournament. And as any Frenchman would tell you, once you've been put in a box, you'll have all the trouble in the world making them get you out of it. They know who you are: save your energy.

As Djokovic hinted when he said he was touched to feel their love in the 2014 final as he knew it wasn't an easy thing to get: good luck winning unconditional love from the French! It's like Nadal had to lose that match in 2009 to be finally seen as a human being and not a bloodthirsty warrior. In 2010, love was pouring down on Rafa... As it took Novak crying in 2014 and 2015? Roger Federer never had this issue: he's been declared a genius, a gentleman, the greatest of all time and most importantly it's been decided he was nearly French. Switzerland is close, he speaks fluent French: it's way enough. Even more when no Frenchman had won here since Yannick Noah in 1983, and when French top players those past ten years haven't always been judged worthy of the French crowd's support. You don't really try to earn the French crowd's love; you just give your hardest on the court and cross your fingers.

As star power is doing its work, the Big 4 starts with an obvious advantage: French people do love their winners. A lot. Nadal, despite receiving a cold shoulder from time to time, still enjoys rockstar status in Paris. He would cause riots when walking the alleys before and after practices, would be chased down by young and less young people for pictures, signed balls, T shirts or even body parts. Yes, I said body parts. Federer needed a full team of bodyguards to step outside in 2015. Things were different for Murray as France was still trying to determine what exactly was going on with him: his dry sense of humor, his impossible to read body language on court, his off court good manners and open mind, his swearing habit through matches, his obvious intelligence, and his sometimes grumpy attitude remained a mystery the French crowd wasn't sure it needed to crack.

Don't forget that France and Great Britain enjoy a love - hate relationship that sports fans never fail to remember and reinforce. But despite all this, kids would run after Andy, people would yell for selfies, and there was barely a match without someone yelling "Andy, dis moi oui." I'll gladly take this chance to solve this mystery for you, non-French people. For each time this would happen, followed by a general giggle from the French crowd, a foreign colleague would look at me in utter confusion while guessing that there was probably something naughty under it. French reputation: you can't fight it.

In the 80's there was a very famous French band called Rita Mitsouko and they'd become as entrenched in French culture as the "pain au chocolat" or the "croissant." There's no party going on in France without one of their tunes being played. Everyone knows all the lyrics. One of their biggest hits, out in June 1986, is called "Andy" and is actually linked to our British friends as it was inspired by Andy Capp, a Reg Smythe comic book hero. So this song is all about a girl following "Andy" everywhere and trying to persuade him to bring her to his place or to accept going to her's. Through the chorus, that will stick in your brain after one listen, the female singer is belting out "Andy, tell me yes!" while calling him specific French nicknames as "chou" or "chéri" that I'll sum up as "honey" and "darling / sweetheart". So if the French crowd is still unsure about the amount of support to give to Murray, obviously some have already decided they were pretty fond of the Scot. Next time you hear "Andy, dis-moi oui!" and the giggles, you'll be able to join.

But what about how Novak had become the crowd favorite in this Roland-Garros? Djokovic and France go way back, and they've slowly but surely grown very fond of each other, everything clicking and culminating in that 2016 French Open. The French were sad for him when he lost the 2013 semi-final, even more in the 2014 final but still it was against Nadal so hearts were divided. In 2015, despite all the appreciation they have for "Stan the Man," (not holding any grudge for the Davis Cup final loss), the suffering of their Djoker was a bit too much to bear to be fully happy. Suddenly they realized that this Serbian had been growing up with them and was now part of the family.

It was then high time to help him get the toy. I told you France loved winners, but among those winners France loves the prodigies even more, those who have the history of the sport on their shoulders and who have evolved and grown to stardom under French eyes. Novak Djokovic was barely 18 in 2005 when he got out of the qualifications here and played Coria in the second round on the centre court, and a year later at 19 he was already in the quarter finals, presented as the face of the rebellion against Nadal and Federer's hegemony. French people take pride in thinking Djokovic was born into the tennis world in Paris. It's a kind of untold narrative, same as when the tennis universe first looked in awe towards the Russian Marat Safin: an 18 year old wonder coming from the qualifications and beating both Andre Agassi and Gustavo Kuerten on his way to the fourth round. The French would never let go of the Russian after that, following his career until the end.

It's the same in a different and more complicated way for Nadal: Rafa is tightly linked with France, and people feel he's a bit theirs. Djokovic shot to stardom in Paris and confirmed his golden child status year after year until finally taking over the world in 2011. France had also lost a Grand Slam title to Djokovic when Tsonga lost in Melbourne in 2008, and a Davis Cup title in 2010. So all in all Novak, or "Nole" and even more "Djoko" as most of the French people call him, is a common face here, someone who has entered many French homes in the last decade.

And not only was he a super talented player but he was also entertaining: if there's a country where Djokovic will forever remain the Djoker, it's France. People loved the impersonations, they loved to see him on French national television wearing wigs to sing along in a karaoke set up. In a land that treats movies and actors like its legacy, Novak's extrovert temperament was right at home. People in Roland-Garros come for the show as much as they come for tennis, and they want to have fun. Here Novak could do whatever he wanted to entertain, no one was going to roll a single eye. After all, it was the tennis country of Noah, but also Henri Leconte and Gaël Monfils: the more mercurial, often the better.

That's again something Djokovic felt right away: he could be himself in Paris, he could be over the top, he could brag, he could be too much if he wanted to. That was fine. So fine that he even tried to break protocol by getting the umpire Pascal Maria to talk on the mic after this late finish against Aljaz Bedene in the third round. The French umpire didn't know what to do with himself and found a way to exit a tricky situation by saying good night. Novak was at home more than ever in Paris that year and everybody was his guest.

On that day where he finally had the last word against Roberto Bautista Agut, he gave up the competitor's mask right after the match point to enjoy the ovation, and after he got his now usual on court interview with Fabrice Santoro. Both have always gotten along pretty well, and the Frenchman doesn't hide that he enjoys those interviews very much. It's a bit show time, and it was again the case that day as he arrived on court in a bright yellow raincoat, welcomed by a laughing Serbian. Without even hesitating, Djokovic agreed to pick the bright yellow hat going with the whole outfit that Santoro was offering him and put it on his head. "It just came naturally," Novak later commented. "I like to do these kinds of things for kids, especially. I didn't know that Fabrice Santoro was dressed like that. We just had a little joke about it. You know, it cannot hurt. Jokes cannot hurt anybody, and it was good to bring a little bit of positive energy in those gray days."

Santoro would later tell me how much he likes those on court moments with the Djoker: "Novak is among the best clients to have an interview with. Pure pleasure. Each time I enter the court to talk to him I'm super focused not to mess this up because I know that I can ruin that interview but he won't. I know that whatever happens, he'll make it great: he's going to be generous, funny, with a knowledge of how to talk back, always having things to say. And he really cares about this communion with the crowd."

Guy Forget agrees that the Djokovic touch fit France very well. "Novak is a splendid ambassador for the sport. He's someone who gives a lot of himself, of time too. He brings a relaxed and fun touch to the game, despite being someone of outmost rigor. He makes the machine sympathetic and accessible. If you compare him to champions of the past, McEnroe or Becker, when they were dominating, they were having anger fits and were more extroverted. Novak has more a Björn

Borg side: you wonder how you can attack him, how you can even take a set from him. He looks unbeatable. But through the years there's also another side of him, which is more open and smiling. He's turning more and more to the people and that makes him somehow more human. At the end, it will also go down with his legend."

And keeping the fun in the game and the Djoker in Djokovic is also something Novak finds crucial for him but also for the game. In a tennis world that's growing more professional by the day, the Serbian doesn't want to lose sight of the human factor. "I guess the tennis and sports world overall has become so demanding in every aspect of that word. The new generations feel like they have to be 100% serious. I understand that. I honestly do. I feel like personally I always try to balance things and to never leave the fun part behind, which is very important for my personality, character, and my life in general. But I understand it, because I also personally feel that there is each year more at stake. It seems like it's getting more serious. But, you know, we should never leave that entertainment part out of the equation, because every sport needs personalities. Every sport needs to see the human side of you as well, especially people who come to watch you play. Of course they come to watch you play tennis, but they all like to see your human side. I think it's always a nice balance to have in mind."

If Djokovic found a way to be more himself in France than elsewhere while playing, it has surely been helped by how at home he came to feel in this country. Living in Monte-Carlo, practicing between Monaco, Roquebrune and Nice, he's a neighbor. More: he's a very interested and culturally curious neighbor. It took him a bit of time, but not only can he now make his way around the south of France, he also has a fairly good knowledge of Paris. He has his favorite spots, mainly parks: "I love parks. Like the park of Boulogne, park Monceau." But the glamour of the city talks to him too: "I also like the area near George V and Champs Elysées obviously. I love Montmartre: it's beautiful, very artistic. It's a bit far from where we usually stay but I like going there. The Louvre is very impressive. There are restaurants too: so many good ones! There's also one Serbian place that we like to visit, where I regularly celebrate my birthday with friends and family."

Keeping a longing for traditions and historical places, he feels inspired by the city and the energy coming from it. "But it took me several years before I actually went to see the Eiffel Tower! As a tennis player you don't have much time for sight-seeing when you're at a tournament between matches, practices, commitments, media, etc. And because it takes a lot of time and energy. So after my fourth or fifth year being in Paris I managed to go to see the Eiffel Tower, the Louvre museum and other cultural sites, and I enjoyed it very much because Paris is definitely one of the most beautiful cities in the world. Every building has its own soul and its own story, architected in a special way. It's also very clean and there is so much to do. As somebody who comes from a country whose culture is very old, goes back centuries and centuries, we nurture that tradition and culture. We respect other countries that have that as well. I enjoy it more because I feel that spirit. There are places around the world that are very beautiful, but you don't feel that ancient history that gives a soul to a country, that gives a soul to France."

Another connection to this was that it was always nice for him to come back to Roland-Garros the year after a loss, which wasn't a given after suffering so much in the same city season after season: "Winning it or losing it, it's important how you feel so yes it's still fun to come to Roland-Garros. Here I feel welcomed, I feel a very positive energy. It's also in a beautiful city, it's very international and there's also this sophisticated spirit of Roland-Garros that you get to feel, especially on the centre court, summer time... When I have this kind of feeling, it allows me to perform at my best, to really maximize my abilities and peak in Paris."

If France has now totally adopted Djokovic, it's also because he has made the efforts to speak fluent French. On court interviews, radio interviews, television interviews or just every day chat once he's setting a foot in the country: Novak now looks like a natural and no one even asks him before starting to chat in French. Even abroad, despite being used to talking to him in English, you'd find French people (players, media, etc) now greeting him and so on in French. Once you've started, Novak, there's no way back, sorry!

And the French crowd has been very sensitive to this: it strikes a good chord in a country that still thinks its language should be known by the whole world. Living in Monte-Carlo, having family in Switzerland and being a total freak of nature as far as learning languages is concerned (English, Italian, German, French, a bit of Chinese, Spanish, even heard him trying Swiss German, and I'm sure the list goes on), Djokovic had no issue making his way through French grammar and common vocabulary. "I'm still working on my language" he insists.

Fabrice Santoro was more than happy to confirm how well Djokovic spoke the national language now: "Doing those speeches in French isn't even a debate anymore with him. Not only can he speak French but I've seen him doing speeches on court in Italian or Chinese and so on. I have no idea how many other languages this guy can speak, it's impressive. And the crowds like it." Side note: Novak definitely nailed it during his live national French TV interview some time after he won the title during an eight minute long interview without any headset or translator. It was really "Peak Djokovic" in 2016 in Paris.

And through this first big language step came all the rest, because the tie kept growing, and in 2016 Djokovic wasn't only speaking French, he was totally a part of French culture and society. Today, no one here has forgotten that in November 2015, when Paris was under terror attacks, Djokovic in London for the ATP WorldTour Finals made a point to say a few words after his first match win, that he was also one of the players who posted messages of support on his social media. Through those same social media, he'd learn that a man who died that day was a huge fan of his, that his friends and family were trying to get in touch with him. Novak would reach out. His tie with France is special and there's no denying it.

That year again in Paris, he was staying in "L'Ile Saint Germain" in Issy Les Moulineaux, a neighborhood really close to Roland-Garros. Parts of Paris got flooded that year during Roland-Garros, Ile Saint-Germain among them as it's close to the Seine. And guess who the neighbors saw one morning coming to help? Yes, Novak Djokovic. The picture went quite viral.

Overall, Novak has probably never been closer to France than during the past couple of years. "I'm getting closer and closer to the French culture. Speaking the language, living in Monaco where French is also the official language and I get to meet French people on a daily basis. Also I've had sponsorship deals with Peugeot, Nutrition & Santé

(Gerblé) which are French companies, because I feel I can identify myself with French culture."

He even passed the test of the French sense of humor and he's pretty proud of it. "French people have a good sense of humor, a bit of a sarcastic one too. Some people can understand it, some don't, but I can so it's funny." He feels it's as specific as the French accent when we French speak English. If Novak has stopped his impersonations of his fellow players, you should still hear him do the "French trying to speak English" one: both hilarious and so accurate. "I love it!" he said while laughing. This French connection indeed also made its way into the Serb's business as sponsors like Nutrition & Santé (Gerblé) and most importantly Peugeot signed him to be their ambassador. It was a golden opportunity for all involved. In Paris for the French Open or the BNPPM, you could see Novak drive a bright red model of the brand. On the Champs Elysées, before the start of Roland-Garros, gigantic portraits of Djokovic would be set on the Peugeot's flagships, and there was no way to miss his commercials on TV. When he arrived for the kids' day, Novak brought a little violin and everybody in France knew why as it's been part of the Peugeot commercial that one would see all day long on TV.

The Serbian knows how to make an entrance, how to entertain and how to mix fun, sports and business. In the daily life of the French, all of this meant that Novak was even more a common figure. And arriving on the Roland-Garros site, you couldn't miss him either as his clothes sponsor Uniqlo had put him all over in the metro stations and bus stops. The Djokovic mania was alive and well.

In Paris, Djokovic didn't only take the support and enjoy being the favorite son. He gave a lot too. And it hasn't been forgotten at all even months after his triumph. When Tiphaine Lauré, a 15 year old ball girl, remembers that French Open 2016, Novak is a great part of it. Having never met him before, the teen was over the moon about the whole experience. Never had she imagined, for example, that one morning, as she was getting ready with the others to get going on their morning run, she'd see the n°1 player in the world join in. "It was amazing! I tried to run beside him but we were so many, we kept pushing each other so it was quite complicated. At the end he stopped and we were

211

all jumping around him like crazy, even the bodyguards couldn't find a way to push us back," she laughed.

Not all players are ball girls' and ball boys' favorites as not all players treat them well. In the middle of highly stressful matches, it's not always easy to remain kid friendly. But in Paris, Djokovic is on those kids' short list, as Tiphaine recalled: "I adore that player because he's the only one to do that with us, like taking time in the morning to come and run with ball boys and girls, it's really nice. And even on court he's super nice, whereas some players treat us like nobodies. Novak is pretty respectful, and even when he gets angry on court it's not against us. Sometimes he even says thank you for the towel which is pretty great."

French players are not always comfortable in Roland-Garros: the pressure of expectations is too much. They're not sure of how to exactly deal with that demanding crowd, not sure fans are always on their side. And those fans aren't always sure of how far to push the support regarding players that more often than not they don't fully understand. French players and the Roland-Garros crowd deserve a full book of their own. And a good shrink. And there came Djokovic: happy to be there, happy to give time, making efforts to fit in, enjoying the French way of life. Being a winner. And asking them for love and support. They were more than happy to take him under their wing. He would be their champion that year, as all was perfectly clicking this time. "I always felt very much at home in Paris: it's so close to Serbia, Monaco where I stay now. It always felt very close to my heart, and I always felt very comfortable and excited to be there, and also because I have family, friends; everybody is an hour away by flight. Also this European feel, European ambiance that I love. This is your identity, part of who you are being European so you feel comfortable. All of this gave me even more incentive to do well."

But he may have avoided smiling on his chair at 5-2. He may have resisted the desire to enjoy that communion at this moment, to celebrate his title before it would actually be his. That was an opportunity his old demons would jump on, sneaking a foot through the door and suddenly crashing the party. It started well with a jumped backhand, yet it would be the sole and only point Novak would make in that game. Murray was still fighting and so refusing to put his knee down with all his heart, and Novak hadn't seen it coming. As the points would turn against him, the pressure was rising and rising to levels he knew well. To levels he knew weren't good news at all. The agony was just about to start when Djokovic hit a double fault to now be down 15-40. A suicidal backhand approach from Novak and a splendid forehand passing shot from Andy later, it was 5-3, Muzz on serve.

The crowd went from wild to more or less silent in the space of a few minutes. Novak's smile was well in the past. The finish line suddenly was further away than thought. He was now preparing to return as Andy had a new chance to get the game and come back to 4-5. Right behind Djokovic, you could again see the trophies standing. Each time he turned to the back of the court, there's a good chance he saw them. Which was really fine until 5-2 in this fourth set. But now, it was like they were teasing him: so close and yet so far again. Backhand down the line...in the net. Murray yelled a massive "Come oooooon!", fist pumped, eyes locked to his box as he had now started to believe again. And, as everybody, he knew his arch rival wasn't immune at all to nerves in Paris, so if he could put some pressure on him....

Novak now had to get away from La Coupe des Mousquetaires and get back to his chair: he was not smiling anymore, was just trying not to think. Scars were burning his skin, heart beating louder and louder, mind doing its best not to go on the dark side, not to let the demons take over. "Again! Double break, up 5-2, serving for the championship... And I allowed it again to play with my mind" analyzed a still astonished Djokovic even months after, before admitting to what everyone had seen that day. "This is the thing: it doesn't matter how many matches you've played in your life nor how many hours you've spent training on the court, nor how many hours you've spent mentally training yourself and working to be the best version of yourself. You're still a human being. It's hard to exclude all the influences. I was up 5-2 and telling myself 'ok focus on each point, one point at a time' but hey, you are four points away from winning the title you so greatly want to win. Those were the kind of circumstances I was in" he ended smiling. We were in January and he was still amazed at the power of the dark force he had to go through in Roland-Garros that year.

So when he got out of that chair to again try to serve out the match, took a deep breath, let go of the towel to hand it to a ball boy as if he was giving up on the last safety net, what was written on his face was surely true: this would be a make-or-break game. Djokovic had given everything he had in those two weeks but mentally he was at his limit: he needed to win that game or there was no way he was going to get his hands on that trophy. When asked about those two games lost in a row, this 5-4 game and the possibility looming of a fifth set if worse had come to worst, Marian Vajda raised both arms in the air, shaking his head as if to chase a nightmare away: "No, no, no! Impossible!"

So when Djokovic stood on the service line again, with the crowd having his back, clapping, shouting encouragement, he maybe knew deep inside himself that if he didn't get that game, it would be over. They had now been playing for 2h57. Novak found his zones but not at full speed, Murray's defense not shaken. Then Andy's backhand broke Novak's first. Out: 0-15. Murray is again yelling his lungs out. Off to the towel, deep breath. "Obviously finishing the match was the toughest thing to do," Vajda well knew. "But he was able to keep his nerves calm."

Now the ball was taken a bit earlier, the shots hit with more intensity: Murray blinks first, backhand in net. 15A, deep breath, off to the towel. I'd swear Novak's face has lost a few shades and is now pretty pale. The crowd was like receiving untold distress messages: more claps, more cheers. Next point would be proof that Novak had been right to give no pass to his backhand for two weeks, as it would be the key. After an amazing crossed backhands fight, Murray went for a great drop shot but Djokovic found an even greater counter drop shot.

He paused to watch his box, then with his arms he turned to the crowd for help. No "Come on," no fist pump, no bravado: just asking for a last push. And he got it, big time: the whole stadium was applauding like mad, chants raining down. 30-15. Becker is still convinced that this point sealed the whole deal, but that even if the worst had come to pass, Djokovic would still have won that match somehow: "I was hoping that he gets the double break in the fourth set, because he was going to get tight. If he doesn't get tight there, he doesn't have a heart, ok. But I wasn't worried because even if it's 5-5, he's still up two sets to one so worst case scenario he's going to go and win the fifth. I was not worried actually. I was so convinced he was going to do it but I still didn't want to go into the fifth set. So when he won that long rally at the start of this 5-4 game, I said: victory is ours."

And after this point, everyone out there, Novak included, were now two points away from witnessing History made. It was like a dome of pure electricity. In the centre, Djokovic was taking deep breath after deep breath, trying to keep his head above water just long enough to get it done. Keeping the emotions at bay, not thinking of what's to come, not looking at the scars: just being in the moment. And this moment, there was pure love and support coming from that crowd: that was a point in play knowing that people wanted him to win, that this time he was the chosen one. Off to the towel, with a smile.

First serve in, crossed forehand and then I'm easily betting many people had an "Oh no, overhead coming" moment. Novak also, maybe, as he hit a very shy one, but Murray missed his forehand lob. It's going out, Novak gesturing with his racquet, like pushing the ball with the air. He's not smiling, he's grimacing while asking for more support, then hitting his heart with his left hand. Off to the towel. Now after three hours of play, he's up 40-15 with two match points coming. Crowd erupting, whistling, yelling, clapping. Surely, the release was now on the way, no? Surely that was the moment his Quest for Roland-Garros would get its happy ending.

And wasn't it just perfect, thinking about it, to get his Career Slam in a country that had never questioned what some call his "wanting to be loved" syndrome? Where he could feed off the crowd in any way he wanted to without second guessing? If there's a place where the "But he wants so much to be loved" critics were sure to encounter blank stares in return, it's in Roland-Garros. Most people's answer would be: "And so what? »

Djokovic was about to fall. From joy or despair, but he was about to fall. Would this safety net created by the crowd finally be there for the winner's landing or again to protect the loser from his distress? At 5-4 40-15, Djokovic had asked for love on every point. Two points later he was still playing that final and things were dire. First he hit a double fault: a look to the sky, heavy breathing, towel. Then a backhand down the line finished its course in the middle of the alley: muttering to himself, mouth opened to grab some air, off to towel. He never had a match point in a Roland-Garros final and now he just had squandered two. He was livid, like about-to-pass-out livid, his box frozen on the spot, his fans close to a nervous breakdown and the French crowd biting its fingers, still doing its utmost to help. They cheered, they yelled some "Allez Novak!": they kept answering every call for attention and care Novak had requested. Djokovic wouldn't win this Roland-Garros on his own and had no problem acknowledging it. "Obviously, as any other year, I was hoping that this is the year. I felt that kind of support and love from the people around that allowed me at the end to be sitting with the trophy. That's for sure. That kind of support was very well present at the stadium again for the final."

And that was the kind of support he had asked for in different ways, and hoped for everywhere. That's what has surely created the biggest debate and misunderstanding around the Serbian through the years. He's not a placid champion, he hasn't embraced "let the racquet do the talking" way, nor the humble gentleman persona. Novak isn't discrete, shy, self conscious or detached from what people might think of him. He also enjoys being the ruler and making rivals feel it from time to time. And once he sets foot on a tennis court, he's there to win but he's also there to be front and centre of a show. He wants to have fun and entertain. He's never playing alone.

Djokovic is a sponge as proved by his talent for impersonations, languages and...tennis. He's also a sponge for energy, good and bad, and everything surrounding him. Even if he has made a tremendous effort to get a hold on this sensitivity, it's still there lying underneath the armor. In this other world of the extreme competitive person that he is, next to the tennis warrior he is, there is an obvious need for feeling included, appreciated, respected and at the very best loved by the people watching.

I totally believe that some of the past great champions have only played for themselves, their teams, those closest to them and, for some, also their country. That they have never cared about their image, the feedback from the crowd, the judgment that would be made on their performances, the recognition it would or not bring them. The love or dislike coming from the tennis world didn't touch them. And that's fine. But that doesn't apply to Djokovic, which should be fine too. Why would it be seen as a weakness, a character flaw or even worse a basis to call him an actor, to be fake? Why would it be so bad to care?

"Tennis is a macho place. You have no idea how much." That's what a renowned coach told me one day while discussing the reactions caused at the time by Andy Murray hiring Amélie Mauresmo as a coach. As well, sometimes when for the umpteenth time someone has been saying something along the lines of "for god's sake, can't Djokovic stop trying so hard to be loved?" And when I've barely succeeded in not sighing or rolling my eyes at this, I wonder if it's not also part of the issue? In this macho place, were displays of this kind of sensibility deemed weak? Was asking for appreciation deemed unworthy of the alpha male status? I mean, I don't hear that when Maria Sharapova is sending kisses to the crowd after a win, or when Serena Williams and Andrea Petkovic were sometimes pulling dance moves. Was there a "you don't show off when you're a male tennis player" line in the locker room bro code?

Maybe it's also the power of reputation building. At the end of the 2016 season, as I was talking to someone who had recently started to work in a big tournament organization, that person said: "You know what? I was really surprised by Novak. He's really a good guy!" I would easily reckon that I laughed at that person's big stunned eyes. "No, but really! I thought he was a bit fake you know, that backstage he wasn't the Djoker you see on court or the guy that claps for his opponents' winners. But actually he's been so easy to deal with, available and accepting to do a lot of things for us. I was completely wrong about him."

Everyone has bad days: players under pressure too, mercurial ones even more, so of course Djokovic can break racquets, yell at his box, send umpires and crowds to hell or rip shirts out of pure rage. He can also complain when ball kids don't bring that damn towel fast enough on a day where he hasn't gotten up on the right foot. He can sit at the press conference desk and make you immediately feel that it's not even worth trying to get something out of him today. And can strike back.

But then most of the time you also see him entertaining the crowd at the next matches, being super fair while playing (how many points is he giving back each season?), or being a gentleman on other occasions.

So why would you call him out for putting on an act? The real issue is that in this case you've missed the point and the in between: you can rip shirts and be a good person, you can have occasional flashes of anger and remain an overall well educated and balanced human being, you can go from a bad day to put on your best behavior the next without lacking sincerity.

Everybody has different layers in their personalities; it just happens that some have more layers than others. And more sensitive buttons to push than others. Also dealing with professional sports stars, there's no way you're going to meet ego-less people. If they were, they wouldn't be where they are now. So after more than ten years of people following Djokovic's career, it should be high time to retire the stereotypes and also to dig deeper on this "He wants so much to be loved" affair.

In this debate, I prefer the reason given by Thierry Van Cleemput, who has been coaching for decades, who met Federer when the Swiss was a 12 year old kid and Djokovic when this 17 year old Serbian was trying to turn his Davis Cup tie in Belgrade into a nightmare in 2005. Nowadays he regularly shares Novak's practice court as he's working with David Goffin who has become one of the Big 4 favorites to hit with. Van Cleemput sees no issue with the way Novak behaves, yet he thinks he should maybe let his talent do the talking and stop caring about being liked or not. "He's a truly fantastic guy. I'm of course not here to tell him what to do - who would I be to do that - but if I was allowed advice, I feel he shouldn't try to do too much to be appreciated. If someone can't like him, so be it. I'm going to make a comparison with wine, as it's quite my passion too. One year in Belgium they did an investigation about champagne and they asked the guys next door to judge high level champagne and cheap ones... And so they made their ranking: but those people knew nothing about champagne! If you don't know a thing, how can you judge? Novak is a war machine, so let's not try to play the nice guy as he won't be when things get rough. Maybe he felt the need to open up to people a bit more... But, personally, I like him as he is. Tennis fans, and sometimes media, need to start learning how to like their champions, to stop being so intolerant of the slightest flaw. Novak is a warrior, a great warrior, and that's his first quality, so he needs to remain one. He's someone I've learned to like more and more by being around him. He's a great professional, someone with rigor, good values and more sensitive than people think. He's not Terminator, he's not a PlayStation: he's a player. Only the court makes you know the truth, only being there with those guys. Novak is an outstanding human being and player: the cream of the crop. He doesn't have to do more. If people can't appreciate what he has brought and is still bringing, it's their loss."

Van Cleemput has a very fair point here: Djokovic shouldn't feel he has to make more efforts or that everybody has to appreciate him. Yet, what if it was not a plan but just a part of his personality? No need to be a shrink to make a link between this desire to feel accepted and a childhood under the bombs, where his country was a pariah for the international community. In his junior years, Djokovic recalls he had to double efforts in order to impress people. He still remembers people taking a step back from him after learning his nationality. Novak probably had more than enough of his fair share of rejection. Years can pass, money can flood a bank account, titles fill rooms, but some things remain engraved. Sure, he shouldn't care about not being every crowd's favorite, but he grew up caring. And in the perfect image he has of a champion, crowds are either on their feet to celebrate him or bowing down in respect. That's in the package. A king needs to have his court. Mix this need to fit in, the desire of a devoted kingdom and an extrovert personality, and you can stop asking me why Novak Djokovic wants so much to be loved. And maybe start asking yourself why this is so much of an issue for you.

I have never hidden the fact that I find Novak Djokovic to be a very interesting champion, nor that I like the whole persona. As many journalists, I have a guilty pleasure for labels, so early on I used to call Novak, "Agassi 2.0." For tennis reasons mainly: the ability to play tennis like it's a PlayStation game and an unmatched talent on the return, added to a devil- may-care attitude. I even got to ask Agassi about that back in 2011 when he came to Roland-Garros, and I was happy to see he also found a lot of himself in Djokovic.

But he was quick to make it clear to me when I asked if Novak was really "a baby Agassi": "No, he's better," was his immediate answer. "He's defending so well, whereas I never felt comfortable doing that. Novak is comfortable when he defends, comfortable when he attacks, his quality of return and serve is huge, and he's so flexible. But sure we share that sense of anticipation, and there's this backhand down the line that we both love hitting (he smiled). But he's more versatile than I was and he's also a much better athlete. And again what about his return of serve! It's like it's an advantage for him to return. Here he looked unbeatable with the level he had, with the feeling it was impossible to hit a winner against him."

With Djokovic, as with Agassi, you could guess the scars under the armor, the doubts lying under the public confidence, the sensitivity beyond the bullet proof thick skin. There was no box in which they'd fit, and no way to tame them or even to fully understand them. People didn't have to like everything about them, but there was no denying that with them something was happening that makes champions have wholly different kinds of brains.

Andre Agassi could come back to Paris every week and be treated as if it was 1999 and he had just won Roland-Garros. Andre Agassi is a French icon: for how many times he failed here, for how many times he suffered, for how many lives he seemed to have, for how public were his struggles, for how massive was his come-back. And also for marrying Steffi Graf, another French legend. Agassi had all the outfits and tantrums of the world here. Started all the polemics. Yet in 1999 when he was bowing and sending kisses to the four sides of the court Chatrier, the main feeling was awe and not eye rolling. No one has ever blamed him in 1999 for trying to be loved. No one after his career has looked back on his antics, tears, outfits or whatever saying it was all for the show, nothing from the heart. No, most of the tennis world and beyond had accepted that it was the Agassi way, with many contradictions. Not an act. And many were grateful to him for being a showman.

In totally different styles, you could also find many approving of John McEnroe's numerous flashes of anger, or of Jimmy Connors' bullying style. Nowadays you even find advocates of current players who not only spend seasons crossing the line, but mainly don't even see there's a line. So again: why is Djokovic wanting to be appreciated and making efforts for it such a big deal for some? Why would his way, that has lasted more than a decade, be an act when others weren't and aren't?

Since Rome, Djokovic has introduced a new celebration to the crowd after each win: he would put his hands on his chest near the heart and then throw his arms to the people. No need to be a genius to understand that it was him sending his heart and love to the crowd. Agassi had bowed down, Serena Williams was swinging with an arm in the air, and so Djokovic was throwing his heart out there. Crowd was happy, TV was happy, photographers were happy, Novak was happy. Harm done? None. Even more, it gave unforgettable memories to the ball girls and boys who were on the court with him, sharing the celebration, being asked to be a part of it.

Tiphaine Lauré, the 15 year old French ball girl, had this chance after Novak won his semi-final against Dominic Thiem. And to say she was thrilled is an understatement. Actually, among the ball kids' locker rooms, knowing if Novak would invite some of them to celebrate the win was one of the biggest questions of the day. Kids had no idea when or if it was going to happen; it wasn't something staged. "No, it wasn't scheduled at all before, but we still all wanted to be on the court for his match because we knew some things already happened in the past with ball boys so we were expecting something, hoping for it. So yeah, really, we were all talking about it in the locker rooms (laughs). We all wanted to be the ones on court at the end of his match, because we knew one ball boy had already done that with him. I saw it on a giant screen in the stadium at the time. So yeah we thought it could happen again, but also that those at the net would have more opportunity. We were very impatient," Tiphaine recalled of that last Friday. When Djokovic had half a dozen ball kids coming to the centre of the court, Tiphaine didn't believe she could join. She was one of the ball kids set up at the back of the court: her hopes were pretty low.

"He first called the ones who were at the net, but then also those at the back of the court. Where I was. When he had us all come to him, I was so happy because I wasn't really expecting it. That was truly amazing." In French, he told them exactly what to do: "We all gathered around him and then he explained: put the hands next to the heart, raise the arms to the sky and that we were going to do that on each of the four sides of the court. He did it once to show us, then he came in the middle of us all and we just did the celebration."

Months after, the French teenager is as happy about it as at that moment on Lenglen. "The most impressive and memorable for me was: it's the n°1 player in the world so it's really kinda weird... I see him all the time in the magazines or on television, and suddenly he's here in front of me and talking to us... We're like right next to him... And after he hugged us all, high-fived us... Treated us like we were his buddies: that was outstanding. And the crowd was really into it too: when we raised our arms, they were applauding like crazy. Being in the middle of the court, that was very unique. Unbelievable." She was still pretty emotional about this, but nothing compared to how she was at the moment: "When we got back in place, I was crying on the court, couldn't realize what had happened to me. It was just crazy! And when we got off the court, with the two other girls that were with me, we were hugging each other, in tears."

Tiphaine wasn't even supposed to be a ball girl for the semi-finals: it was the terrible weather that made it happen. "It was a huge amount of luck! It was my day. Maybe it'll never happen ever again so for me those are unforgettable memories, to be like that with a player you only see on TV and who is talked about all the time. To be with him in the middle of the Lenglen court right after he qualified for the final of Roland-Garros...There are no words. It's truly unbelievable."

When asked why he was now inviting the kids with him, after doing this at the end of his quarter final against Berdych, Djokovic answered in French, smiling: "C'est plus joli come ça" ("It's prettier this way"). He was in a sharing mood that year as he felt people were finally fully ready to support him. And he has a pretty good sense of what works to make a good show. So why eye rolling?

There's this famous story showing anger of a part of the locker room when Monica Seles, for her first Roland-Garros at age 15, decided before her third round against Zina Garrison to give flowers to the crowd. It was 1989; she'd go all the way to the semi-finals, beaten by Steffi Graf. Garrison refused to take one flower, didn't like this show at all. Others would say it was all made to get the crowd on her side, despite not always being that nice to her colleagues on the court. Seles would say she thought it was just fun and a common way in Europe to show respect. Crowds aren't stupid: they will know when it's too much, when they're being played. But until the line is crossed everybody is happy so....

Seles, who by the way had been discovered by Jelena Gencic just like Novak, would end being one the most beloved champions in Paris.

A connection that is still there, very emotional: you don't create that by fooling people, you don't build this on an act. You don't get minutes-long-standing-ovations that bring you to tears if you haven't been genuine. Many would say that neither Federer nor Nadal have ever done the kind of things Djokovic does on court. But neither had Graf, and that didn't prevent anyone in Paris from loving Seles too. Champions come in different forms, with different fragilities, egos and needs.

Marian Vajda and I suddenly laughed in between sipping our tea and coffee in Monaco. Why? Because he had started to tell me about Novak and the love from the crowd, and went "I always gave him the example of Monica Seles..." Me: "Well, I basically just wrote that..." "No way!" "Yes, way."

The Slovakian also felt it was the perfect point of comparison for Novak to really get to the point where he'd let go totally until he'd be totally connected with the people. And so after laughing, he started again: "I think he became very popular among the fans. People love him. And I was very happy about the French Open because I always told him, giving the example of Monica Seles on the how can you get these people, because the French are really tough to get, believe me! But once you get them, you get them forever. And it was like that with him that year from day one! The best Grand Slam for him, it really was."

For Djokovic, the show is part of the game, not to forget that we're talking about someone who in his first years on the Tour stripped to his underwear to walk a runway, just because why not. Since when has being an extrovert been labelled a bad thing? Novak has put to rest a lot of his past habits, has stopped his famous impersonations to avoid the wrath of some of his fellow top players. He took this as good fun, he was putting on a show, but they were taking it as new proof of lack of respect. Novak even retired the habit that would see him put on a mask in Bercy for Halloween. But he remains a showman and someone who needs that kind of energy. Someone also liking the attention, liking to be under the lights in the middle of a stage. Harm done? None. When a player like Nadal arrived on Tour and started to make waves, he did it by still bowing down to his eldest, Federer. He would beat him but would still call him the greatest ever, keeping it humble.

He's also a matador on the court, but a very discrete legend off the court. He's not rubbing most people the wrong way, even if he had to deal with his fair share of criticism for the pirate look, the loud "Vamos!" and those shining biceps. Described, wrongly, as a bull and a bully. Djokovic arrived on that Tour saying out loud that he was there to take over, that he wanted to be the n°1. And he came with all his flashy personality. Djokovic entered a well "socially organized" tennis world, but bowing down and gently asking for a place at the main table wasn't an option he'd even think about. Fitting in, yes, but playing the third wheel: sorry, not in the plan.

So Djokovic would be loud, on and off the court. He would be the entertainer, he would try to seduce the crowds, he would make people and rivals notice him. The shock of the "How dare he?" was real and became a case of love it or hate it for many who for a long time associated his colorful personality with the defiance showed towards Federer and Nadal. The contrast of tempers between him and the Nadal - Federer duo was huge right from the start and it got amplified by their rivalries. It continues to this day to be a polarizing one, and so it says a lot about what it took for Novak not only to take his fair share of tennis glory but to also become one of the people's favorites despite not coming from the same widely approved mold of his two rivals.

But France had accepted right away that Djokovic didn't have to be like the two other rockstars of the game: they let him be, they enjoyed what was a kind of rebellion, a mark of independence. And the Parisian crowd didn't question nor mind too much his flashes of anger. That wouldn't go that far anyway, as they would also see him sign for every kid around, with cameras rolling or not. The extrovert side of his personality is more than welcome in Paris. Let him be flashy, social, joyful, chatty and loud as much as he wants to, as it's not an on court persona he'd activate: it's totally who he is. You can sometimes track his presence at players' restaurants or lounges just by his high-pitched laugh, or his recognizable deep voice. I still remember the struggle it was for me this 2016 season at Indian Wells to listen to my recording of a Marian Vajda as during this interview, one floor down, Novak was chatting to Goran Ivanisevic. One floor down.

That's the "Novak way of life" and that seems hardly the basis for the character assassination you sometimes witness. Was dislike really the price to pay for having dared to come to power in the Federer - Nadal era, where the "Fedal" narrative was welcomed with open arms and tagged so bankable? Yes, his way is also to try to put on a show and entertain when he can, and of course he's smart enough to know the effect it's going to have on TV and in the crowd. That doesn't mean it's not genuine, just that it's how and who he is. I don't have all the answers as to why he's still sometimes made to feel like he's disturbing, but I am glad that this 2016 French Open finally left no opportunity for anyone to write or say that Novak Djokovic had been an unloved winner.

In Paris, it was his whole persona that triumphed, and it demands curiosity and an open mind to try to get it. Because if not, you might actually miss the heart of the whole Djokovic success story. And one day after Novak's career is over, one will watch a player win a Grand Slam semi-final match with a tiny smile on and a discrete wave to the crowd, before packing his or her stuff and just leaving the court, thinking that roses and celebrations with ball kids weren't that bad after all. Same for drawing hearts on the court.

Great first serve, super accurate inside out forehand and a forehand drive winner: Djokovic was now hitting that heart with his racquet, eyes closed. That's how on theory the champions should play the big points, by being bold. Go big or go home. Easier said than done. But at this moment Novak did it. Reward? A third match point. Deep breath, off to towel. The cheers are getting tough to control, the majority of the crowd sounding as stressed as Novak was looking. As he's about to serve, you can see people behind him and on the side taking pictures: third time they've tried to immortalize the moment tennis history would be made. Up there in the Djoker's box, Gebhard Gritsch was also waiting for deliverance. "From 5-2 to 5-4, it was like 'please, please now it's time. Don't do that!' (Laughs). But obviously he was nervous and all kind of thoughts got into his brain. It's not easy to win these matches... And he wanted it so badly, and sometimes in life when you want things so badly it doesn't work."

Andy Murray was actually counting on Novak's nerves to come back into that final. "Obviously when you're trying to do something for the first time and you've not experienced it before, that can throw you off, you know, a few extra nerves," he would say after the match. "In that game I was close to making it I think very interesting." That's also why from 5-2 on, Miljan Amanovic was in complete denial, basically expecting things to go wrong. "Until the last point, until he has won that last point, until it's written on the scoreboard that he's a winner, I do not believe he is a winner. Because things in the past had changed just for one ball!"

And Amanovic takes the role of the team in the box seriously, whether Novak needs to yell out of frustration or share a comforting look, the team needs to be there and efficient. So from 5-2 to 5-4 up there in the box, it was intense. "Emotions, emotions, emotions," Amanovic summed it up. "And you are trying to control it because he's looking towards us in the box, so if we are upset then this energy is upsetting him. If we are able to motivate him and to push him, he's pushing himself. If we are calm then he might think 'oh they are calm, I should be calm and continue.' Many times this happened. He gets the frustration out at certain moments and of course he can't pick up somebody in the crowd: he's turning to people that he knows, to people that understand him. We're spending 24h/7 with him, we know how he breathes. Every one of his looks: I know. Every one of his reactions: I know what it means. It's a body language and an automatism now."

So there, after 3h02 of play, Djokovic threw himself into probably the biggest point of his career. And so did his team. Big serve on Andy's forehand, then a battle of backhands, then of forehands and then it was just about the one who would blink first. Get this ball over the net and between the line, over the net and between the lines. Then Murray hit a great crossed forehand, Djokovic on it, sliding and losing his footing a bit. A tiny blink. But Murray blinked harder: crossed backhand in the net. Game, set and match: Novak Djokovic! Had Andy seen Novak sliding? Did he push harder at this moment thinking it was the opening and overdo it?

Djokovic now couldn't care less about why: he fell, but he fell out of joy and release. The crowd was on its feet, cheering, yelling, applauding. On his back, on the clay, throwing his racquet behind him in the fall, finally Djokovic knew. He knew what it felt to win Roland-Garros. He wouldn't be the Great Loser this time. He wasn't cursed. He didn't choke. He made it. He made everything. He wouldn't get a lot of moments just with himself now so he was taking all this in: eyes closed, arms and legs spread wide. You could see his stomach going up and down heavily. A ten years' quest had ended. Scars had stopped burning. He reached the summit of his mountain. Hard to imagine what one must feel in this moment, as the crowd was also going wild. Those are the gems players are chasing throughout their careers. And as I thought in Melbourne, Novak had no coping mechanism for such a feat: now all emotions were out there and raw. Nearly freezing him on the spot.

People wanting to know what Roland-Garros really meant for him, how much he had suffered there and how deep it had touched him, had it all condensed in the next minutes of this win. When he got up again, he could barely walk or run so he kind of did both. The first person he saw was Murray, who had crossed the net to meet him. Djokovic and Wawrinka shared a great moment in 2015, and there would be another one in 2016 between Novak and Andy as after a handshake they would just fall in each other's arms, exchange a few words, Novak putting his hands around Andy's neck in a very brotherly way.

Muzz, hating defeat as much as any other champion, was still giving friendly slaps on the back of Djokovic. Not sure Novak heard everything Andy said as he looked absolutely on another planet, trying to keep it together while emotions were running wild. Right after Murray let go of him, Novak gave a teary, not smiling, look to his box: in the flash of an eye, everything was in it. There was no smile for now as it had been so hard to get there that it seemed it wasn't sinking in. The shock was way too big. Novak couldn't even stand anymore. As Andy shook the umpire's hand, Djokovic was folded in two behind him, hands on thighs. He stood back to clap for Murray, then it all started to make sense so he smiled wildly, looked at the sky and let it all go. Both arms in the air, he could hear the crowd going absolutely nuts. As wild as the emotions inside of him, as for a few seconds he had no idea what to do with himself.

Folded in two again, out of pure joy and also because the body he had requested so much of, was releasing all this tension. The crowd was still giving him a standing ovation, and Novak was walking the court like a disjointed puppet. Somewhere in his brain he remembered how he wanted to celebrate that win but something was missing and he wasn't sure what. His racquet. His senses were telling him he had left it at the back of the court but his eyes couldn't see it. So Novak was lost. But that's Novak Djokovic we're talking about so the loss of control wasn't going to last too long. Realizing he was losing it, Novak shook his head a bit, left hand to his forehead and got back to his chair where his racquet had been brought back by a ball kid. Why did he want his instrument so badly?

Because a much younger Djokovic had seen Gustavo Kuerten draw a heart on the Roland-Garros centre court to celebrate his win, and had since dreamed of doing the same. Novak has always said how much he liked Kuerten and always told that heart story as one of the most beautiful moments he had witnessed. He didn't do it because it had been staged in a Peugeot commercial, as some would write after. Reunited with Guga for that commercial shooting, he was asked by the Brazilian how he would like to celebrate his win if he was to finally get it. And the first thing that came to Novak's mind was this heart.

So Guga and Novak made a deal: if the Djoker won, he was allowed to borrow the heart. Kuerten even got to talk to Djokovic again about it when both did the "Drive to Tennis" video for Roland-Garros, as he recalled after the final after saying how nice he felt it was to see Novak drawing that heart on the centre court. "I suspected it because he asked me permission. He said 'if I win, can I do it?' And I said 'of course, man.' But my heart was a little bit better I think. I'd tell him you need to improve. On Saturday I drove him to his place as we did an activity here. And before driving him I went to fitness and he was there working out, and Boris and Vajda - a great friend of mine because of Dominik Hrbaty (that Vajda used to coach) at the time as we were practicing together - asked me 'what can you give us as advice?' And I said: 'Heart.' And today you could see it, because in the end he got nervous and he needed to express himself a little bit. And that's how you get the emotions to dissipate a little and you can survive the nerves."

For Novak, this heart now on court was like completing his story with Roland-Garros. And if there's one image I would also keep from this 2016 Roland-Garros, it's the one of Gustavo Kuerten with tears in his eyes while watching Djokovic drawing that heart and then lying inside of it. He also wanted to be loved, so he knew how one feels when it's clicking and you're adopted by that world while you've reached the peak of your career. Had Novak, who was now sending kisses to everyone, thrown his racquet into the first rows and gifted his wristbands to kids, not put efforts in connecting to that crowd over the years, he of course could have also ended with the trophy, but it's highly doubtful that he would have felt as fulfilled as he did that 5th of June. Everyone goes after what one needs, and it really doesn't look that bad to add love to the list.

CHAPTER NINE

Triumph Of The Holistic Approach

Novak Djokovic winning Roland-Garros after a decade of trying was also the triumph of his beloved holistic approach. And he was off to celebrate it as he wished to. In the way he reacted after the match point, you saw many of the Serb's traits. It was like waves going from super emotional back to under control then back to the boss. When he was making gestures towards the staff who apparently weren't sending the ball kids fast enough, it was hard to repress a smile: bossy Nole was in the place again.

As he had a fixed image of that heart to be drawn on the red, he also had one of how his final celebration should go. He had spent the past two years explaining how he found his balance in a specific approach to life, and this 'I'm sending my heart to you' celebration seemed a symbolic ritual for all of it. So he got his ball kids in the middle of the court, actually a dozen ball girls for what looked like a choir, briefed them quickly as now every French Open ball kid knew the drill, and off they went. The crowd echoing each heart wave by an "Olé!"

He exchanged high fives with the girls, threw his arms one last time in the air, then a fist pump and he sat on his chair: job done. Holistic approach: validated. His head now deep into a towel, he took a bit of time for himself, to enjoy the end of such a long and eventful quest. When his face reappeared, Novak looked elated. So much that he had a laugh attack. A few minutes after that match point. Also after Novak Djokovic had gone to hug his parents who had appeared at the entry of the court, coming down from the players' box, unable to resist touching their eldest to really celebrate that win, the sun decided to show up. It made Novak laugh as he gave his first on-court interview.

A ray of light: something we hadn't seen for two weeks. The last touch for his coronation.

Novak Djokovic is probably not a personality one would read like an open book: he comes with a lot of layers. He has also delved a lot into self-development and positive thinking books. Had done a good measure of soul searching work and a big one of professional mental performance too. For anyone not really into this nor at least a bit curious about psychology, there was a good chance of not having the slightest idea of exactly what was going on with him. But everybody needed to admit that the man who was now preparing himself for the trophy ceremony, putting a clean white T-Shirt under his immaculate red jacket, smiling to the world, had come too far since his rise to power in 2011 to reject how efficient his new approach to tennis and life had been. Not in order to copy and paste it on every budding champion, but to understand how Novak found the path and tools that he needed to fulfill his potential.

"Is he different? For sure!" said French coach Sam Sumyk who'd won Grand Slam titles with Victoria Azarenka and Garbine Muguruza. He was there with the Spaniard in this 2016 Roland-Garros which she won the day before Djokovic's coronation. "He's obviously different because here's a guy who found a way between Nadal and Federer. And those two didn't give anything and still don't want to. So here came that guy who created a place for himself in spite of them, won as much as those two legends. This is admirable. We knew how strong he was but the evolution and the drive are outstanding. He doesn't look like someone who made many mistakes along the way. Where did he find that energy? Day after day!"

The Frenchman was very curious about the Djokovic way of things: "What he has now achieved is out of this world and it's been a bit underestimated in my opinion. And surely on the mental work side, he's maybe been ahead of the rest, but that's what the best do: they're always ahead. He wasn't scared to get out of his comfort zone, and for that you need a huge desire. I know Djokovic's team a bit, I know Novak a bit, it happens that we all chat. And now I want to go and talk with them even more. I see the work he's accomplished over many years, I've appreciated following his evolution. So yeah, now I'm ready to share a beer with him, or to go meet him in his restaurant in Monaco! (Laughs) Novak is among the Greatest ones, but all I care about is the way."

My colleagues and I have developed a kind of Pavlovian reflex each time we hear Novak saying "Holistic Approach." That's what happens when you've been on Tour most of the last seasons and spoken and listened to Novak in press conferences. No way you'd get out of the room without having heard about it at some point. After a while I would have basically been able to answer in Novak's place! Joking aside, it's the pillar of The Djokovic Way, the only software you can use to get the best shot at deciphering his persona. If you refuse to try to understand how the wheels are turning inside his brain, there's indeed no way you're going to understand Novak Djokovic. Which is a pity when you happen to write about him week in week out. And when he's one of the greatest players of all time.

Telling the Djokovic story in Paris made no sense if one didn't dwell on Novak's psyche a bit, because one of the reasons why it finally clicked for him there after years of struggle, one of the reasons why he achieved the 'Four In a Row' where everyone else for nearly half a century had failed, surely rested in there. Tennis is a mental game; everyone on Tour agrees on that, so as much as his obvious talent with a racquet in hands is responsible, that mindset is also how Djokovic propelled himself into the top ranks of the Greatest-Of-All-Time list.

To non-tennis people who would ask me "So, what is Djokovic really like?" or to some colleagues in a "But really, he's weird no?" moment, I'd often end summing it all up by saying Novak was a bit New Age, that was all. And when I say New Age, it's with the French cultural idea of what it means: a peace and love mindset, being one with nature, developing one's spirituality, improving the planet, focusing on a bigger picture, etc.

I was actually thinking about that a lot through an interview we did in Monaco in April 2016, as he was talking about his passion for nutrition, saying it had become like a "quest" for him since 2010. He went on to say that he wanted to take the opportunities he had, thanks to his success, to "grow" himself and his family" in a human perspective, not just financially" and that what he wanted was to "keep this consciousness about others in the world, to improve the planet. Making a positive change." Probably only Novak Djokovic in the tennis world could decide he would be up to changing the world! Watching him virtually send his heart up to the crowd in Paris was totally in sync with his evolution, where this holistic approach was also adopted to remove what he felt was chaos.

That's basically been his quest for peace, where he'd call trees his friends and go for hugs regularly, like feeding off nature's energy. That would make many people roll their eyes, but he didn't care. As an insider told me without wanting to be named: "He's different, but that's who he is. Issue being that people don't like difference. He's not playing a part, he doesn't pretend to be." Through any tournament, he would go to parks, into nature, to temples, to anything taking him out of that tennis bubble that maybe would drive him nuts if he remained only there. Maybe it was that which had actually started to drive him there when he was losing those Grand Slam finals or when he kept missing the last step in Paris.

Since 2010, that's definitely been the most obvious change in Djokovic. Many players are now committing to meditation, yoga and sophrology in order to get better on the court, but few have endorsed it all this much in their general lifestyle. Surely having also to change his diet completely and learn about what exactly he was putting in his body had an influence as well. When you start going gluten free, dairy free, processed sugar free, vegetarian or vegan, or whatever else, you're opening a whole new page of learning experience compared to what you were used to if you weren't that much into eating organic food before. I've gone down that road myself since 2013 and I guarantee you that after only a few weeks, my friends and family were looking at what was on my plate wondering if I was now soon to be off raising goats in a deserted part of the country, or to a hippy community somewhere.

The answer of course, is "no, I wasn't." And Djokovic is surely not either. But, with all of this innovative mind set, this need for spirituality and that new nutrition focus, he ended up taking a different road and, Novak being Novak, he made a point of visiting every stop on the way. When he finished, there's no doubt he wasn't the same guy that had started it: not because he's impressionable or anything, but because there he found tools and answers to something that was probably lingering somewhere in himself.

All of this had found a way into his daily lifestyle but also into his business as he has opened a vegan restaurant "Eqvita" in Monte-Carlo. "Nutrition is a huge passion of mine," he told me back in April. "Ever since 2010, it became my quest to see how I'd react to certain changes, and all of a sudden it became a hobby, a passion. I see people today saying of people like me who have a passion for food that it is obsessive, that you shouldn't be that crazy about what you eat. I respect that but I don't think that's the right way of thinking. You are taking care of yourself, fueling yourself in the right way so of course you care about what you want to eat and there's nothing wrong with that. The more you do it, the healthier and better you will be. Plus, I'm a professional athlete so this is a kind of responsibility, part of my every day routine to take care of myself, to give my body strength and power."

He wasn't just verbalizing some points waiting for the next question; he was making a statement and could have gone on for hours about that philosophy. It mattered to him in a way that was now inherently tied to how he saw his career. Finally physically totally fit and raring to go in 2011, he would then discover around 2012 - 2013 that his mind needed a mandatory update to avoid continuing to lose those Grand Slam finals. That's the thing with Djokovic: he doesn't lie to himself. I'm sure at the end of the 2013 season, he was able to look in the mirror and say "ok, you've now messed up enough Grand Slam finals. You're better than this. You're off to get fixed."

Djokovic's issues weren't just to get to those finals, weren't to be doubting he had what it took or whatever. His issues were to manage that stress level, that frustration too, when pressure would be at its peak. That little negative voice that had started to take over at this time whereas it was shut down in 2011. Professional athletes spend their time in self questioning, and it's impossible to imagine where it can bring them. Individual sports also mean that when the pressure is at its worst, the athlete is alone out there: no one else to blame, no one else to lean on.

Tennis season starts in January and finishes in late November: pressure is non-stop, expectations are non-stop, travel and separation from family non-stop. So, even if they're super ambitious and awfully gifted, if they don't find their own internal balance and a way to put sense into the life they're living, there is just no way it's going to work in the long run at the highest level. For Djokovic, Nadal, Federer and Murray to be dominating the Tour for more than a decade without mercy, it takes not only a fabulous tennis level but four amazing minds and wills. And each of them has found what was best for him to get and stay there. They've bettered themselves until finding that last version of themselves that would unlock the last door. And probably each time that last version faltered a bit, they've gone for an update.

"New Age Nole," in my opinion, has been the latest Djokovic transformation to succeed in all of this, and also to find more purpose. What came first? The tools to manage his stress, and that helped him connect to what he would adopt as a new lifestyle? Or the desire he already had to evolve in that direction, and that found a way to open the last door?

There's something he told me that year in Monte-Carlo that struck me. I asked him why he had worked so hard on his mind, if it was all about sports performance or more a general curiosity. "It's just important overall to dedicate time, energy and effort to yourself, to what you want to achieve for yourself, who you want to be," he answered. "The worst thing that can happen is for you to be in some kind of stage of stagnation, being nowhere, not going forward, backward... God or the universe is giving us the opportunity everyday to do something with our lives."

It all clicks with his ambition, his perfectionism, his sensitivity and the fact that since he was a child his entourage told him he was bound to achieve great things. He found a higher purpose to aim at, a purpose broader than just him hitting tennis balls, so that winning tennis matches would just be the way to get there and build. And this whole process, added to the hard work on his game (better serve, better at the net), had eased his spirit enough for him to stop losing when it mattered the most. His career is just part of a whole, so if he takes care of everything else around it, it's going to reflect positively on his career as well. In order to solve his tennis problem, he basically took on his whole life. The only issue to be seen here is that it was widening the territory and the intensity of his perfectionism. But for Novak, the risk of constant discontent is much smaller than the benefits gained from this approach.

"He's an unbelievable perfectionist: If before I was surprised with his approach, now I'm shocked," Miljan Amanovic told me. "Really. Shocked. He is taking care of every single thing. About fitness, tennis, recovery, food, mental stuff, emotional stuff. Also knowing that he became a father. All of this had a big impact on him. But he put this in the right place so he is calm. He's so hungry for learning, but also for sharing his experience. He never stops learning. As I said, I am shocked because maybe he could say 'I reached 12 Grand Slams, 30 Masters 1000s, I am full and sick of everything.' But no. This is his style of life, which still applies to his profession. He can go on vacation and spend two or three days easy on himself but then he's going to wonder 'maybe I should stretch, maybe I should bike, maybe I should swim.' He's been dedicated to doing much more than he needed and he's been doing this with joy and pleasure. And I know he's enjoying (himself) also because after three or four days of vacation he comes back at it despite the fact that he could want not to see nor think about a scoreboard or results or pressure and so on. It's a lifestyle."

"New Age Nole" is also probably one of the most spiritual World n°1 tennis has ever had, and that day in June was like the meeting point of everything. He's not being a weirdo, he's having a view of the world and sharing it, and maybe we're not used to it in the tennis world. Through the years I've been able to ask about anything from politics to culture and religion, which isn't that common, and this spiritual side is actually quite fascinating, whether you agree with him on everything, part of it, or nothing at all.

Also because, yes, he's determined to change a world that in his opinion isn't taking the right path anymore, as he would think each time he'd see the news: "It's a global problem... With terrorists, the violence that goes on, with some disrespectful manners of some individuals, nations or whatever. We all need to try to first of all work on ourselves: change our micro-world in order to change the macro-world. As people we have evolved a lot, and money has become one of the values of society, as well as fame and power, which is very dangerous. When you give power to a man, you can judge his character you know...Greed has conquered many parts of the world, and business has become the top priority of many country's societies. Then you forget about family and what life really is: to make yourself peaceful and calm and happy. And to be surrounded with positivity, and not with chaos all the time. I love nature you know: everybody needs to shift their attention a little bit to what's surrounding you. What made you? You come from nature. And you will end up in nature as well, you'll go back to the ground, right? So if you don't take care of nature and yourself, which is the same thing, then you might very well end your life before you even plan to. You might not see your children get married, or other milestones in life that make everybody happy and that you'll remember forever. It all starts with mindset, nutrition, a holistic approach. Then the planet will change slowly. But as long as we only think about 'let's succeed, let's create feisty rivalries, let's fight against each other....'"

And it's not like he suddenly became a totally different person, as he would root this all in the way he'd been brought up. And of course tied to the life he's had since early childhood: moving to Germany at the Pilic academy, then traveling the world for the tournaments. I told him once that he actually looked more like a citizen of the world and it made him laugh: "All the tennis players are! I'm glad that I was allowed by my parents and my family to have freedom to experience new cultures, new countries, to actually approach this in a positive way, in such a way that I have no prejudice, that I'm able to learn and understand what's best out of these cultures and study it, enjoy it, learn. Of course I am Serbian and I'm proud of that, but as well I'm a citizen of the world. I don't make too much of differences between people."

He could have stopped here that day but he didn't and went by himself to a topic many would run away from. "Talking about religion is a sensitive subject but I am Serbian Orthodox, this is my religion, but I'm one of the people that is more pacifist in this way. I believe that we are all basically praying to the same God through different names," he'd say, smiling. "I believe we are all the same, and if we have this kind of altruistic approach to one another we're able to respect one another better and to live in more peace than we have today. Today, unfortunately, religion is one of the biggest issues and one of the driving forces behind the wars that we have."

You put all of this together and you would think it could be the start for a political program, no? Novak often said he didn't want to go into politics, despite many people convinced he could decide to go for any position in his country at any point. For now he seemed to have decided to use his power in another way to achieve his goal of changing that world. "With the political system that is in place right now in my country, I don't see myself in politics," he explained to me back in 2015. "If something changes in the future... Never say never. I don't think about it right now. I see myself helping my country in a different way through my charity and other ways using my name, contributing through my influence in bringing the important and influential people in Serbia to help our country. Of course politics is something that is part of everybody's life, not only about political parties and so forth, it's about your life because it influences everybody, that's why it interests me but I don't see myself right now in this system."

Again refusing to trade his peace for chaos? He actually has the same approach to his tennis rivalries. "That's another thing: I believe that the men's tennis era now is sending a great message out there, because we respect each other and have a very friendly relationship off the court. Wawrinka, Murray, Roger, Rafa, me: all the top guys, we talk, we laugh... Of course on the court we want to win against each other, but it's all in the spirit of good sport and fair play. At the end of the match, we hug each other, give congratulations, respect and this is important because it sends a good message to many kids who want to start, who want to become tennis champions or sport champions tomorrow. No disrespectful comments, no humiliating others or creating rivalries not based on sports values but on success or ego."

So it should now be easier to understand the deep importance of the notorious Djokovic holistic approach to life, so that next time he brings it up it doesn't sound as a new hippy vibe trend. And actually when he puts it in words, it sounds totally "Djokovic-ian." The day he succeeded making it the clearest had to be in 2015, in Melbourne, when he came back for a press conference on the Monday after his latest victory there: "In terms of a holistic approach to myself, to my body, the mental side, my regime, my recovery, my training, I'm very much dedicated to that discipline because I know that it brings me success. Over the last couple of years, people were trying to make me reveal my 'secrets' but there's no one special thing that I can say has contributed the most to my success: it's a combination of things, everything has to fit together. It's really holistic approach as I've said before. Your mindset, your life philosophy, the way you work with yourself from this psychological point of view, the way you grow physically, the way you train and recover, the food regime. At the end of the day all these things play an important part in order to play at the highest level for a whole year. It's a very demanding sport in every aspect of your life. I'm not the only one that takes care of my life on and off court to that extent. I'm sure Andy, Roger and Rafa do the same in their own way. Self discipline, private life, handling your emotions: the way your private life is arranged reflects directly on the tennis because I don't believe those who say you can separate the two. You're the same person so if you go into tough mental times it reflects on your results and your feelings on the court."

This self discipline and holistic approach have set Djokovic apart from the other champions, in Guy Forget's opinion: "He masters every parameter. When you see the time Rafa dominated, the time Roger dominated, or Agassi and Sampras back in the day, you feel that those players at some point were like musicians who had so often repeated their so complicated musical score that they didn't need to look at it anymore. Novak is like that and that's beautiful to witness. You can feel such physical control, a stunning ability to defend and attack, such a variety in the game and an iron mental strength. Everything has been taken care of and that leads to this kind of virtuoso performance where mistakes seem impossible. It comes from such hard work...I tried when I was playing to reach that excellence, but Novak is able to repeat it month after month, year after year." And Boris Becker still marveled about the Novak way of doing things: "Novak doesn't leave one stone unturned. He really thinks about which area he needs to improve. I think Murray picked it up from him. But I think Novak was the first one to see it as a whole."

Those top champions' brains are wired totally differently from yours and mine. That's something that becomes so very clear when you get to work around them. And inside the top champions' category, there's also no doubt that the Djokovic brain has a very different way of processing things than the others. It could also be that through this total acceptance that the French Open crowd gave him in 2016 and the performance he then achieved he found a validation not only of his method but of the champion he had become, away from the image of an unbeatable machine that was too often associated with his name.

There's also something reassuring and inspiring to see a professional athlete, one of the biggest sports stars, caring about something other than his bubble, being that passionate about the world he's living in. So this 2016 French Open hasn't consecrated that machine that some associated with Novak Djokovic. It had in fact crowned someone that couldn't be further away from that robot. Something the crowd had obviously agreed on when it gave him another remarkable ovation the moment he raised the French Open trophy above his head. It's possible that this holistic approach helped Djokovic express himself more and so to connect more, as much as those 2015 tears had also paved the way for this connection.

The ovation didn't stop after Djokovic raised the trophy above his head. It went on as he enjoyed the moment, eyes closed and, with a sigh of relief, totally fulfilled. He thanked them, gave a few thumbs up and then it was time for him to enjoy the Serbian hymn.

Up there, Miljan Amanovic was busy doing one thing: "I was crying," he told me one evening at Indian Wells in March 2017 after his day of work. That's how much it meant for the whole team to see Novak finally getting the win in Paris. "And I could cry again now... Because it was really something...(He pauses) Look, wow, I really could cry now... (He laughs while tears actually really look like they are about to come) It's something which he was looking forward to. Something that he was missing. Like you have a puzzle and you are missing the last part to have the most beautiful one ever. And at some point you find it under the carpet... That was the missing piece. And accomplishing this, and then the Serbian anthem, wow wow wow..."

It was like all the irrational surrounding that tournament has finally gone so all could click. "He had already played three finals so he had all the experience getting through all of this," Amanovic went on. "It was just to have one more thing to add. What was it? I can't pick one. He knew everything already. Had already 11 Grand Slams on his back. Everything was there and finally it comes (laughs). It was like a dream come true after waiting for so long." A feeling Gebhard Gritsch also shared: "It was such a huge relief after so many years!"

On court, Novak was visibly struggling. With the trophy. His reward was so heavy that Djokovic was having issues keeping it in his arms. But he wouldn't have let go of it for all the pain or money in the world. He even had to be told to let go of the trophy for a bit so he could hold the mic for the victory speech. This time it was really happening! There was nothing robotic then, and there had been nothing robotic in the way he had finished the match, nor in the way he reacted right after it sunk in that he had finally won. A machine would have closed it out at 5-2 for sure, and also at 5-4, 40-15. There would have been no emotional panic.

"In the last point I don't even remember what happened. It was really one of those moments where you just try to be there. It was like my spirit had left my body and I was just observing my body, you know, fight the last three, four exchanges, going left to right and hoping that Andy would make a mistake, which happened. A thrilling moment. One of the most beautiful I have had in my career." That's how Novak, who to general surprise and laughter actually arrived early at his post-final press conference, described what was going through his mind when trying to serve it out for the second time, also stating "we're all humans."

The last moments had felt like a sci-fi movie for the Serb: "Kind of an out-of-body experience. I felt it very few times in my career where I actually felt that my body was just on autopilot. Because of the emotions, because I realized the importance of the moment that I was in. And also, we played for three hours and I had had a long season so far. We were both exhausted. That last point was the moment where you get into this autopilot mode, basically. I felt that maybe for a bit longer time with Nadal in the finals of the 2012 Australian Open where we played for almost six hours. Usually it happens when you don't have much fuel left in you and you have long exchanges. But, yeah, between 5-2 and 5-4 and actually closing out the match a lot happened in my mind, in my soul, I think. But I guess in order for me to win this trophy I had to go through that. To achieve big things in life, you need to push yourself above the limit and really make the best out of your abilities on a given day. And you need to be ready for it, because when it's coming, it's coming hard."

So, yes, most of the time now with Djokovic, emotions are filtered, analyzed and dealt with to bring him to the highest level of performance. But they're still there and they often escape and reappear. As he achieved his quest in Paris, in that way, and after going through so much in this town, how was it possible to still hear and read that machine comparison? He had now won 28 matches in a row at Grand Slams, achieving The Consecutive Four, but in the process it hadn't been a walk in the park, it hadn't been cool. So how had he succeeded into making some people think he was that winning machine, into make some say "oh look he's human after all" on some occasions as if it hadn't been a done deal? Why put that tag on him? That very emotional Roland-Garros chase coming to an end also felt like the right moment to put an end to the myth.

"That's nonsense! Comparing him to a robot is ridiculous. Novak is a really emotional person" said Patrick Mouratoglou, disagreeing strongly with this vision of a robotic Djokovic. That had nothing to do with the guy he knew. So he tried to see what could have been the origin of that legend, and as many others would tell me, it was probably mostly his game. "I think this gap between who he is and that image is mostly due to his game style," the French coach would decide. "He's a player who commits very few mistakes, who covers his ground really well, who is also very steady in his results. And his game is made of an amazing accuracy. He's all about playing close to the lines, and has a fantastic hand. That doesn't make him a robot, but just someone with a great touch and really an unreal hand quality. Maybe sometimes it's not as elegant as others, like his drop shot: not that clean but lord the touch... And when he defends! The touch he has while defending is outstanding. No really: not a machine at all."

And that was also the point of view of another experienced coach, Darren Cahill: "I think they say that because most people only see him playing on television and that at times he makes it look like he's playing Wii Tennis. He makes it look easy. But you have to look back at his career: he struggled a little bit with acceptance at the start, struggled a lot with heat and injuries. But he's been able to make many changes to his game and turn himself in one of the great professionals, one of the most world-like players on Tour but it hasn't come easy and it doesn't come easy for anybody no matter how good you are."

Christopher Clarey, who has been reporting for so long, found it even "totally unfair" to try to put Djokovic in that inhuman kind of box. "I never thought of him as a robot," he'd tell me. "I think he's been clinical at times in his career but I never saw him as a robot. And what also made this whole French Open so fascinating in the lead up is that you could tell he was under a lot of pressure, even in Rome. And the crazy thing is also that we all know he could have been disqualified with the racquet incident. There were a lot of signs of external stress, things he was fighting through. His quality was still there but that's the fascinating part: he's anything but a robot. But I think it's because his game is so balanced that when he's playing well he's taking the ball very early, he's dominating exchanges, serving well: there's nothing about his game that says 'hole.' In other players you see the effort more: Nadal is always moving around his backhand, Federer too. Djokovic can play very simply and make it look easy and straightforward, and dominating, and it may not be spectacular. Although I think his movement is spectacular. But I agree that to the average sports' fan his game is less accessible and looks more robotic, but the person isn't robotic."

Gustavo Kuerten would even point to the Serbian's heart as much as his head to find the key to his Paris - and overall - success: "Always here there's one match you need to put out more, one day where things are not working, or you're tired or sad but you need to go there, get dirty and sweat, run for three hours, run for ever and win. And I think for him it happened here against Bautista Agut: he had to put his heart there. And even in the final as he wasn't feeling himself freely at the beginning. It can take time but it doesn't matter for him if he has to stay one hour or two hours waiting for this turnaround point: once he gets it, he doesn't doubt anymore."

Could Djokovic actually pay the price for the other face of his discipline coin? Mouratoglou thought it could be possible, yes. "The only way it could be said that he is a machine is, maybe, about the way he can mentally discipline himself in a very impressive fashion. He's by far the most professional one, even if Murray isn't too shabby there either. But Novak went all the way, even for food."

As I previously said, there's discipline and then there's Novak Djokovic discipline. Mouratoglou witnessed a few examples of it and still couldn't believe how far it went. "When you start knowing him better and share a lunch with him, you'll see him count the salad leaves, wanting this many carrots, inquiring about where the products are from... He's a Martian! I took a coffee with him in Monaco one day: he asked for a tea and said 'I want a mint tea, but I want the leaves inside and I want you to squeeze them.' (Laughs) And in his nutrition business, I know he wants this plant which is in that location and nothing else! One needs to go there to get it. He's the real deal! A total purist: he goes to the end of what he believes in. I love it." The Frenchman rather likes the Novak way of life: "He's a visionary. Someone who knows where he wants to be in 5 years, then in 10 and who works for it. It's just how he functions. He's very committed to anything he sets his sights on. He's brilliant."

Djokovic found a way to win Roland-Garros at the end of an incredible streak, not because he had somehow removed all emotions from his being, but because he was now much better at controlling them. And his former coach Niki Pilic praised him for it: "Novak is mentally very strong although he's also very emotional but I think he can control himself. Without this control anyway, he'd have never reached this level. Thing is, if you can't withstand pressure and you're a top player, go play something else."

Something Novak himself was totally aware of: he had worked hard enough for it to know, as he'd say after the final. "It's many years obviously of commitment, hard work, sacrifice and dedication, not just to training sessions, but also to a lifestyle, trying to devote most of your time, energy, thought to making yourself the best person and the best player possible. Something I've found out in the previous years in my career is that you can't separate yourself professionally and privately. You're the same person. So all these emotions that are maybe trapped, you know, that occur in your private life, the issues, the problems that we all face, you need to make them surface. You need to find a solution. You need to face, encounter these particular issues privately in order to maximize your potential as a player, as well."

Those matches where the stakes were blowing the roof off demanded that of him in order to win: "When it comes down to very few points, when you're challenged in every aspect of your being, if there is something under the surface, it will come out and it will play against you. It will be your worst enemy."

An enemy he's been relentless in fighting and also been very public about how the mental fight was done. "I believe in power of mind very much. If you train it as much as your muscles, you maximize your potential. We don't all know how much we can go and achieve until we have this kind of mindset of always wanting to evolve and improve. Power of mind and visualization are a big part of my everyday life. I know I can't physically influence the future but I can send good vibes, and then do everything in my power to get myself prepared and then when the time comes I'll try to seize the opportunity. It's mindfulness: I try to get disciplined to all the kind of exercises that I execute on a daily level, that make me feel good, present, calm and happy. That's something that works very well for me."

It isn't common at all at this level to be that vocal about mental preparation. Some players who are obviously doing some would deny it, others admitting to it would just refuse to give any details at all. Yet it's spreading more and more into the professional tennis world and even in the junior ranks to work on the brain as much as on the forehand.

"I think it's more prevalent these days with more players, but the importance is as relevant now as what it was back in my day," said Cahill. "Many players in my day used sports psychologists: it's the same pressure, the same expectations, the same media, maybe not the same money. Today I'd just say the difference is that more players are looking to make sure to turn over every stone to be better. No one wants to look back at the end of his career and go 'what if.' More players now have been able to do that because they're making a little more money and can afford to invest in themselves."

For Novak it wasn't something to hide at all, not something so private that it couldn't be put out there for all to see. "He's not the only one to do that mental work: many have also done it before him, but Novak is the first one who isn't trying to hide it, who has no shame about it," said Mouratoglou. "He explains everything, is totally

246

transparent and I find it very good. Then people are free to believe in what he does or not, to try to copy him or not, but at least he's honest about it." There's indeed nothing wrong in admitting you need help to handle the pressure and the life of a professional tennis player.

Marian Vajda, who himself said it had been the toughest preparation and fortnight he had gone through with Novak, was smiling. On the court, Novak was talking to his close ones, apologizing a bit about what he had put everybody through. "My family, my team, my loves, thank you so much for tolerating everything on a daily basis. There are plenty of things that I can talk about until tomorrow but you know what I'm talking about so thank you for being able to manage me in a way (laughs)."

So Vajda was smiling. A smile that also praised the long journey his pupil had made, mentally, from ten years ago. "He worked so hard," he'd tell me months later in a Monte-Carlo morning before joining Djokovic for practice. "It was his best improvement. When he was young, ok, those emotions he thought could help him and they did lift him up for a little time, but then four games later he would crash down. I remember that."

The Slovakian had no issue recounting that at some point he let Novak find other people to help him deal with this whole mental approach. He had been honest enough to know when it had reached the limits of his coaching job. "I'll tell you frankly, when he was young I emphasized these things, but then he decided to work with other guys through yoga, tai chi, psychology. I have my opinion that as a coach I do all the stuff through the tennis because it's the healthiest thing when you find the mistakes on the court and analyze them, try to change things. But obviously for him it was important to find the balance and I don't have these techniques, to tell him 'listen, sit down, meditate a little bit, etc.' He needed to find someone. And that's good to have somebody who guides you through exercises, focus and everything. To find the techniques."

Kent Katich has been spreading the yoga word with lots of success in the NBA ranks for years and can testify that the trend just keeps growing for a different kind of preparation: "When I started teaching, athletes were more interested in the physical (stretching and strength) and now more athletes are interested in the concentration, the meditation, the relaxation aspect of yoga. It changed, and now they're more open and receptive to the mental aspect of yoga. Yoga has become normal now and people aren't afraid anymore to try it. They also understand that they need to work on the mental side. But now that famous, high profile athletes are doing it, others are becoming more receptive and saying 'ok I'll try it too.' In tennis, you have so many opportunities to pause and think. So some can get upset and lose concentration. If you get stuck in the last feeling, in the last thing that happened, you're not present for the next move. The physical is connected to the mental. Staying in the here and now: it's the only way, otherwise you think too much, you anticipate too much and your body can't do all that."

Vajda would add that, in Novak's case, there was also this need of help because his life wasn't anybody's life. "People tend to forget that around those guys it's sometimes like a hurricane. And he's not a machine; he's one of the most emotional players you can find. That's why he worked on the mental side and improved a lot the last four years when he became World n°1 and it was his biggest asset. The mental side. That's why he finally achieved this in Paris."

Thibaut Venturino can testify how dedicated to that mental work Novak was through that 2016 French Open, and has no doubt how it played a huge part in the success of the Serbian through the years, until that point where he had totally perfected the method. "He's a very emotional person, but at the same time he has learned how to control all this and you can see it. He's doing a lot of yoga, a lot of meditation, which is very obvious. When we were practicing, there would often be some breaks. We wouldn't make more than two sequences without a pause. He'd take his time to come back on the line to start again, would replace his strings, take a deep breath, wait a few seconds and go back at it. You could see that something was going on, that there was a lot of work behind, like meditation, yoga, sophrology. It's impressive, really. You feel he's working on himself constantly. He'd do that sequence, would turn his back to me, do his breathing routine, close his eyes. It had become a routine and that helped him to improve like crazy on every side of the game."

I'm a bit nosy - please fake the surprise here, thanks - so I asked Catherine Aliotta what could be behind that practice habit, and here was her theory: "These are people who are extremely focused on their senses. At this level they don't feel the racquet anymore: it's just the extension of their arm. They're at such a level of perfection in the motion that their only way to anchor it is to anchor the feeling it creates. Those motions are now so automatic for the brain that sensations are gone, hence the reason if they do a beautiful motion or a great point at practice they need to anchor it. That can be done through breathing."

Novak's quest to win Roland-Garros came with his overall quest to get better and better all the time. By chasing that little piece of land that kept resisting him, he'd also go on a personal adventure that actually totally suited the way his brain worked: non stop. "How do I recover and disconnect? Well, I don't disconnect. I'm always connected. I disconnect probably only when I sleep. But aside from that, I assure you my brain works 300 kilometers per hour," was Novak's answer when asked, in Madrid, how he'd switch his brain off from time to time in. Easy: he wouldn't. "I like to have a right combination or balance between passive and active recovery, I would call it. By being involved in some things that are not related to tennis or sports. I enjoy many different things and try to get my mind off the tennis. That's how I recharge my batteries actually. You also always try to rationally spend your energy. Not too much outside and going around, because you need all your awareness and concentration for the match."

And this discipline he's been committed to would be displayed in Paris as the decisive part. As it had been for months and months now. "Before he would lose track during a match, would get annoyed and frustrated," said Guy Forget. "Today it can still happen but it lasts way less. He's always in control, and breathes power and mastery all the time. What's astonishing with him is that he keeps improving. If you watch his matches from a few years ago, you'll see that he's now better everywhere. He's faster, he's serving better, he comes to the net more often, he misses less."

If the method, and the rigor to apply it are praiseworthy, Thierry Van Cleemput insisted on the fact that at the heart of all of this there was an extraordinary individual. "Novak pushed his mind to the maximum, that's for sure. But the mental potential, no one created it: it was inside of him. You don't create champions, you get to grow the champion that the player already has inside of him. Champs, they go and search for what they need."

Something that Niki Pilic fully agreed on: "Novak is very talented and intelligent. He was brought up with both feet on the ground and now deserved to be what he was the last five years, that is: the best player in the world. He improved all the time, knew he could jump into another gear even in that final. And he bounces back all the time. He's always been like this: most of the time he finds the right solution because mentally and physically he's very stable. And when you win so many matches, you have such confidence in yourself...When Novak was 14 and a half, I said something I couldn't believe I was saying because this isn't my way. Goran Ivanisevic was at my academy in 2001, six months before he won Wimbledon - he was in bad shape - and I told him 'look, that guy with the black shirt, I think he will be in the Top 5.' 14 and a half, Novak was, and I'm too experienced to say something about a guy that age, but I was so surprised at how coachable and professional he was. It's so tough to say when someone is so young but I believed it."

And that was something you either have or don't: "He's always been so professional. He was just about 13 years old and I was supposed to play with him at 2pm. I was eating and my wife was drinking coffee there, but Novak arrived 25 minutes early. She said 'where are you going?' and he said 'I'm going to warm up.' She told him 'I think that's very good,' and Novak went on: 'I'm not going to risk my career.' 13 years old! And he never forgot something, never was there anything missing in his bag: all was under control. The key has always been that he's 100% focused on what he's doing, that's his big quality. His desire to win is incredible and so intense. If he had lost the French Open this year, it'd have been tragic because he was in the final three times so if he had lost a fourth time, he'd have been very sad."

The Djokovic way, like that of many great champions is quite unique. "Maybe he wanted it more than many other players," wondered Gritsch. "He had all the ability, mentally and physically to push through, but to stay there for so many years... The demand from himself every day to be fully focused, it is quite amazing. I guess sometimes it's not pleasant because everybody is focused and quite intense, but without that, you can never reach that level."

With this French Open triumph as a testament to it. His road had been bumpy before finally getting his hands on that Coupe Des Mousquetaires, but it was the last test to pass before greatness. And Guy Forget is convinced that it'd be an error to think that a player like Djokovic has been built step by step by some all inclusive method to create a champion. He insisted that people need to understand that players like the Serb are the exception of the exception, the tennis not even 1% but 0,5%. "You can 'make' a professional player if he's got the talent, but a champion like Novak... Those are out of this world, exceptional people: they can repeat these performances as others do but for smaller tournaments. And yet I'm not sure someone like Novak is necessarily working that much harder than others: for him it may not be "harder" to win a Grand Slam title than it was for me to win an ATP 250 in my days. Same for Federer... They have such a high quality of play! But again I'm not sure they've practiced harder than Alex Corretja or Arnaud Clément. They also have extraordinary physical and mental abilities. And sure they've worked very hard to get there, but like Pelé, Mozart or Michael Jordan, they sometimes touch the grace and are able to keep it for a long time. And luckily it's not due to a training program! It's like when people say we need to change things at the FFT so a Frenchman finally wins Roland-Garros. To those people: you just don't get it! A federation can produce really good young players, really good professionals and that's the case nowadays. But the players ranked between 1 and 5, it has nothing to do with an academy and a system. It's a unique individual, with this innate part. And it's for the best or that would be pretty sad to manufacture those players like in a supply chain."

There's one female tennis super star who has always had a really good relationship with Djokovic: Maria Sharapova. They've been friends since their teenage years, have shared the screens for sponsors commercials and the courts for exhibitions. You could even see the Russian in Novak's box for his first Grand Slam final, at the US Open 2007. Novak's impersonations of Maria have also gone viral and famous, to her amusement. And they have both a liking for interrupting each other's press conferences for some banter.

She completed her Career Slam at Roland-Garros as he did, a tournament she'd win twice despite the struggles she went through on clay at the start of her career. So it was interesting to get her take on what she felt best defined him. Funnily enough, when I asked her about it in March 2017 in Palm Springs after an interview, she had actually crossed Novak the day before at a restaurant in Los Angeles. "I always liked the fact that he's very close to his family and that's kind of how I got to know him with his parents," she would say as we were seated in an amazingly pretty garden at the back of the hotel she was staying at. "He was a kid and he is still a kid. People think top players are super heroes and super humans, and yes some of the moves we're able to do or shots we're able to hit look like 'wow' for someone who doesn't play the sport, but at the end of the day inside of us we're kids, we're young, we're happy with the smallest things in life. I feel he's been able to maintain that. And intellectually I feel he's grown as well. Even the way that he speaks now, his use of words and language, I'm like 'OMG! What books are you reading?' (laughs) He's someone that is a learner. In order to be interesting you have to be interested and I think he's an individual that is."

Those exceptional players weren't super heroes, sure, but they were still probably the only ones able to experience what Novak had in those last few points of the final. Something quasi-mystical that came at the peak of Djokovic's fusion with who he was and how mentally hard he worked. An "Altered state of consciousness," was the pragmatic name Catherine Aliotta would put on that moment. "It's a pretty special one. That's also what players would call 'zoning' or 'being in the zone.' We call it the 'flow.' It's the perfect harmony between what I think, what I feel and what I'm doing. He was realigning himself: motivation, focus, goal. It was not conscious, it was just happening. Same thing when one transcends oneself. Or under a huge scare or stress: I needed to do it and I did it. Those are moments of grace and it's nice to see they can happen from time to time. But it's not luck: it's all the work done ahead of this moment that made him able to go and reach that energy." But in this perfection of a moment was also maybe the seed of the price he would have to pay for achieving this dream: "The issue comes when you fall in the quest for those moments. Some people just quit everything:

'it's over, I don't want to do it anymore, I'll stop at the most beautiful victory because I know it's going to be too difficult to do it again.'"

Djokovic put all of his focus, spirit, physical abilities into winning the 2016 French Open. Not for two weeks but for a year. And it came after ten years of chase, after the last five seasons where he kept arriving as a favorite in Paris. For nearly two years he kept touching perfection on Tour, but on that day in June he not only touched it again, he reached Greatness and Fulfillment at the same time. It's impossible to understand or even try to imagine the shock it must be. Even Novak didn't see it coming.

Roland-Garros had been the one shaking him even deeper than he thought possible through his whole career, and finally winning it wouldn't change this. As the French Open kept another trick in its Major pocket: its trophy would not only be heavy on Novak's arms, it'd also be on his mind and body. Conquering the Holy Grail would come at a cost. One that was also lingering in Djokovic's own spirit as he was no robot, as he never did anything without needing a higher purpose. He'd be left, after Paris' celebrations, suddenly waking up and thinking: but what's next? Like entering Greatness Land but discovering that to again start climbing there too, he'd need to open his own Pandora's Box.

CHAPTER TEN

The Price To Pay

The whole tennis world seemed to be under Djokovic's thumb once he conquered Paris. What could happen to him now? Nothing, right? He would have so much confidence and ease of mind that this time people could already see him doing the calendar Grand Slam, and of course winning the gold in Rio. Why would his rampage stop? No reason, right? But making history came with a price to pay, and it came quickly.

Everybody, Novak included, had underestimated what would come along with the Parisian triumph. When you've been running after something for years, when you gave everything for it, when finally your puzzle is complete and when it comes after months or even years of domination, sure there's a good chance you'd feel so free that you'd still surf that wave. But there's also a big chance that you're suddenly going to wonder what's next, that suddenly the focus that came to you so easily, so perfectly mastered is going to rebel a bit. That your body and your mind, pushed again and again under loads of stress, are simply going to tell you "You know what: I'm taking a break."

Usually after Paris, Djokovic was asked to bounce back, to forget about a loss and to go and catch new glory at Wimbledon. He knew how to do that. But this time he had won Roland-Garros and he had no experience for how to deal with it. It was unknown territory for him as would be this whole end of season. His job and tennis history were asking him to move on, move on, move on, so he tried. But it wasn't working. And if it wasn't working, it was also because you can't move on from a page that isn't ready to be turned. Djokovic and the French Open weren't over, so how could Novak move on? How could he turn his head to Wimbledon (which he had already won three times) when he still needed to pinch himself to believe what he had achieved in Paris? It wasn't human. It wasn't possible.

We were talking since a little while about that final match, about the emotions that were running through him, about the joy and the fulfillment it brought when I had to play the "Debbie Downer" a bit and ask him if it had sunk in, if he had time to realize what a historical feat he had accomplished, and if it played a part in his complicated end of season. A heavy sigh came as he thought about the answer. "Honestly..." he started before pausing, "No, I didn't. And the reason why I didn't realize what I had achieved and it didn't sink in, is because I didn't give it time. And all those issues I've had in the last five months of 2016 are because after such a great roller coaster ride and after giving so much effort in the 15 months leading up to Roland-Garros and then winning it finally, if I look back now... I don't regret anything, because I really believe everything happens for a reason. But you know it would have probably been better if I had taken some time off, maybe even skipping Wimbledon because it just required more time for me to recharge my batteries, and I didn't. So I had to (he snaps his fingers) kind of switch back my mind and Wimbledon was around the corner."

And it wouldn't go well as Novak would be beaten by the US player Sam Querrey in the third round (7-6(6), 6-1, 3-6, 7-6(5)), in two days, after way too many ups and downs, after unusual mistakes too, after the rain again coming into to play, and against an opponent who was among the trickier ones to play on grass with his huge serve and forehand. A match not played on the centre court but on court 1, where maybe it had also been tougher to really get into the feel of the event. Everybody thought he'd again get out of this "right before the cliff moment" when he served for the fourth set but it wasn't to be. He would himself call this loss "a shock," and that was the right word for someone who until then had looked unbeatable in the first weeks of Grand Slams as he hadn't lost that early since the 2009 French Open. For someone who had made history again at this Wimbledon after clinching his second round win: he had now won 30 matches in a row in Grand Slams, the new record of the Open Era.

But truth is that, if physically Novak and his team were in London to play Wimbledon, mentally they maybe weren't totally there. And at this level it's about close margins at the top so if you blink, you're done. Djokovic was blinking, and he couldn't stop it even when he wanted to. The three weeks between Paris and London hadn't helped that much, especially as the week after Paris had been a sort of coma. "After that win I went to the sea for holiday with my family," Marian Vajda told me. "I was just lying there, and they were saying 'Come on, move!' but I stayed like that basically for one week (he lies on the couch, arms wide open). Completely out." And, like Novak, he couldn't compute exactly what had happened in Paris.

He knew it was big of course but it was so huge that his brain couldn't fully take it in. "Had it sunk in? Probably not because next was Wimbledon, next was Rio and the US Open. Always something. We had a party and Boris was like 'let's go for another!' and we were like 'Boris, calm down please, we have just finished the French Open, I am tired, I can't speak, I can't even walk, I can't lift anything, it was amazing, and you're talking about Wimbledon!' (Vajda has a laugh attack) That was Boris' personality. But Novak wanted to enjoy what he had achieved. Up to that point we did excellent, but I think it's normal that then he released himself completely. Too much, a little bit, but it's normal."

Sure, Becker wanted to think about Wimbledon, wanted to get ready to roar there too, but it wasn't the complete image. Becker, too, was in a way stuck in Paris. There was this little voice in his mind that started to talk louder and louder. So maybe by pushing for Wimbledon, it was his way to fight that little voice. "After the final I wasn't too emotional," he told me. "I almost felt that it was the end of the road. I was alone at the hotel Molitor, having a last whisky, and then I was emotional because I felt also this 'what's next?', 'How can I motivate him or myself?' Sure we got to Wimbledon, but it had this different vibe so I also felt that this is the end of the road." Their road would end months later as Becker wouldn't be head coach anymore at the start of the 2017 season. The little voice in his mind and probably Novak's as well had won.

They took some time to fully understand each other but once it was done, around the 2014 Wimbledon victory, they became one of the most successful associations in tennis history. But their relationship was also intense, as Becker doesn't hide the fact that coaching Novak Djokovic isn't a walk in the park. "Novak is always very challenging, which keeps it fresh," Becker told me with a smile. "There's not a dull moment, there's not one thing that we'll do the same every week. That's exhausting, stressful but that's the exciting part: you never know what you're going to get. You, as a coach, you have to improve as well, because whatever I said two years ago doesn't work now. So it really keeps you on your toes." There's still a true fondness when Becker talks about Novak, something bordering on admiration too. Tennis legends recognize each other, no doubt about that.

This Wimbledon exit was a shock for Novak and the team, so it brought them brutally back to earth. Waking them up from that Paris dream. Like shaking them by the shoulders to open their eyes. And still they had tried their best to keep them open since Paris, but it was too hard, as Miljan Amanovic also recalls. They were swept into an emotional tornado and even if they knew it, they couldn't really find the way out. "The day after the final, I was not aware of this, of all we had achieved... You're already packing, going to the airport, coming back home. Then next day you are ready to jump into civilian life and then you forget it until you get people messaging you. And they are saying you can rest now, but in fact you can't because Wimbledon is just around the corner. We didn't have time to enjoy, to really feel it. People were calling me, sending texts saying 'do you realize what you guys did! You must be proud!' But there was no time! The momentum for feeling and for joy was not in that moment because next is Wimbledon and you have to refocus again. For me it's easy. But for him, looking back at all he's done...This took so much energy and it's really hard to focus again. We tried our best for him not to feel we were nervous in Paris, and here now we were a bit more relaxed but at the same time, how not?" Indeed.

Yet, Novak did bounce back when he won the Canadian Masters 1000 in Toronto at the end of July, after some time off taken after Wimbledon. He looked good to go again and the timing was perfect as the Olympic Games in Rio were coming. But that's when his body decided it had enough: left wrist injury. Bad luck struck too at the Games with a first round against Juan Martin Del Potro, back this season from a long injury and among the best players in the world. An overall nightmare for Djokovic who would end losing 7-6(4), 7-6(2), leaving the court in tears. He won the bronze in Beijing in 2008, then lost the match for it in 2012 in London against...Del Potro. For sure, he had dreamt about getting a gold for Serbia this time. But Paris had taken everything, and what followed would be much worse than the Wimbledon shock. Djokovic now had both feet deep into the red zone, and we were only in August. The season ends in November.

Left wrist injured, he'd withdraw from the Cincinnati Masters 1000, the only one he has never won. He started a time trial to be ready on time for the US Open starting at the end of August, barely made it, then got an unbelievable scenario with the Czech Jiri Vesely withdrawing in the second round, then the Russian Mikhail Youzhny retiring in the third round and Tsonga in the quarters. That was an even more good news as he had also injured his right arm after only a few games in his first round against the hugely powerful Pole Jerzy Janowicz. So he made it to another Grand Slam final, which is a huge achievement for anybody but had become what people think is the norm when your name is Novak Djokovic. Yet, he would totally implode here against Stan Wawrinka, mentally and physically.

From 5-2 in the first set, he would just lose it: shouting to his box the whole time, missing, shaking on big points. Against "Stanimal" who was on his short list of "do not want to face in finals" and who again was playing out of his mind, he was unable to keep his own mind in the present moment, and so got overwhelmed like I hadn't seen him for a very long time in the big finals. And lost in four sets (6-7(1), 6-4, 7-5, 6-3): mind burnt, right arm sore, feet bleeding. The warrior just couldn't take it anymore, and was spending so much time fighting himself that it was pushing him into very dangerous territory. That would be the last straw: he had pushed himself to the limit but this was it. When I met him again after this New York final, we were in Shanghai for the Masters 1000 and despite all the efforts he was making, Novak wasn't back to being Novak. He may have even been further away.

Only he knows what he went through that summer but obviously it was hugely painful. He would be on court playing but the game was off and, more worrying, the mind was off too: this control and this confidence in everything were like gone. He was nervous, he was getting easily angry for nothing. He was fighting things that had nothing to do with being on a tennis court in Shanghai. But he was still trying not to sink so he tried different things like humming a tune after committing an unforced error so he wouldn't yell at anyone or destroy anything. The difference was so huge that people kept asking him 'what the hell was going on,' but it wasn't the right moment as I'm not sure Novak even fully knew what was happening to him.

To add to his problems, his lead in the rankings, that had seemed impossible to lose, was now melting. Andy Murray was coming back at him, playing the tennis of his life while Novak just couldn't get back on his feet. But even that race for the number 1 wouldn't matter enough for Djokovic to help him be himself again on the court. He'd try coming to Paris without any coach, but would lose in the quarters and then see the number 1 go on Andy's back. Still, he'd be a win away from keeping it in the final of the ATP World Tour finals in London, and after giving real signs of being in a better place. But, in another shocking fashion, he'd play one of the worst matches I've ever seen him play at this level in years to lose against Murray (6-3, 6-4). Abdicating without fighting, his mighty backhand so off it would kill him game after game. Finally the season was over for him. The last five months had been like a black hole but it felt that he had started to climb out of it, as he at least looked in a better state of mind in Paris and London than in Shanghai when he appeared at rock bottom.

"Those people are so able to forget what they've done well as soon as the next day in order to move on..." Patrick Mouratoglou, coach of Serena Williams, wanted to point out with his usual direct way of stating things. Never count on him to mince his words. "When Novak lost Roland-Garros in 2015 despite being on an amazing roll, he totally forgot that roll and felt as if he had failed at everything. It's back to scratch, and that's terrible. But here in 2016 there's the Wimbledon loss and then the Olympic Games that totally messed him up. Once again he was on an unreal run, but felt he had failed and hit rock bottom. I felt he couldn't wait for the year to be over. He needed to just do something else, get some fresh air. He just couldn't go on anymore. The final at the O2 was abysmal."

Winning Roland-Garros made Novak both reach legendary status and self destruct as the new box opened was full of new demons and questions. It was a much nicer box, bigger, shinier, unknown to most of all the other champions that walked the tennis world. But it was also heavier and even more demanding than the previous one. Able to make him reach even more glory from now on, but Novak needed to be ready to own it and to be sure that it was what he wanted.

That may have been part of the issue lying around the words he'd utter through that summer and that would also shock the tennis world: that he had lost the joy of playing. It'd be like an earthquake through the ranks. Djokovic losing his drive and saying it publicly? It became the biggest deal. But there was a touching honesty in him coming out there saying he was suffering. Because that's what he was saying. He wasn't whining, he wasn't being unreasonable, wasn't searching for excuses, hadn't started to take glory for granted. No, he'd come even before hitting the first ball of a tournament saying he had lost the way and was suffering.

"My approach is just different," he would try to explain in Shanghai. "Especially after the period following Roland Garros where I had a little bit of difficulty enjoying being out there, really. Maybe I was exhausted mentally and emotionally. I didn't know actually how I was going to react after winning the French Open because it was very emotional. I was obviously very content, but on the other hand I was also very exhausted and I needed some time to recover, to regroup. But overall since then I didn't find that kind of satisfaction on the court, which is the very reason and the source of my motivation to play tennis. So if I don't have that kind of inner joy of playing... I know that every day obviously is different and it's not easy to always feel at your best and always enjoy being there at 100%, but, you know, in the last period there were just too many of those days where I felt like I was spending too much energy and mental effort in my training and matches. So that's my priority now: to get back into that inner joy and really feeling happy for being on the court and everything else comes second and behind that."

The Inner Joy. That would be the topic of many discussions backstage. People acting as if it wasn't normal that he had lost it, as if it was a new ordeal never faced by champions before. The brutal arrival of this crisis, added to some comments Novak would make about personal issues, took this whole struggle into a much bigger and complex battle lived in the public eye. It obviously didn't help. Everybody had issues understanding how suddenly Djokovic couldn't cope with things he had mastered for years: how could the pressure now be too big for the guy after what he had achieved in Paris and after all he had won in the past years? Because it's a story of balance and sacrifices. And that suddenly the bowl was overflowing. Novak wouldn't back down, wouldn't play pretty: his motivation was fading, things were rough and that was it. Demons identified and challenge accepted.

He was deep in the battle when he found the words to explain his struggles in China: "I understand that people have different perceptions of what I say, and of course you can look at it from different angles and perspectives and say I'm doing that just to release the pressure, I'm doing that because of this and that, but I'm honest and I say what I feel. And at this moment I sincerely feel that that's something that I should take care of. It's not the first time that I've said I play tennis because I really enjoy it and because it gives me that happiness on the court, holding the racquet and playing because it's a game. But if I don't have that feeling and if I put too much (pressure), not just on myself but on people around, you know, and if you impose too much stress and expectations, then you start to lose that balance, and balance is everything in life. So I try to find that optimal state of mind and balance which gives me that joy. How long that's going to take, I don't know. I'm a different person than I was maybe three months ago, maybe six months ago. You constantly get to know yourself and what life is giving to you as an opportunity to grow."

This kind of sudden crisis Djokovic found himself in actually resonated with many players. Those who look at the top of the game to learn how it's done were sort of surprised and fascinated at the same time. They were all reading the articles, searching for Novak's quotes, as I guess no one felt willing to just sit down next to him and go "So Novak, what's up with that crisis of yours?" I was talking to Emmanuel Planque in Beijing, curious as to how he saw Novak's situation. Planque is coaching French new wonder Lucas Pouille, and he's a very respected French coach. There are interesting similarities between him and Vajda when the Slovakian started to work with Djokovic. That's maybe why the duet was especially intrigued by what was going on with the Serbian.

"Lucas and I read Novak's interview together, the one where he talked about losing the joy to play. And he said one sentence that for me was very important and also constitutive of how demanding the highest level is. He said he wasn't clear anymore with his goals and mindset. He was polluted by external things. He played a lot, won a lot, so it can be tough to keep the appetite when, added to that, he had finally won Roland-Garros. Now he has his Career Grand Slam, and I don't know how many Masters 1000s. I guess there can be a little depression, a sort of a letdown when one has achieved amazing things in his professional career. We're reading what he says with some kind of envy actually as it's a rich people issue. We don't have them! (Smiles)"

His tennis twin, Andy Murray, was also asked about this whole thing in Beijing and he wasn't worried for his nemesis, or surprised. After all, he himself went through rough patches of months several times in his career after a loss in a Grand Slam final. And he had also chased Major titles for a very long time. He knew the high of being one of the best players in the world, and he knew the low too. "A lot of players have gone through that," he'd say. "It can happen at different stages. When you achieve something that you've wanted to achieve for such a long time and put so much effort and thought into that, and come close a number of times and not quite done it, I think when you finally do it, you feel incredible for a number of days afterwards. But, you know, there can be a low after that. It would be completely understandable to have those feelings. I'm sure a lot of players have experienced that at different stages after big wins in their career. I think it's quite normal."

That was also the opinion of Roger Federer, who knew quite well what it was to handle the pressure and expectations of having no other choice than winning. The Swiss was surprised but could still understand as he told the Tages Anzeiger[22] in October 2016: "He's going through a

22. "Roger Federer: 'J'espère encore gagner davantage qu'un tournoi'", 24heures.ch, October 20, 2016 (*http://www.24heures.ch/sports/tennis/Roger-Federer-J-espere-encore-gagner-davantage-quun-tournoi/story/30144851*).

mini crisis, I'd say. I'm still surprised because I was expecting him to win another tournament than Toronto after Roland-Garros. But when you won the last Grand Slam title you were missing, a new age starts. After Paris, he might have wondered: 'Why am I continuing to play? What does it bring to me? What are the goals?' That state can last a week, sometimes a month or a year. Sometimes also that good feeling never comes back."

There was another side of the tennis world that was reacting in a different way, maybe the same folks who also thought in 2015 that Rafael Nadal shouldn't have started to say how stressed out he was feeling on the court, how the anxiety was hampering him. I remember coaches saying at the time that it was a mistake to show one's weakness like that, to verbalize doubts that much in public. Remember the "tennis is a macho place" line? Yep. They are all strong and confident men. If some were privately confiding their issues to shrinks and mental coaches, fine, but they should keep it to themselves. It's all in the "Bro code." Hence why if you'd ask a player if he was doing mental work or seeing a psychologist you wouldn't be that well received most of the time. That's also why it was a big thing for Murray and Djokovic to start talking about the mental work they were doing, for Andy to say he had also started to see a traditional psychologist. It was one more gate opening.

So Novak Djokovic, the confident showman, the guy that all knew not to mess with too much, was now telling people he was struggling so much mentally that he couldn't win the biggest matches anymore. That was like killing the dream a bit and for Thierry Van Cleemput, it maybe could have been avoided, also to protect Djokovic. "He should have kept it to himself because when you're such a great champion you don't have to justify yourself, and you let kids and tennis fans stay in the dream. When you have just won Roland-Garros, you don't have to say you don't want to play anymore... Go and take some vacation. At some point there's been a dip in his motivation... But I think he shouldn't have said that. Everything is a cycle. So probably Novak put so much energy into his desire to win Roland-Garros... And also, I don't believe it: he's going to recover the motivation at some point, when he'll have enough to have enough." Van Cleemput smiled at this last line. But with his experience, he may have also feared that digging too much into one's mind and letting people know about it would open a can full of worms.

Someone like Sam Sumyk wasn't surprised at all at what Novak was going through. The coach was more surprised to see all of the tennis world questioning Novak and focusing on the wrong topic. "Why would it be surprising?" he asked me. "Maybe instead of focusing on what's not been good, people should just realize that what he's been doing has been amazing. Of course at some point there's a little letdown. But as he's among those who have set the bar so high, if he doesn't win the tournament it's like he's not been good. No, no. The guy is still there and everywhere. He won a few less trophies but after so many years and triumphs maybe people could just let him breathe! People don't get how much it takes out of those guys to make it. Life is great, for sure. It's Ritz Carlton and business class. But it's not that easy. People forget the difficulty and the road to get there." Christopher Clarey had seen many tennis Greats through his career, and he's not one who easily gets ahead of himself, so maybe he was stunned at how much he hadn't even thought it could happen to Djokovic. Which confirms Sumyk's take that at some point: we've been spoiled with too much greatness. "I was totally shocked because I think we got used to the abnormal," recognized Clarey. "But yet I don't know who could have predicted it."

Marian Vajda and I were searching for a free room in which to talk. I met him after Novak's practice in the O2 Arena in London during the ATP World Tour Finals. I just went to ask him when he'd be free for the interview we agreed on, and in a typical Vajda way he threw his arms in the air and said "Well, what about now! Ok? Let's go!" Bag grabbed, a short look given at Novak to see what he was up to, and off. It was November 2016 and this season was coming to an end. There was a "finally" swinging in the air. He was his usual jumping and smiling person, asking me when the hell I was taking my vacation as he joked that it seemed I had done more weeks than he did on the Tour this year. Marian Vajda wasn't worried: not for Novak right now, not for Novak in the future. The Slovakian knew better. And he also knew better than to push his charge too much now, as he feared he could do more harm than good.

Vajda, with his father-like relationship to Djokovic, was starting to have enough seeing his boy presented as this unstable champion in this weird existential crisis. He also had enough reading that Novak working on the mental side with Spanish coach Pepe Imaz had turned him into some weirdo. Imaz had been there for years, Novak was fine: nothing to see there, leave him alone. So the coach, who more often than not prefers to stay quietly behind and not talk too much to journalists, was this time in the mood to take the time to tell it like it is. And he wanted to remind people of one thing: Novak Djokovic completed the Grand Slam in 2016, so don't try to erase it.

"We have to take the year in its all complexity," he said. "Because he completed the Grand Slam which was amazing and hadn't happened since Rod Laver. All the focus was on winning the French Open: it was double focus basically with the Four In A Row and the French. And I'm pointing it out: it's a very unbelievable year! Four Grand Slams in a row and Paris which he had never won. You cannot make as if these things didn't happen because then it's not nice... Ok, people want to see him winning, winning and winning but it's not possible every time. What he has achieved is amazing and we have to take it this way, in a positive way."

No doubt it was also the speech he was giving to Novak. Same for this US Open final disappointment. "He lost in the first round in Rio and it was a tough moment for him. Got injured too, so for me to see him reaching the US Open final was a miracle. The final didn't go well but we have to always remember that he reached a Grand Slam final and remember it in the positive way: that's the way he should think and never forget that."

If anyone needs a let's put-both-feet-down-to-earth-and-please-put-your-brain-back-in-place, stop-the-non-sense, you can always go to Marian Vajda. He wouldn't find one word to summarize Novak's situation at the moment, didn't want to go into this burn out world. He just knew that it was like at some point after the French Open, everything started to pile on Djokovic and that it ended up being too much. "I don't know how to name it but it's the consequences of everything." And he would take the concrete way: if Novak could get his focus back, all would be solved.

"Obviously after that the level of focus went down," Vajda went on. "He wanted so much to play the Olympics but I think this goal,

Roland-Garros, drained him so much already that he lost focus during the end of the season. You can't push too much. He's been competing for so many years so lapses like this can happen. So he loosened up a little, and suddenly his focus wasn't enough because to stay at the top level you need to work all the time with high focus. I don't think the main issue is his love of the sport, I think the main issue is his focus. Without it, you're not sharp enough. It's not only one match, it's complex and you have to take it like this. But Novak is now enjoying it again. This year was very tough and we were expecting it: but we've had things happening in a very good way, just that it happened at a cost."

The coach would also say that at some point after the French Open, Novak wondered "What's next?" without finding an immediate natural answer. He would also hint that in a way not having Federer and Nadal around anymore felt weird for Djokovic motivation wise. And stated what should be obvious but wasn't: what this Big 4 has done for years now isn't normal and that people should understand that lapses are going to happen. "You can see it with Roger, Rafa, Novak and Andy: they are on top all the time, their focus is amazing and not many players can keep it up. For me it's amazing to just think of how many years they've been staying there at the top, all the time. I suppose they have something special, they don't need to convince themselves because it's inside of them. But they're human beings and also they have a life so outside things are happening which is normal. You want to be all the time professional, but you can't always, it's part of the life. I can't name one thing only, as I see it as a combination of factors that can happen. And I'm not worried."

Not worried but he was also trying to protect his player a bit, to make people understand Novak couldn't have gone on and on winning everything. He had seen in the past how those situations ended, so he'd try not to let Djokovic fall into this. "Novak just wants to be the way he wants to be. They see him always winning, and the media are very tough on every athlete: obviously they make a lot of money, have a lot of success, etc. So they want to see him that way but it doesn't work. So maybe he's changing something, which is good for him. People need to see that it's amazing to be an athlete at this level for so many years. A guy like Björn Borg ended it at 26 because he couldn't handle the pressure. This pressure is amazing. It's very tough to play every week and win, win, win. But I don't think we need to dig that much and to make a drama out of it. It happens, that's all."

And as Federer himself would say about that: the issue was that people started to take that success for granted. "When I hear people talk about what a shocker Novak's second half of the season has been... Just because he had been dominating everything until this...It's not easy to play well every week. People get used to it and expect it but that's not easy. What Rafa, Novak, Andy and myself have done, that's not really the norm."

Vajda hadn't said the words "burn out" but bringing up Borg's retirement in the conversation couldn't be a coincidence. That's why he wasn't pushing Djokovic or lecturing him: who knows what would have come up in that case? So Vajda let it go. He obviously kept some thoughts to himself, and accepted Novak's decisions to go and find some other people to help him. That's one of the things between Djokovic and Vajda: loyalty and respect being a done deal, one can disagree or try another way without the other feeling betrayed. Vajda had wanted more time with his family since 2014, Novak accepted. Djokovic wanted to work on his mind with other people: Vajda had let him do it for years. And at the end there's this kind of knowledge that, whatever, they'll be sitting on the same bench sooner than later.

"Novak is just finding a way to go through this," explained the Slovakian. "He doesn't want to go through this much emotional stress anymore. He wants to release that stress in some way. It's not an experiment, because the game is there. And he worked with Pepe before in the past. He's using him for this goal of reducing stress. You need to find something. He was learning through meditation to reduce this stress. But there's no reason to start talking about manipulation of his mind: he's fine! That was exaggerated too much: he worked with him already in the past but suddenly everybody's like 'wow, who is this guy?' They're trying to find a story... Tennis is entertainment... Novak is fine with it."

In Shanghai in 2016, a colleague told Novak he didn't look himself on the court. And Novak didn't like it at all. So it said a lot that in March 2017 in Indian Wells, when asked about what achieving the Four In A

Row had meant to him, Novak went for it by himself: "Winning Four Grand Slam titles in a row is definitely a life and career achievement for me. But it took a lot of emotion and energy out of me, so obviously it took some time to reflect on things. I had to motivate myself again, getting back on track and I feel that right now it's much better than it was, especially after the US Open. I had those couple of months where I was just not myself on the court. Now I'm at a better place and I hope and believe I'm on the right track." He would lose in the quarter finals, revealing a bit later that he had a right elbow injury and had played under pain killers. Pity as he had displayed some vintage game to beat Del Potro that week. But he looked in a much better mindset overall: you'd see him joke around, being open to silly questions or tough ones. Good old Djoker.

With the eye of the professional, Catherine Aliotta considered that Djokovic might have escaped from a more dire situation. That his struggle at the end of 2016 could have led to a more painful crisis. "He was even lucky, because he could really have done a burn out," she told me. "Often the injury comes first: over training, because the goal is so high that 'I can't prevent myself nor listen to myself.' It's surprising as they are aware of what's going on. So it's all the difficulty: the brain can last longer than the body. Often then it's a depression phase born from the fact that you can't get motivated again, you can't find the strength to go again. It's of course made worse by having run for years after something and now reaching it."

So it was normal and a good sign that he had started to work differently on his mind in order to fix what was going on, that he hadn't been afraid to talk about it and search for solutions. "There's a whole lot of mental work to do in order to get over this," Aliotta would say approvingly. "Because if he can't anchor another goal after this, the risk is to retire. Federer's 18 Grand Slam titles record? It becomes a new extrinsic motivation. Sure, it's great. But when he's connecting himself to the kid inside of him, he's being asked why he's doing all of this, and that wasn't part of the original story. So running after victories: he doesn't care. He needs to build another challenge. There can be a transition phase, for a shorter or longer period. When he talks about losing the inner joy to play, it's exactly what it is about: at some point, 'I reached my Grail, that was the basis of my intrinsic motivation and now what do I do?' At some point there's no joy anymore in the idea of hours of work, of the personal sacrifices to make. What for? An athlete isn't all about the sport, there's a balance to find. He needs to get this joy back. And to remember that at the beginning, it's a game."

What about those fits of utter rage he had gone through the past months, leading to many judgement calls? "At some point, it's just too much," explains the sophrologist. "We're typically in an emotional management of self-sabotaging. 'I can't go on anymore. I've had enough of having to control things.' That's not the point that is happening out there, nor the match, it's a lot of anger towards oneself most of the time: 'why can't I have fun anymore? Why am I not succeeding to go on? Why can't I focus?' But also a lot of guilt to be in the 'I just can't do it' phase because behind him there's his family, his team, his country, his fans, his sponsors, so many people: 'if I stop, there are a lot of consequences.' And at the same time, there's this last breath, as when one has his head under water, this survival instinct that tells me 'Just stop!'. They're human beings."

That's actually something Djokovic himself hinted at right after losing the 2016 US Open final. In some way it was amazing to see him able to calmly reflect on this when such a short time ago he was going nuts on the court. "Of course everybody is playing the sport because you want to make some kind of success in life. What defines success now, that's different for each one of us. For me, success is not just winning tennis matches and winning trophies. It's more than that. I guess my main source of motivation for playing tennis is because I really like it: it's my choice to do it. I still have that intrinsic satisfaction and passion when I play tennis, just when I hold the racquet in my hands. But, you know, over the years I had to always find ways of motivating myself. To be honest, trophies are not enough, because that's something that -- that's not sustainable. Surely you're going to feel great if you're No. 1 and you win Grand Slam trophies. Part of my inspiration is related to that surely. But on the other hand, as you grow older, as you play more tennis, you're on the tour at a high level, of course, you need to find new ways, find other meaning and purpose for why you're playing it. Life is a big lesson. It's a big book. You know, we keep writing the stories. There is another story to be written."

For now he was still rebuilding after the tough previous chapter. Which was the mandatory thing to do: recapture this now famous inner joy. As it was the key for everything else. "At this level they need to still take pleasure in the game," explained Aliotta. "When I start to play a sport, it's because I like it, then little by little and through victories, the trophies reinforce the desire to win. The issue comes when the result takes over the pleasure of the start. In those cases once I've reached and fulfilled the extrinsic motivation, my engine is empty." So, then, it's back to basics.

And if you definitely felt a kind of "let's wait and see," of uncertainty as to how long it would take him or of how he'd find his way back to this best version of himself, when talking to his team, not a single one of them had any doubt that it would happen at some point. Amanovic was adamant that Novak was still enjoying very much what he was doing, that the fire was still burning. So whatever else he went through after that French Open had been the proof of something many wanted to put aside: he's a human being before being a great tennis player.

"It's not human if you're not having those emotions," Amanovic stated. "You're what if not? Machine. Many people are comparing him to a machine but Novak was doing all these things with such enjoyment. He was doing something which he's born with. It's drive, fire, like surfing the best wave and also using the energy of the wind. Yes, we faced some difficulties, when he'd be really tired. But still he was able to digest it, to get over it. We had the best period ever since 2011. And even last year! Ok he lost Wimbledon and the US Open, but you could feel that he wanted to take a little bit of the weight off his back. He was all the time in gear 6. All the time. He put it on gear 5 and that wasn't enough. And that's it."

What was Boris Becker thinking about all of this? He wasn't that sure. He hadn't seen the collapse of the O2 Arena coming and had been rather shocked to see Novak losing early in Melbourne. The German was in Australia even if not on the Djokovic team anymore. He was there for Eurosport Germany. But he was keeping an eye on Novak, as he did when the Serbian won in Doha at the very start of the season. He had seen there a sign of him being back on track. Obviously not everything was fixed though.

Becker knew about this state; he went through it himself of course. So he could guess the issues faced by Novak, but he was also thinking that those recent struggles could help in the long run. "You have to redefine your priorities," would be Becker's first words. "When you have a lifelong dream and you reach it: it's tough. Where is the next hurdle? Where is the next goal? And it doesn't happen overnight. I think what happened over the summer last year probably has prolonged his career. Other top guys stopped when they reached their pinnacle, like Borg. I started playing less, Agassi went through many ups and downs. Novak is a very smart guy so now he needs to intellectually understand what the next goal is. And once that is clear, success on a tennis court will come back."

People could talk to Novak about records all they want to, be astonished that it didn't seem to sink in that he had every record now within reach of his racquet. But you couldn't convince anyone about what should be his or her personal motivation. Becker kept total trust in Novak's abilities and will power. "I think tennis is always his first love apart from his family. He's a real tennis player: he loves the game, he loves to compete and I've never seen anybody defend better. The points he gets, you can go through history, I've never seen a better defense player. And yes he's unbelievably resilient, which is always going to be in his favor." Because actually Djokovic, in this whole new post-Paris triumph world, had come back a bit into a known territory: now it was the time to be resilient again, to brace himself and to go to battle.

It wasn't about a tournament, it was searching for that long term goal that made him wake up roaring in the morning. Gebhard Gritsch could feel that Djokovic was still wandering a bit. You can't fake it with Gritsch, one feels it right away: he has this straightforward and focused look that seems to be analyzing everything all the time. And he tells it like it is. Gritsch, who worked with Thomas Muster (1995 Roland-Garros winner), didn't believe in multitasking at this level of the sport so for the Austrian, as for Vajda, it was all about Novak's focus and what he now wanted to do with his life. "What happened after the French Open had to be expected," he told me with the utmost calm.

"Novak looked for motivation, really. The real issue was that he didn't have an immediate objective anymore... What do you need to prove now? I believe he felt so strong as a player that he wanted to reach out more, to see what life was about. He ventured into nutrition, things like this. It's a normal reaction: if you've mastered one part of your life, you think now you're in control and want to see what else is there for you, to find out what you're interested in. But the air is so thin in high performance sport that the moment you take 3 or 4% into some other direction, it becomes different very fast. I asked him many, many, times: 'How do you feel?' And he'd say 'I feel great, better than before, happy.' So now let's see what the future brings." As Vajda told me back in the O2, many things were involved in this tough spot Novak was trying to get out of, and obviously little by little, piece by piece, they were all putting the puzzle back in place.

But there was one thing that whatever happens would not change: the joy Djokovic was feeling each time he'd be thinking of this 2016 French Open. Not a single loss nor injury could damage the memories and the pride he had of having finally won Roland-Garros. I remember that through the end of 2016, he would sometimes be asked if winning in Paris had been like a curse, or if he had now mixed feelings while looking back at it, or if after all it hadn't been that much of a blessing to win that title. His answer was always the same: no, no, no. "I'm thinking about it as one of the greatest moments I have had on the tennis court in my life, and that's how it's going to stay," would be his answer in Paris in early November during the Masters 1000 event. A little while after, I'd learn that no one on the Djokovic team could even understand how people could wonder about that.

Of course they would all always smile about that French Open. Of course they would never blame it for anything. You'd pronounce the words "Roland-Garros 2016" to Novak and you'd see his eyes light up, the smile coming. That tournament was now part of the family, and you do not question the worth of that new family member. "Whatever happens, it's a positive anchor," stated Aliotta, agreeing that there was just no way it would ever become a negative thing. "It's something he always wanted to get and now he has it. With all he had to go through to win there, I think it's more a relief. It's self-fulfillment. It's a career peak." For Patrick Mouratoglou, the struggles met after that win had to be differentiated from the achievement. Champions, they bounce back from feat to feat. They collect pieces of glory and then put it in the past to get the next one. That's just how they are and that's why they're never going to be happy ever after. And that's why they're the best.

"They're never satisfied and that's why they're champions," he told me. "Some players win a tournament and party for ten years. Champions like Novak are all the time kept under pressure and need to bounce back right away. No time to enjoy. Champions don't look back, but ahead. When Serena won in Paris in 2013, after having chased a second title here for a decade, she got out of the trophy ceremony, told me she wanted to stretch and after two minutes she said: 'Ok now we need to win Wimbledon.' She went to dinner and off to sleep. It was already over, forgotten. I find it great! You live all the time with goals. If you're not under pressure, you're not a champion. They live with it and it's also their personal engine. If they don't have this, they're not motivated. They need that all the time. But there are very few like that."

It had been the Djokovic Way of Life for years and years. But after that French Open, the engine got stuck. Novak opened his eyes and took a little amount of time, for once, to enjoy it more than a couple of hours before thinking about what's next. And when he was ready to think about what's next, he couldn't find it. That's all it took to get out of this zone and to struggle to come back into it. But that zone is his home and the door remains open. The door back home, and the door to the new world contained in that new shiny box he earned by winning Paris. Because now, and he probably had to accept it once and for all, the only land remaining to conquer was Greatness.

He may not always like it but that's the only measuring tool that was left for the tennis world when it looked at him, a world where everything is competition. Where the conversations week in and week out are about the stakes. Federer had chased his n°18, Nadal had his n°15 in sight for a little while as he was for now stuck at 14 with Pete Sampras. Novak was behind at 12 but he had considerably reduced the gap since 2011, created his own records, and had now achieved one huge thing that none of these other Greats had ever accomplished. He still had everything within reach. He had transformed what was supposed to be a two player race to the GOAT title, to a three contestants' one. One more time, he had made himself part of the conversation, this time of the highest one, the only one remaining. Only the future will tell how he finishes that race, but for now the fact that he was running it was a performance in itself. When he left Paris on that Monday the 6th of June 2016, after the photoshoot of the winner at Place de la Concorde, that was the golden bonus of his victory.

There was for me one huge sign that Novak would soon be game for the task: that he was still refusing to reflect on what he had achieved, of what it meant for tennis history. He was still in this "what's next" state of mind. It was still there lying low, trying to peek out of the fog. It appeared when I asked him if he realized the scope of what he had done in Paris, and he just couldn't go there. He knew it was huge of course and he'd say it was a life achievement, but you couldn't go past that. He wouldn't pause on it and dissect how much it meant to him and tennis history, how it opened a whole new chapter. "I didn't really have time to reflect on that," he said. "So I'm glad we're talking about it because a lot has happened in my life, professionally and privately, since then and I just didn't have time to comprehend the achievement. I did, but not to the extent that I would like to. There will be a time I guess when I will have a bigger gap, just to sit down and reflect." We were in January 2017. He could have sat down and reflected all he wanted to during the off season but he didn't. And he wasn't planning to. Surely this little voice had started again to talk in his mind: the one promising him that more could be achieved.

CHAPTER ELEVEN

Only Playing For Greatness Remains

As we're being spoiled by an era of Greats, it's unfortunately easy to just look at an achievement, say "wow," and move on to wondering what they could or should achieve next. But that's not how it should go. One should pause and reflect on what had just happened under his or her nose. So let's pause. We're on June 6th and I'm back at Roland-Garros one last time to be driven with other colleagues to the place where Novak is supposed to have the champion's pictures taken. A photoshoot that by the way ended exactly as the image of the tournament that year: rocky. Going from the "Jardin des Tuileries" at Place de La Concorde to the middle of the Place de La Concorde in a bit of a joyful mess, with photographers running, then tourists who started gathering while wondering who we were all waiting for.

Then of course photographers had to wait for Novak to arrive and, yes you guessed it, he was late. Anyway, someone had the nice idea to bring an umbrella and then give it to him when he was finally there, everybody working on the best way to set it all up: it looked so fitting that he also ended up pictured with that umbrella, another symbol of this 2016 French Open.

Back to that morning: people were already hard at work in the stadium to remove any sign of the Grand Slam event that just took place. I was early so I wandered around and ended on the players' lounge terrace. And I smiled. On a white table, there was an empty champagne bottle. The only remaining proof of the party that went on there after Novak's triumph. The other proof would have to our recordings of the interviews done in the place after the victory, with the voices in the background of Novak's family and friends celebrating their Gladiator. It had all been like a tornado of clay, rain, cold, nerves but now that it was all over it had to sink in: tennis history was made here. Not only one page but several. This forgotten champagne bottle had been toasted for many reasons; no wonder it was now lying empty.

If, surely, accomplishing the Four In A Row is by far the biggest achievement, I felt and still feel that for Novak and his team it was and is still more about winning the French Open. Sure, the rest will follow. But mainly, had Novak only won one Major that year and had it been Roland-Garros, the elation would have been close to the same. "This one is right at the top with my first Wimbledon in 2011 when I clinched the number 1 and then managed to achieve my dream of winning Wimbledon. And now this one is right there," Novak would say on court that Sunday during a quick interview with John McEnroe. This trophy in itself meant the world to him, because that was the missing piece, because he had wanted it so badly. Because maybe sometimes he had also lost hope about it.

Each time Novak talked to me about those moments of his 2016 Roland-Garros, he exuded more than joy or pride. It was a sort of closure, relief and appeasement. He was so serene but also gave the impression he still needed to pinch himself to believe it. He could go back in time in a snap, about any moment of that fortnight, and would recount everything with the passion of someone who finally arrived at the end of his personal quest. Empty but happy. It reminded me how he had watched and touched this trophy through the press conference after the final, as if to make sure it was real, that it wasn't one of those many dreams he had about it. In 2017, Djokovic was still amazed by his 2016 Roland-Garros.

The feeling I had back in January 2016 in Melbourne had been confirmed: Roland-Garros had been the one to shake his world again on a tennis court, to bring back this pure joy, this touch of innocence, this sense of "let it go" as well. I also wondered - not if - but when Novak had thought about Jelena Gencic after this win. It was after all her last tennis wish[23]

---

23. "Youth Coach Helped Djokovic Fulfill Many of His Hopes", NYT, June 2, 2013 (*http://www.nytimes.com/2013/06/03/sports/tennis/03iht-coach03.html*).

for him to get the Roland-Garros title, to own the four Grand Slam titles. Her "special boy" as she used to say when recalling the kid she taught everything she knew about tennis. He has exceeded all her expectations.

His set of Grand Slam titles was now finally complete and it was a huge performance. One of the biggest any player could achieve, as only seven other men in all tennis history had succeeded in doing it: Andre Agassi, Don Budge, Roy Emerson, Roger Federer, Rod Laver, Rafael Nadal and Fred Perry. And that's it. No Pete Sampras, no Björn Borg, No Ivan Lendl, no Boris Becker, no Stefan Edberg, no John McEnroe, no Jimmy Connors, et al. Novak was also the one who had waited and suffered the longest to get that French Open win as he clinched it on his twelfth try, one more than Agassi, Federer and Wawrinka. Why had so few players done the Career Slam? Because it's awfully difficult to be, not that good, but the best on each surface after a two week tournament.

One needs to be an extremely special and complete athlete and player to achieve that: different techniques to master, different fitness abilities to possess, different kinds of tactical approaches, different mindset between aggression and patience, between being a risk-taker or someone that build points. You needed to switch brains and games. We all know those comforting words: "You can't be good everywhere." In tennis, some could. Not only be good, by the way, but be great and be the best. That's what Djokovic did in June 2016: he officially proved he could be the best everywhere. No more asterisk to his résumé, no more "but": career complete. He wouldn't end in that "cursed" bunch of amazing champions that had lost hope facing that clay challenge. A better natural clay player than they were, he found a way, pushed a little harder, believed a little stronger.

And Boris Becker, winner of six Majors, knew intimately how hard it was to clinch at least one of each Major. Now he saw Novak achieving that, and that might have been an interesting feeling for the tennis legend to have helped the Serbian do something he himself never succeeded in doing. Becker had won the three others but the French Open would remain the elusive one forever, with three semi-finals (1987, 1989, 1991). Yet, the feeling was different for him as he knew right from the start that Roland-Garros and he weren't a match. So, yes, he had been annoyed not to win that one, but not heartbroken.

"I had a similar scenario to Novak's: not winning Roland-Garros despite winning everything else. So I knew how frustrating and really annoying it was," he told me. "I wasn't as good as Novak on clay so for me to get into the semi-finals was already very tough. But you're still annoyed because you're going to get asked the question: 'why couldn't you win the tournament?' So I had to be honest with myself: my game was always about hitting more winners than the opponent, and on clay you have to hit less unforced errors which is so totally against who I am. I'm somebody that steps forward and clay is about who defends better."

Roland-Garros was against his personality: he tried but it wasn't meant to be, as he explained in 2013 to CNN[24]. "Psychologically, it was always difficult for me to play on clay. Trust me, I tried everything to win. I reached finals, semifinals of big clay-court tournaments and the semifinals of the French three times but I wasn't good enough. I lost to Mats Wilander, who was better than me on clay. I lost to an Agassi who was better than me. It was just about the quality of play, and my quality of play wasn't good enough to win a major on clay. I can't complain. Wilander, Agassi and Lendl were better. It wasn't unlucky: they were better."

So one can imagine how "full circle" and special it had been for him to be with Djokovic that year. "It was a very emotional two weeks," he'd readily admit. Mostly because he was putting himself in Novak's shoes and could feel the meaning of what they were all fighting for. "He won everything else. He won the three Majors before, so it was not only for him winning Roland-Garros but also winning the Grand Slam, four in row, even in two years. It was very unique."

Pete Sampras wasn't made for the French Open either, but unlike Becker he never really tried that much to see if, at least once, there could be a common ground. He himself would say in that same CNN feature that he "could have worked a little harder." Sampras took the stubborn way in Paris: his way or the highway. It would never be his

24. "French Open: The grand slam that got away from tennis legends", CNN, June 7, 2013 (http://edition.cnn.com/2013/06/07/sport/tennis/french-open-becker-sampras-edberg-tennis/).

way. Edberg would have a shot at the title in 1989 but lost against Michael Chang, and so gone would be his only chance to complete his set of Slams.

All of this gives even more praise to what Djokovic has now achieved. Just to look at the names of all those monsters of the game who never got to the point where he now was. There will be no "what if" with him as he had given everything to get a chance to win everything. One could argue that grass maybe wasn't ideal for him, but as Wimbledon was his childhood dream and as he knew the aura of the event, he found a way. There was no "I like it," "I don't like it," "if only" or whatever with the Djoker and the Slams: only four titles needed to be owned, and the knowledge that he had the game to unlock every surface and every opponent. There's never been any limit to his dreams and ambitions, simply because there's no limit to what he can do on a tennis court.

The feeling that continues to emerge from Novak's triumph in Paris is: relief. And it's telling enough that it's not coming only from Djokovic and his team, but from many people in the tennis world. Like when Federer finally won it in 2009, or when Agassi touched the grace in 1999. For everybody, it was like righting a wrong.

Guy Forget also shared that relief. Of course, as tournament director he was very glad that Djokovic wrote history on French soil: this 2016 French Open will forever remain a reference. But he was more emotional for what it meant to Novak and his team. He had seen for so long the commitment, the will and the pain in their eyes. Enough to know that this win in itself was the biggest thing. "For Novak and his team this win was such a relief. They tried so many times to get that trophy, from Nadal's hands most of the time. Each time he failed, even times when he was so close. In 2015, there's no Nadal in the final in front of him but Wawrinka: Novak is the overwhelming favorite but Stan prevented him from achieving his dream. So really this year we had the feeling that he was again the massive favorite and that after each match and despite the weather conditions he was like on a mission to win. It really was a quest for him. And when he finally won, you could really feel that relief, that joy, that emotion. That was moving to watch."

Even journalists who had covered this whole "Is it finally going to be the year for Djokovic in Paris?" saga were relieved for the Serbian. "Novak was such a good clay court player and he was certainly getting into Nadal's head, and you got to feel it coming so I was really surprised it didn't happen earlier," Christopher Clarey told me. "But that was a great set-up for that year. Talking to Novak before, he was kind of wary of the whole narrative because he knew everything he was going to be asked, knew what he should say, what he ought not to say, what he had to do. So I think everybody was just kind of relieved for him, for us, for everything at the end." Without even noticing it maybe, this Djokovic quest had grown on everybody, becoming a part of many people's routine too. One of the best storylines ever in tennis had just come to an end.

And there was of course no way for his colleagues not to have an opinion about what he had just achieved. From Germany where Roger Federer was about to resume competition in Stuttgart, he congratulated the Serbian, as reported on June 7th in L'Equipe newspaper: "Well done to him. He joins the very closed club of players who have won each Grand Slam. Djoko deserves it fully. It's everything but luck. It's a huge performance. And that's excellent for the image of our sport, it allows us to speak well about tennis and that's a good thing. I'm very happy. Everybody benefits from it." I asked Stan Wawrinka what he thought when Novak won, after all they were sharing a special French Open story together. "To finally see him win..." he started with a smile. "I thought it was just huge, as huge as everything else he had done the past few years. Until Roland-Garros he had won nearly everything, was going at an unreal pace. So much respect."

"Respect" would be also the word used by Maria Sharapova when we talked about it in California in March 2017. And she would just go back in time recalling the Novak Djokovic she used to see around when they were both at the start of their careers. The respect she has for him comes more from how much he worked and how total his will power was than anything else: "When you've accomplished greatness and victories and with the streak that he had: it's so impressive. It's also remarkable, from a physical point of view, like the determination he had. He knew what his weakness was: being able to play long matches, long tournaments, doing it daily, weekly, monthly. He couldn't handle that when he was younger, something would shut down and the physicality would turn mental. The fact that he was able to acknowledge that and to address it and to work on it to change it: that's the determination that gets you success. I have a lot of respect for people that acknowledge their weakness or insecurity or something they're not comfortable with and turn it around into one of their strengths. That's respect."

And that win in Paris in itself was for her, who at the start of her career had just no clue of how to tame that clay before she gave everything to find a way to win twice at the French Open (2012, 2014), the proof of all of this: "It's always interesting if you have a challenge... You've accomplished something on three surfaces and then there's that one in front of you that people always say, 'you know...' And on the surface that's the most challenging and unpredictable because you can come to the tournament as confident as you can be, as ready as you can be, but whether it's a feeling, or the pressure or the conditions, sometimes you feel it's almost a different tournament. And then you have a heavy day, you have a windy day, you have a day where you can't hit through the court, and so maybe from Novak's perspective when you get to that point you're like 'I'm ready for it, and I'm waiting, and I'm waiting.' So, yes, what an achievement!"

Nobody is entitled to anything of course, but after all those years of chasing and with all the talent he had, many would say that Djokovic had deserved this French Open title. That was a story in need of a happy ending, and that was even bigger than the Career Slam and "Novak Slam" stakes. "I'd have found it very unfair if he hadn't won Roland-Garros," Fabrice Santoro would say without hesitating at all. "He deserved it. He had to win Roland. Same as for Federer, it would have been unfair as he's been one of the greatest clay players of all time but the issue was that Nadal was there too."

This notion of "he had to" was overwhelming from every side of the tennis world. Patrick Mouratoglou shared the same opinion: "Winning Roland-Garros was essential for him, and it could be the door opening to winning two, three or four because there won't be that stress anymore. It's like a player who takes 6-0 in the first set: winning a single game is now an ordeal, he feels he's never going to win one.

But you'll see that when he finally wins a game, nine times out of ten the match switches. Now that it's unlocked for Novak..." But someone like Sampras never "had to" win in Paris to complete his collection, and he's still considered one of the Greatest. Why had Novak to win in Paris, outside of the obvious fact that his talent deserved it and that he got so close so many times?

Maybe it was also a case of people wanting more, of people feeling there would be a never-before-seen race for Legends among Federer, Nadal and Djokovic if the Serbian could finally complete the set. That was maybe the last sign that Novak's career had reached another level of expectations. And for a tiny and strange side of the tennis world, the last proof they needed to declare and accept him as one of the Greatest of All Time.

Rafael Nadal has been Djokovic's biggest rival in Paris so he knew how much it meant for Novak to finally win there. And he was sincerely happy for him, and for the game: "I think it's great...For me too and the tennis in general that three players competing together won all four Grand Slams. That makes our era a little bit, even, better (he smiles) and I am happy for that. Even if in terms of ranking and titles it goes a little bit against me, it's not all about competition: I think it's fair that Novak won, after playing the final rounds of Roland-Garros a lot of times, after competing for the title. I think it was great for tennis, great for him, and at the end of the day I am happy that people who really feel the passion for the sport, who love what they're doing and work hard to make that happen, achieve what I believe they deserved. And I think Novak deserved to win Roland-Garros."

But once everybody digested the fact that "Nole" was finally a French Open winner, a 12 time Grand Slam champion, and one of the few players in history with a Career Slam in the bag, the last mind blowing fact could grow: the "Novak Slam." This amazing period of domination imposed by Djokovic over the whole Tour had created a masterpiece that no one in half a century had achieved. The biggest feat in that sport for those who are amazing enough to be allowed to dream of it: winning four Grand Slam titles in a row.

There's a reason why no one had done the Melbourne - Paris double since Jim Courier in 1992. Between the Australian heat and the

Parisian clay, coming after many big events, it had to be one of the most physically demanding feats. There's also a reason why no one since Rod Laver (1962, 1969) had won four Majors in a row: to dominate the Tour this much had been made impossible by a competition getting tighter over the years, by a physical demand made stronger and stronger, and even more impossible by what would be remembered in the decades to come as the Big Four Era. But that feat had still been approached, and by three players in the last decade or so!

It was in itself remarkable that three players had succeeded in winning three Grand Slam titles in a same season in a very short tennis period. Roger Federer did it in 2004, 2006 and 2007, each time failing to complete the set because of Roland-Garros. Rafael Nadal did it in 2010, missing the full set due to the Australian Open as he would again in 2011 for the non-calendar one. Then Djokovic came close twice in 2011 and 2015, being each time denied by the French Open. But after this French Open 2015, there were signs he could still be the one making the Four In A Row, despite so many observers being unable to conceive that he could succeed where Federer and Nadal had failed.

Talk about a crime of lèse-majesté. His domination was total: both Nadal and Federer were either struggling or unable to find a way to beat him in those events: the rest of the rivals sounded at his mercy. In 2011, Vajda coined the phrase "cosmic tennis" to describe Novak's level. In 2015 until this French Open 2016, it was most of the time simply out of this world.

"He's worthy of that," Rod Laver would say about Novak winning the four Majors in a row. We were at the 2016 US Open, in the players' restaurant situated in the centre court building. An ear infection prevented him from going to Wimbledon but he was now back on his feet for New York. He was at every major tournament, displaying amazing energy even at his age. When we met at the entry of the players' lounge, he smiled broadly and shook my hand, looking me in the eyes. And when we made our way to the restaurant, I saw what a rockstar Rod Laver still was: at every step he would be stopped by a coach or a player that just wanted to shake hands or ask how he was doing. Younger players would quickly set their stuff out of his way, obviously impressed.

At 79 years old, Rod Laver is still as passionate about the game as ever. He even agreed with Roger Federer and the Swiss' manager, Tony Godsick, to create a new event, the Laver Cup. He said "yes" right away when I asked for an interview about Djokovic achieving the Four In A Row. He's always game to talk about tennis and the generations of champions as I would discover. So how did it feel to be in Paris on the Chatrier when another man did the Four In A Row? "I think it's good for the sport if someone does win a Grand Slam. This is not a club that I'm a member of: It's an open course (smile). It didn't need to take this much time, but competition now is tougher and tougher. You look at some who got three legs in...I'd say it was quite a feat, even if it still wasn't in the calendar year. But Djokovic's performance was unbelievable. To be the defending champion of all four titles is quite a feat. Yes, he's worthy of that."

When you judge an achievement, it's always a good measure to see who else did it before and for how long it hasn't been done. Also to look at the surrounding competition. Then you have a better idea of what you've witnessed: a great performance or a historical one. For what was at stake in Djokovic's case in Paris, it was quite obvious: he won the chase after one of the Giants of the game. Each feat he achieved in Paris was huge in itself, but combined they made the difference between enforcing a superstar of the game status and rendering a place in the GOAT debate unavoidable.

"I think he and I have both made extreme history," Serena Williams would say about the "Novak Slam" that echoed her two "Serena Slams" (2002-2003, 2014-2015). Don't go and talk to her about the real Grand Slam or not-the-real Grand Slam. Calendar year Grand Slam or non-calendar year Grand Slam, she was the holder of the four titles at the same time: that was it. Same for Djokovic. Steffi Graf - who even did the golden Slam by winning the four titles in the same calendar year and the Olympic Games - and Rod Laver were still flying above, but there was no denying that what the American and the Serbian did was in the same category.

Not forgetting that in Djokovic's case, between 1969 and 2016 tennis had changed dramatically. And also that the Serbian did it on three different surfaces. For Rod Laver himself, it was like talking about a different face of the same initial sport: "It's a wooden racquet against a metal / graphite racquet. How do I understand both? The game has changed so much. What they're doing now wasn't possible with a wooden racquet."

In case some would still try to make the non-calendar Grand Slam a way easier thing to achieve: do you know how many male players did either the calendar or the non-calendar one in all of tennis history? Three. You can only add Don Budge to the list of Rod Laver and Novak Djokovic. Budge did the non-calendar one in 1938, before going on to do the calendar Grand Slam.

Three guys in the whole of tennis history, despite all the amazing champions who played the game, despite the Big 4 era, despite Nadal and Federer. That's the spot in the history books Djokovic earned in Paris to set himself apart from nearly everybody else. "He was well prepared, did that under an enormous stress: he did something great, amazing, out of this world," Miljan Amanovic would say with eyes wide open in admiration. Yet he knew that if one guy was able to do it, it could very well be the one he was working with for a decade. "He's able to switch from surfaces, dedicating everything towards a goal, towards something he was doing with pleasure. Results came at the end."

Andy Murray understood this very well, as his speech during the trophies ceremony showed. Muzz didn't win on this June 5th but he surely made one of the nicest speeches that day and showed one more time that despite the rivalry, he and Djokovic really shared a special bond. "This is his day," Andy started to say on the podium about Novak. "What he has achieved the past twelve months is phenomenal, winning all four Grand Slams in one year is an amazing achievement... This is something so rare in tennis, it hasn't happened for an extremely long time, and it's going to take a long time for it to happen again... so everyone here who came to watch is obviously extremely lucky to see it... Me personally being on the opposite side, it sucks to lose the match (general laughter and applause, Novak laughing too) but I'm proud of being part of today so congratulations, Novak: well done."

After Djokovic would lose at Wimbledon, instead of joining the bandwagon of negativity, it would be this same Murray who would ask instead for praise of the streak. "Novak's run has been incredible, so everyone expects him to win every match. But, you know, history suggests that that's not going to happen. There's going to be a match where maybe you don't play your best, and your opponent plays great tennis. But rather than it being sort of a surprise, it should really be sort of almost celebrated now, what he's actually done. I mean, it's incredible. He broke a number of records, winning all four Slams, what was it, 30 consecutive Grand Slam matches. It's amazing. Looking back, it's been probably the best twelve months in tennis for years. His performances over the last 18 months to two years have been exceptional."

I also discovered through the discussions I had for this book, that for the players and coaches, what was exceptional in what Djokovic achieved was not only that he had played amazing and had beaten every other top player, but more that even when he didn't feel his best through this four Grand Slam events, he still won. Every person I talked to said the same: through those 28 matches, he must have had bad days and, look, he still found a way again and again. "It shows how much of a special athlete and competitor he is to be able to do that," Darren Cahill told me. "And also in an era where we have some all time Greats playing with Rafa Nadal, Roger Federer, and Andy Murray in there as well. It sends a message that it is possible. Over time it's proven how difficult it is to do. Not only winning on four different surfaces, but also you need a lot of luck, professionalism, talent, mental strength. 28 matches, best of 5 sets: a lot could go wrong on any given day, you've got to work yourself out of tough moments in the course of those 12 months."

That was also why Fabrice Santoro was amazed at the Serbian's performance: "It's at four different moments of the year with totally different conditions of play, with inevitably some complicated periods, moments where you're close to defeat, moments where, through those 28 matches won, you wake up with stomach pain, with a stuck back, where potentially you've gotten into an argument with your wife or have some personal issues. And each time you find a way to rise above it and to win. 28 times in a row... How many times has he woken up without feeling any pain or sore muscles, with being totally fine mentally, with playing his 'A game,' having great sensations in every shot? Twice, maybe four times? So that's where I'm admiring those champions so much: each time they do with the means of the day. If

I had to train a kid, that's what I'd tell him: what matters isn't to win when everything's fine, but to win when it's not because you're rarely going to have everything at its best at the same time. It's an amazingly huge performance what he's done."

David Goffin had played two Grand Slam quarter finals at the time (Roland-Garros in 2016, Australian Open 2017), and also entered the Top 10 for the first time in his career. The very gifted Belgian was already a great player and was now entering the world of the top ones. He could testify about how hard it was and was stunned at Novak's achievement: "Four in a row, it's outstanding, incredible. And I know, from reaching the quarters twice, the energy it requires and how long it is as there's the week of preparation before the Grand Slam event, then two weeks of tournament with each time a lot of stress, intensity... You need to hang in there. I reached the quarters of Roland-Garros that year so when I think that I would have had to win this quarter then the semi-finals and then final, each time pushing again mentally whereas you're already a bit tired and the legs are hurting more and more... Doing that through four consecutive Grand Slam tournaments where the body reacts differently, it's truly unbelievable."

Funnily enough, "incredible" was also a word frequently occurring within Djokovic's own team. "To accomplish four Grand Slams in a row... I never had that in my mind that he could really do it. It's amazing because he always had such motivation to be number 1 but priority was to win the Grand Slams, but I never expected to win four in row, never" admitted Marian Vajda, eyes lost in the distance as if he was again trying to mentally pinch himself. And it was again telling that however big this non-calendar Grand Slam truly was, the coach would still always come back to the French Open crown.

"The Four In A Row was the incredible cherry on the top. The goal was the French Open," Vajda insisted. Was it Novak's greatest win, that 2016 Roland-Garros? "In some ways yes, definitely," Vajda answered. "This was the toughest one. And for me Paris is my n°1, always! I dreamt of winning it as a player all the time. And then when Novak was there, well it's difficult because I don't enjoy as I'm in a very stressful process but when I looked back, pffft it's unbelievable memories now. It was a huge relief. It means a lot because it's been ten years, so it's one of the sweetest tournaments for me. Finally!"

And the Slovakian wasn't even sure Novak totally understood the scope of it all: "I don't think Novak really fully enjoyed nor realized what he had achieved and that it will only happen after his career. He'll look back at it and would say 'woah, I did that!' But yeah the best was finally winning the French Open." Even Novak himself was a bit at a loss for words when asked after the Roland-Garros final about that Grand Slam he just did. "It's incredibly flattering to know that Rod Laver is the last one that managed to do that, of course. There are not many words that can describe it. It's one of the ultimate challenges that you have as a tennis player. I'm very proud, very thrilled, obviously. But it's hard for me to reflect on what has happened before and what's going to happen after. I mean, I'm just so overwhelmed with having this trophy next to me that I'm just trying to enjoy this moment. Winning this trophy gave me so much happiness and fulfillment. I'm trying to grasp and I'm trying to cherish these moments right now."

Rod Laver smiled when I told him he was still a bit of an icon for those guys. He's not hiding that it pleases him, not for his ego but for the recognition it shows of what the previous generations brought to the game, even decades earlier. "I think they realized that yesterday's players were important to the game of tennis," he said. "They know where tennis was and where it's got to with them. They appreciate the past generations."

So why, after all of this being said did I, and others[25], get the feeling that Novak Djokovic winning four Grand Slam titles in a row didn't provoke the shockwave it should have? Or that this shockwave wasn't highlighted as it could have been? That the logical "wow" factor of the first days after his win faded too quickly and that very few took the time to look back at what just happened and just give it the full recognition it deserved? Christopher Clarey from the New York Times knew well about the situation as he of course covered both periods where Serena Williams did the non-calendar year Grand Slam. But he was still convinced that the praise would have been bigger for the calendar

25. "The Djoker Slam", NBC Sports, by Joe Posnanski (*http://sportsworld.nbcsports. com/the-djoker-slam/*).

one. It was for him the main reason, alongside the fact that the French Open in itself had been the huge story here with Novak.

"I do think it's fully appreciated but I don't think it's the same as the Calendar Slam," Clarey said. "In this era especially where it's becoming a huge deal, it's as much a mental challenge as it is a physical and tennis one. And I don't think the mental challenge is the same in a calendar year Slam. I saw Serena do it twice: the first Serena Slam was a big deal, but it's just not the same. And you can appreciate this so much also by seeing Serena crumbling under the pressure of the real Slam. It's a bit arbitrary but it's a big pressure. In Novak's case it also coincided with the French Open and all we cared about was him winning it, not doing the four in a row. Maybe if that had been at another tournament, it would have been more of a talking point."

Djokovic was also obviously again paying the price of this era of greatness: people were getting used to history being written, and were having issues realizing the scope of each performance. Preferring to ask for more, more, more. Last but not least, praising the "Novak Slam" was also felt by some as a kind of betrayal of the "Fedal" cause. You know how parents come to the elder children to explain to them that they have such a huge heart that it's fine to get new siblings as they're all going to receive the same amount of love? There would nowadays be the need for this pep talk adjusted for a tennis world torn between four corners, and that sometimes seems to be tempted to sweep some achievements under the rug depending on which favorite child is involved.

And there was nothing tennis related that upset Gebhard Gritsch more than hearing some of the things people would say while commenting on Novak's abilities. "I always wonder when people say he's by far not so talented and things like this... These people have no idea what they're talking about! No idea about movement, hands, anything. Sometimes you wonder..." The Austrian had worked with enough athletes to know, had also been there with Muster earlier in another tennis era. He was working day after day with Djokovic among this Big 4 era for years. After the "Novak Slam," he had thought that finally the Serbian was going to get the huge and fair recognition of his actions. But it didn't come as strongly and widely as he thought.

In his opinion, Djokovic was again treated like one interfering. "Many in the world grew up admiring Roger Federer, all fell in love with his game. We all love him of course, but then for these guys Novak was more like...not the enemy...but: he crashed the party. And they would never forgive him for this, never change their minds. It was also an advantage because he had to work hard, as he knew there would be no easy way to get there. He got motivation through these things. But once he achieved all of that, he was still not recognized as much as Federer or Nadal were. It'll come later maybe. But you know when we travel around the world at the tournaments, I'm amazed to see all those young kids who are really his fans, maybe also because they didn't grew up with Roger Federer."

That's also the power of the "Novak Slam" story: despite all this context, Djokovic still created his own mark in tennis history and still came first in that "Tennis Avengers Pack" to put his name next to Rod Laver's. That feat also changed the power of the conversation around him for that famous GOAT title. It pushed him up the short list where he was already standing, and also sealed his future tennis fate: Greatness would be the only company he could ask for from now on. Even if it wasn't his driving force, even if it was sometimes reductive and that it would be better to already admire the path made. But tennis is a competition, and it just never stops. That Grand Slam title n°12, that Career Slam and that non-calendar Grand Slam had set up Djokovic in the last part of the legendary road. But mainly it was already a huge reward and a massive achievement.

Novak Djokovic found excellence by running after perfection, so there's a good chance he could find many more Grand Slam titles by chasing Greatness. He loves the game for the game of course, but I remember Toni Nadal telling me in Beijing 2015 that even if those champions refused to admit it, after winning so much, the only thing that they want to do and the only thing they can accept is to continue winning. Djokovic, being the competitor that he is, and with the mindset that's been described through this book, can't get away from the fact that he's within reach of the sky now. Chasing the GOAT title may be the only thing left for him in the game, even if he may not like it as he said in Melbourne 2017, where he insisted he didn't want to be prisoner of those things. Which at the time I found a very interesting wording, meaning that those records ahead of him were already really more a burden maybe than this crucial intrinsic motivation. Greatness probably asks him now to enjoy that chase too, whatever he has to tell himself to get there. Here is certainly one of the keys to his future career.

Roger Federer himself didn't deny the place taken by his Serbian nemesis in tennis history. In Roland-Garros 2015, the Swiss said so when asked where he would put Novak on the GOAT list: "Well, very high already. He's still got some way to go. You know, maybe he doesn't have as many Grand Slams yet as others, but he's got a ton of Masters 1000s, which not many people talk about, which I find extraordinary. It just shows how his head-to-head is as well with top 10 players overall, and that he's stayed injury free now for some time, and clearly that puts him very high on the list now. I think the last three, four years have definitely changed the game for him."

But that he even reached that point says it all about Novak's achievements as of today. Deemed condemned to watch the GOAT's title battle between Federer and Nadal from third place on the podium, the Serb has turned this duet into a tennis version of a ménage à trois. This in itself is colossal. Djokovic being debated as the GOAT inside a very short list is a testimony of his tour de force. Winning the French Open, completing his set of Slams and achieving the "Four In A Row" clearly set "Nole" on a path of his own, where the "Novak Slam" is a huge bonus up one's sleeve in building a case for "GOAT-ness." Not to forget his for now 223 weeks spent as the World n°1. So where will this path land Djokovic? Only the future will tell. But instead of constantly looking for more, let's just appreciate the case as it is now. Novak has created a mould branded "Djokovic," his own mark in the game's history written in golden letters in probably the toughest period of the game.

It takes one Great to recognize one of his kin, so when the legendary Rod Laver speaks, you listen to him. When I asked him in September in New York what Novak's place already was in the GOAT debate and what his legacy could become, he didn't hesitate at all before answering. "He's got to be up there pretty high. And his career isn't over, he has a long way to go. You hope that he doesn't have injuries... His chance to win a lot more titles is very high." And the very interesting part was also that Laver had set Djokovic high in this debate even before the

French Open triumph, as he told ESPN[26] early May. "When you look at Djokovic's performances and his results, you just have to say, 'Hey, this guy's unbelievable, and how can you look past him when discussing who is the best ever?'"

Someone like Guy Forget was even a bit stunned at his own answer when I asked him in July 2016 about how Djokovic was challenging a spot many thought would remain a Federer - Nadal affair. "Yes, maybe he's now taking a place in history that few saw coming! Besides, in the last five Grand Slam tournaments, he was the favorite: for a whole season! Even when Nadal and Federer were dominating, they would come to some of those events (Wimbledon, Roland-Garros) not being the favorites. So yes if he goes on like this, he can reach Rafa's record and beat it, then go after Roger's one. It's unbelievable to have those three players in the same era. But what's for sure is that today, in the history of the game, Novak is one of the most complete ever."

I'm known for not being a fan at all of the GOAT debate. I found the topic borderline disrespectful when one sees the achievements of all those champions through the years. Then again, I don't believe in comparing such different eras, especially nowadays where the material has changed so much, when the sport has become so much more professional. Too much subjectivity. Blurry criteria sometimes as well. So I'm used to staying away from that debate and all the extreme reactions it brings. But I reckon that tennis being a competition, there's a place for this debate. And that even when you're talking about the best of the best, the temptation to still elect a champion is unavoidable at some point. After what Novak did in Paris, it was impossible not to voice it out loud. So be it.

Yet I loved Darren Cahill's reaction when I raised the topic: "I hate this conversation..." You and me, both. "I think we're very spoiled and lucky to be in this era of the game," he'd go on. "And when you start talking about the GOAT, there are so many factors...Also that most of the guys back in the 60's, 70's, 80's didn't play most of the Majors. It's

---

26. "Laver: When it comes to GOAT, Djokovic is Federer's equal", ESPN, May 3, 2016 (*http://www.espn.com/tennis/story/_/id/15452386/tennis-rod-laver-comes-goat-novak-djokovic-roger-federer-equal*).

an honor to be called one of the GOAT and an honor for us to have at least three in this era and, depending how Andy finishes his career, maybe four." And then there was this utterly logical point brought by Thierry Van Cleemput who shot me his nicest but still biggest "oh no, please" look when the topic came up.

"I'm not interested in comparisons," he'd start. And off he was to explain why it was useless: "You know, there's good wines everywhere but for it to be good and balanced it needs to be associated with the notion of soil. It's the same in tennis. If Rod Laver hadn't come up with hitting from under the ball when everyone was going from the top, topspin wouldn't have happened. Then Borg came with this physical side, then a mercurial kid decided to take the ball at the top of the bounce to upset Borg, it was John McEnroe. It's a game based on opposition. Those players feed off each other: that's very important. They're links of the same chain and have to be grateful for each other. Sure, each time there's a genius in that champion but he also uses what others have done. It's a never ending story happening in that soil. We are unbelievably lucky to live with this Big 4: four outstanding champions happening to play at the same time and it brought something amazing."

That brought me back to wonder if with that "something amazing" these four guys had created, it hadn't also blurred the usual lines so much that we may have missed a point. At the end of the 2015 season, I wrote in one of my features that tennis might have already found the next Roger Federer, and actually for years already. And after this Roland-Garros 2016, and after all these talks for the book, it was still somewhere in my mind. What if it had always been Djokovic? Don't reach for your panic button right away, please. Sometimes with a genuine but provocative thought you can widen your thought process, reach another layer and get a bigger picture at the end. Roger's longevity is fooling us, but there's a six years age difference between them. That's the difference, let's say, between Novak and Dominic Thiem and the Austrian is still presented as the next generation. So where does that leave Novak and Roger, and why do I still have this idea in my French brain?

Well, when is the last time there was this impression of a constant and inescapable domination on the Tour if not through Federer's best years? When Rafa was at his best, let's say in 2008 and 2010, he didn't look omnipotent from January to November, week in and week out. His body didn't let him. Djokovic and Federer didn't let him. And he wasn't a galaxy ahead of the pack in the ranking. On June 6th of this 2016 season, the Monday after his Parisian glory, Novak Djokovic held a record 16,950 points in the ranking while his n°2 Murray counted 8915 points and the n°3 Roger Federer, 6655 points. The Scot and the Swiss combined still didn't reach Novak's number. "It's the Mont Everest!" Niki Pilic would shout about this feat. Not a single World n°1 had ever accumulated 16,950 points in the ranking.

Yet, I can hear some yelling from where I stand: "But the game, the game? How can you even compare the game, Carole?!" Well... I was used to hearing that no one could play as fast on his baseline as Federer, then Djokovic arrived. I was used to hearing that no one could destroy any opponent as Federer would dispatch them on any surface, then Djokovic arrived. They both suffocate their opponents in their own way, with a PlayStation like kind of game. And I can still hear Rafael Nadal saying after this French Open 2012 final he won, talking about the amazing momentum Novak had in this match at some point that it was like with Roger, that when they start to play like that, there's nothing to do. Just wait for the storm to pass.

Also genius is subjective and comes in many forms. Watch again any of the battles between Federer and Djokovic in Grand Slams without most of your partisan feelings: you'll see a speed of play never seen before, winners at angles you didn't think humanly possible, shots sent down the line or crossed court without being able to even see the ball bounce before they hit it... Try also the 2011 US Open final between Novak and Rafa in the "Shock Of Wonder" saga by the way.

When you debate best tennis seasons ever, you come down to two: Federer 2006 and Djokovic 2015. And then you read Rafael Nadal's quote[27]: "I played against a player who did everything perfect. I know nobody playing tennis like this ever. Since I know this sport, I never

---

27. "Djokovic touches perfection in crushing Nadal in Qatar final", The Daily Mail, January 9, 2016 (*http://www.dailymail.co.uk/wires/ap/article-3391790/Djokovic-crushes-Nadal-Qatar-Open-final.html*).

saw anybody playing at this level. When I say perfect, it's not one thing in particular. It's everything. It's difficult to imagine anyone can play that good." Who was he talking about? If you ask around, I'm sure many will say: "Federer of course." But no, that's what he said after losing the 2016 Doha final against Djokovic (6-1, 6-2). So...

And there's no "but" to find or invent in this domination story. For any of the Big 4 guys. Ivan Ljubicic, who is now working with Federer, was helping Milos Raonic when we had this talk on the terrace of the players restaurants at Indian Wells 2015. The Croatian, whose best ranking was n°3 in 2006, was coached by Riccardo Piatti and has shared the Italian technician with Djokovic when the Serb was a teenager. Ljubicic retired in 2012, so he has seen from a front row seat how the Big 4 took over to turn the field into a kind of inferno for the other players. "They don't give you anything. It's not like 15 or 20 years ago when Sampras and Agassi could go through some bad weeks. Nowadays, guys are at their very best every week. It's also fascinating how they always try to improve and to constantly find ways to indeed get better. For the others, it's exhausting to chase behind especially when those guys are setting the bar higher and higher." Nothing has ever been weak in this era. Nothing was ever given on a plate or helped by circumstances for Djokovic. Novak's first victories on Tour over Nadal and Federer happened in 2007, a year after his quarter final in Roland-Garros: the threat was there right from the start. No weak era, no late bloomer.

Drawing a comparison between Djokovic and Federer has also become more and more frequent backstage, less and less a sacrilege, something one would mutter after checking that nobody famous was around. That's probably also why it made its way to my brain cells. I didn't even suggest it while talking to Paul Quétin, the French fitness trainer. We were discussing Djokovic's footwork on clay, and it's the only point of comparison he found.

"When Djokovic started he was more into power but now the two words that for me define him the best physically are fluidity and balance. When you see him evolve on the court, it looks so easy, so effortless... You don't see him move, you don't see him struggle. He can absorb the power of his rival and send it right back. His timing is simply flawless. And when you think about it, when you take a step back, you can actually see the Federer of his vintage years. When he was at his best, you would forget about his physical abilities despite the fact they were amazing. It's just that everything else was so perfect, every positioning so accurate. Yet his movement was equally outstanding. So nowadays, if you take the last months of 2016 out, Djokovic is moving with the same ease, the same looseness so it looks easy. But for both of them, it's been hours and hours of training, on for sure an amazing basis, to reach that level."

Djokovic was blowing minds in a way rarely seen before: "When Novak lost that French Open final and came back the next year to win it, added to the way he dominated the Tour for the next 12 months, winning the Four Majors... There, he really impressed me," Cahill said. "It's rare to see such domination in our game against such quality opposition. Federer did it, but it is very rare." Oh, look, a Federer comparison. It also used to be forbidden to say the words "best ever" for anyone other than Roger. Still, some are now openly wondering if anyone ever played as well as Novak did in this 2015 to Paris 2016 period. If Novak's 2015 season wasn't the best ever? And no one has been struck by lightning, or laughed out of the room.

Nadal's résumé as of today is already amazing and worthy of the GOAT debate. He is also two Majors ahead of Djokovic and five years younger than Federer. But my brain wouldn't think of Rafa as the next Roger, because, I guess, of the differences in the style of play and personalities. But between Novak and Roger? I couldn't help it, maybe also because of how they enjoy ruling, of how much they owned their ego and ambitions, and of that game that matched so well. Growing up differently but from the same regal mould?

And there was something different in the electricity one would feel in the air when they were facing each other. A case of a room too small for two Kings? Maybe. And of course Federer didn't want to be "the next Sampras" and Djokovic doesn't want to be "the next Federer" as he didn't want to be "Agassi 2.0": both want to be the first Federer and the first Djokovic. And they sure are. But sometimes it's just nice to think out of the box, search for bonds, just for the sake of it: it brings you to interesting places. So I'll forgive my French brain for that one.

One thing for sure: at the end of this French Open quest, and of this next elevation of his game and then of the domination that Novak showed since 2011, his mindset had changed. If the doubts came from time to time as with every other player, one thing was gone: the fear. The fear of failing, the fear of not reaching his potential, the fear of not being good enough to reach the sky, the fear of not knowing where he was standing compared to the other Greats. Now, Novak knew. I remember a press conference at Roland-Garros when he was asked about Tsonga who would be his next opponent. It had to be in 2014, when they met in the fourth round. Novak accepted to answer in French for the national radio, and someone asked him if he feared the prospect, having in memory the four match points saved in 2012. Novak raised both eyebrows with a smile, looking around the room as if he didn't get the question. So we all went into translating mode, but eyebrows were still up. Then he said, laughing: "No, no I understand what it means. But I don't fear anyone." Case solved. He had said "fear" as if it was a strange word for him to even pronounce.

Asked about any opponent nowadays, he would answer with a variation of saying his next rival was a quality player, that it was going to be a tough one but that if he could find the good focus and play his own game, he liked his chances. There was a time from his Australian Open win in 2008 and his 2010 US Open semi-final win over Federer or his Davis Cup final win the same year, where Djokovic would cross fingers and toes before facing any of his biggest rivals, hoping he'd have his greatest day and his opponent an average one. His 2011 season put that to rest, and every season since then confirmed that now Djokovic would always like his chances. He proved to himself he was able to beat anyone in whatever situation so many times that it was deeply engraved. Confirming what he had been feeling forever, and what he had been promised when he was a kid. "I don't want to sound arrogant," he said after the French Open final, "But I really think everything is achievable in life. Winning this trophy gave me so much happiness and fulfillment."

With Djokovic, you have someone who has never ever believed there was something in tennis he couldn't achieve. That even if he knows his career could stop tomorrow and still be judged as one of the greatest, he can't get past the fact that maybe there's something even better waiting for him. His former coach Niki Pilic was convinced he could do it as long as he was willing to make the sacrifices required: "Novak has a chance to catch up with Federer's Grand Slam titles number if he's hungry, if he's not injured. But nowadays you need to be ready to take the maximum out of yourself. There are a lot of sacrifices. Today, the guy who refuses to make them isn't going to be successful. No way."

Something Gustavo Kuerten would also emphasize. "He achieved one of the highest ever possible feats in tennis. He's able to break all the records, able to get better every single year and that's scary. He's dedicating himself 400%, he's doing everything to play better and that's how he's improving. Even fitness and then you are better on the strokes and you are faster and your mind gets stronger. Once you get to that stage, every single move reflects in all the competence you have in your game. The hard thing is to wake up every day and give your best, while being the best. Sometimes you say it's enough but for him, it's not: it's his dream, it makes sense so he keeps going."

In my young tennis days it was all about Agassi and Sampras. About how Sampras was so very amazing. About his record, about his 14 Grand Slam titles. It looked like the top of the tennis mountain. Then in my young tennis working days, the Big 4 landed and nearly wiped it all out. The Sampras mountain wasn't the biggest. And not only one player was climbing a taller one, but three. Mind blown. The American's superstar's mind too, as he'd say to CNN[28] in March 2016. "Roger not only passed me but he has 17 (18 now as of April 2017) and Rafa has 14 and Novak has 11 (12 as of April 2017). Literally three guys who passed me in one decade or in pretty much 15 years' time. It's incredible: I didn't see it coming."

Sampras was Djokovic's idol when he was a kid, which has always been funny to me seeing how their games and personalities are naturally different. Sampras wasn't hiding how impressed he was by Novak's evolution: "He's so good, moves so well, has the whole package," he said again to CNN. "Mentally, physically he's so strong. You can tell that he's so focused on being the best in the world and he's dominating at a time when the game is strong. His run in the last couple of years has been incredible. To beat Roger twice at the US

---

28. "Pete Sampras: 'Novak Djokovic is one of the all-time greats'", CNN, March 18, 2016 (*http://edition.cnn.com/2016/03/09/tennis/tennis-sampras-federer-djokovic/*).

Open and Wimbledon, to beat Rafa at the French. Truly he's one of the greats of all time. If he keeps this up over the next three, four years, he could very well pass me and get to 16, 17."

Thierry Van Cleemput remembers a specific practice on clay in 2016 of David Goffin with Djokovic that for him showed what kind of champion Novak was. And why he already achieved so much and entered the All Time Greats territory. He was still smiling by the way, remembering how it went: "It was in Monte-Carlo, right after Miami. A very important session as it was the first one on clay. Novak had just won the title in Florida, beating David in a great semi-final. Right away we felt Novak really wanted to show who the boss on the court was, so that was a very friendly practice but very intense too. You can see the touch of the great champion he is in those moments. There's a lot of ego going on there too, just because when you reach that level, you have no choice than telling yourself that you're here to win the tournament and nothing else. One needs to have a really specific mindset and a tremendous amount of confidence."

One needs indeed an extreme belief in ones' self to achieve all of this despite the odds and despite being told repeatedly that, as Fabrice Santoro put it when we were talking of Novak's popularity, "Cards were already distributed when he arrived, and people were taken, not single anymore." We're French, you won't get a lot of metaphors without something evoking love life. Sorry. So Djokovic fought for every title, every feat, every bit of attention he got, every slice of glory and he succeeded in creating a nice and shiny spot for himself. Was it actually really something he always felt he was born to do? I asked him that as I always had that impression, and many people told me the same.

So, had he always been convinced of being destined for great things? "I have to admit that from a very young age I dreamt and envisaged being the best and winning Wimbledon. Those were two pictures I had in my mind. But other than Wimbledon, I really didn't see myself winning all of that. Obviously you have one dream that you stick with, that you want to achieve one day. Then everything else comes along: as you grow, as you mature, you start to develop yourself as a person and as a player and you start to discover your own advantages and disadvantages. You go through a learning process, through this curve where it depends on you as well, on your choices: going the wrong way or the right way. And also the people you have around. Life offers so many different options, and everyday there's something new to learn and to explore. It depends on how you look at life, and I always try to see the bright side."

The bright side was also basically what Novak was for Serbia. A light even brighter and more powerful after that day in June. It was more than his success in career and life: it was about how he had set a new and more favorable light on the country after the dark times. Something Serbian journalist Sasa Ozmo explained to me: Novak Djokovic is crucial to the country nowadays. Both an absolute icon and a savior.

"He's one of the best ambassadors of a region that's still a bit torn. It was harder for Novak coming from Serbia, and we can identify with that. He's an example of the good that we have in our people, that there are good sides to Serbia. We love to say we're a sports nation and we live it really emotionally. We follow it very passionately. When he plays finals, 90% of the population is watching. And 100% focus is on the screen. No jinxing thing, like 'don't move from that chair!'... 'He was playing better when you weren't in that room, go away!' It's totally crazy. He said he could feel that energy, how much they cared, because he was the same when he was a kid. And during matches it would occur to him like: all Serbia is watching, I have to do this." His colleague Vuk Brajovic shared the same opinion: " Novak has been the symbol of a better tomorrow, a new hope, a new vision, new perspective for everybody in Serbia, not only the sports people. He's been like a positive revolution in many ways."

In Rio for the Games, a legend like the swimmer Michael Phelps got a bit star struck when crossing him in the Olympic Village: "I was walking back from an interview this morning and he was walking past me," he explained[29] at the time. "And I was like, 'Hey, that's Djokovic.' You usually give each other the nod and the smile, but I was like 'I'm going to say hi'. We kinda ended up just talking. Took a photo. Wished

29. "Michael Phelps meets his sports idol Novak Djokovic in Rio", Yahoo Sports, August 3, 2016 (http://sports.yahoo.com/news/michael-phelps-meets-his-sports-idol-novak-djokovic-in-rio-175411567.html).

each other good luck. He's super down to earth and easy to talk to. For me, it was something that was cool to see. I've watched a lot of his matches on TV, and he's had some epic ones. Definitely a very talented athlete and someone who was fun to run into."

It's nice to be a rockstar, it's nice to be writing tennis history like few ever had. But it also means there are millions of eyes on you each time you step on the court: all those eyes expecting that you'd win. That's also huge pressure. But after achieving everything he was wishing for in Paris that year, Novak felt that in the scale of things it was more an inspiration than a burden. As said previously through those pages, Djokovic never plays alone. He doesn't want to, and he can't.

"I have many people around the world that are with me and supporting me," he'd say after the final. "First of all, my family and the closest people I have in my life. Knowing that I'm not alone, even though I'm an individual athlete and on the tennis court I'm playing by myself, but knowing that I have that many people behind me, I don't take that for granted. It's an incredible fact that keeps me going day in, day out."

When you work with the cream of the crop, you of course know it. But do you think about it? Like, would Novak's team sometimes pause and think they were maybe working with the GOAT? That's also what I was wondering while talking to members of his team because it'd be human to sometimes think about it. When anyone reaches the highest possible position at one's job, there's pride that emerges. There's the feeling you reached the pinnacle of your profession. That's rewarding. Also, people working with Steve Jobs back in the day surely often paused and thought "wow, I'm here working next to the GOAT." No way Michael Jordan, Serena Williams or LeBron James' coaches or colleagues never thought about it either. Or was the key to actually block it out?

"It's a mix of emotions," Amanovic would start. "People often ask me 'do you know what you guys are part of? Do you know what you've done?' Only in those moments do I realize it. But I don't feel it on a daily basis. I've known Novak since 2007: he became family, he's the godfather of one of my daughters. All the team, we are normal people. We're friendly with everybody. Really. And I do believe in this." I guess it's also better not to feel you have a short-listed GOAT between your hands when you're tweaking and bending his muscles and joints every day. Imagine the pressure.

Yet, Gebhard Gritsch would be thinking about it. He wasn't trying to block the fact that he could be working with a future GOAT. "I'm aware of that, yes. I have worked with a lot of athletes through my career and I can clearly say that he is absolutely amazing. At every Grand Slam tournament there are moments where he impresses me: in some matches, he'd play for a while in a way that you think is not possible."

Marian Vajda had seen the teenager he first met becoming one of the greatest players ever. Would he sometimes think "wow" when looking back at the journey? Would he sometimes believe that at the end of the road there could be the GOAT title? "Frankly I don't know... I never look at it this way," he'd tell me. "The great feeling was right after the French Open: it's a moment. But then you don't live with it: you have your family, you go back home, you relax. Because if not you'll only think of it... For me as a coach, I really enjoy the moments. But obviously what he did was unbelievable. Insane. Historical. As for the GOAT debate, this will come down to history. But he's there, for sure he's there. One of the best now for sure. Tough to say greatest but he's getting closer to Federer and Nadal: that's what the results tell. We'll see what the future brings."

In Melbourne in 2015, I asked Novak to what extent he was thinking and caring about his legacy and he didn't shy away from what it meant to him. "Most of the players, especially from the top, will tell you that it's important to have the kind of mindset that keeps you in the present moment and once something is done you move on and you try to focus on the next one. Not thinking too much in advance or too much in the past. Because that allows you to work and to kind of reset your ambitions and your goals. But I think you have to be honest and frank and say that you think about the amount of Grand Slams that you've won, about the number of tournaments you've won and what your place in history is. I definitely have that in the back of my mind."

If Djokovic would check his Wikipedia page nowadays, he'd see two words recurring with his records: "stands alone." Was Novak, with his

"Four Major In A Row" crown, now tempted to take a step back and enjoy how he'd been able to best all his rivals? From what he had said in early 2016, that wasn't something he'd allow himself to get into. It was actually more something he'd keep his mind away from in fear of what karma could do to him if not. "I don't want to allow myself to be in that frame of mind. Because if I do, the person becomes too arrogant and thinks that he's a higher being or better than everybody else. You can get a big slap from karma very soon. I don't want that. I try to follow the same kind of lifestyle and routine, you know, things that I've been doing all these years that have been helping me to get to where I am. This is kind of approach that helps. I don't want to step away from it."

Whatever the new situation faced since this 2016 Roland-Garros. Whatever the new obstacles and struggles. The belief that Djokovic was still "history in motion" or "legend in the making" as Federer called him during the Hopman Cup right before the start of the 2017 season when asked to sum up his rival, was still around. "It depends on him now," Boris Becker would tell me. "How much more does he want? He can win on every surface: who has this talent? Who has this determination? I think history is still being written as we talk and it really depends on him"

What a journey it has been for Djokovic, someone whose career has so often been about defying the odds of a moment in tennis history that wasn't at first supposed to be his. In Paris in 2016, he proved that one can't write history in advance. And that the Djoker wasn't to be denied. We were finishing this Roland-Garros talk and were about to leave when I couldn't resist asking Novak one last thing: had he in his off time since June 2016 watched this final? Novak said in the past that he didn't like to watch his matches, that he would rarely do it. But this one was maybe different, that's why I asked.

"I've seen, not the full match, but highlights and many points. Many times in the period of two months after Roland-Garros. Ever since then, no. But yeah two months after, I've seen them many times," Novak recalled. And then again this 2016 French Open won him over. He smiled and admitted to something he looked quite stunned about: "Literally, 80% of the time when I'm watching I feel tears in my eyes. I feel again this kind of goosebumps and emotions, and my all body is like... All the chemical processes inside are happening. (Laughs) It's like I'm on the court." He paused before concluding. "It's a beautiful feeling."

Be it "Nole," "Novak," "Djokovic," "Djoko," "The Djoker," however you're used to calling the man: it's someone who in this 2016 Roland-Garros succeeded in closing one of the most successful and moving chapter of his career, and of all tennis history. Respect.

Made in the USA
San Bernardino, CA
28 May 2017